DEATH
SPIRAL

DEATH SPIRAL

THE COLLAPSE OF CINAR, NORSHIELD AND MOUNT REAL

WILLIAM A. URSETH

The Inside Story of One of Canada's
Largest Financial Failures

ECW Press

Copyright © William Urseth, 2008

Published by ECW Press
2120 Queen Street East, Suite 200, Toronto, Ontario, Canada M4E 1E2
416.694.3348 / info@ecwpress.com

LIBRARY AND ARCHIVES CANADA CATALOGUING IN PUBLICATION

Urseth, William A.
Death spiral: the collapse of Cinar, Norshield and Mount Real / William Urseth.

ISBN-13: 978-1-55022-844-1

1. Weinberg, Ron. 2. Cinar (Firm) — Corrupt practices. 3. Norshield Financial Group — Corrupt practices. 4. Mount Real (Firm) — Corrupt practices. 5. Chief executive officers — Québec (Province) — Montréal — Biography. I. Title.

HF3226.5.U78 2008   338.7'61791456523   C2008-902384-6

Cover and Text Design: Tania Craan
Cover Image: René Milot and Norshield Financial Group
Interior Images: Courtesy of the author
Typesetting: Mary Bowness
Production: Rachel Brooks
Printing: Friesens

This book is set in Garamond and Interstate

The publication of *Death Spiral* has been generously supported by the OMDC Book Fund, an initiative of the Ontario Media Development Corporation, and by the Government of Canada through the Book Publishing Industry Development Program (BPIDP).

PRINTED AND BOUND IN CANADA

ECW PRESS
ecwpress.com

This book is based on factual occurrences and uses the names and likenesses of real people. When I was not present for an event depicted in this book, the scenes were related to me by people who were there. Some incidents, while representative of actual happenings, may have taken place at a different time. Some information was provided to me on the condition of anonymity and I have respected my sources' request. Finally, the information contained here was accurate at the time of printing; no doubt, the circumstances of some of the key players will change.

TABLE OF CONTENTS

Successful entrepreneurs have become the royalty of first world society: the princes, dukes, viscounts and count-esses. They gain access to the courts of power, rooms of greatness and halls of influence. Investment bankers court them, analysts seek them out, politicians hope for their advice and support, writers interview them and old friends remind others that they "knew them back when." Entrepreneurs, especially the self-made type, have a special place in today's world.

While they vary widely in their interests, backgrounds, businesses, methods, tone, nationality and motivations, they all share certain elements of commonality. Among these are knowing what it means to make a payroll, be a guarantor, sign a financial statement and that oftentimes the most important decisions are made in the quiet of their own mind.

In an evermore complicated world full of regulations and regulators, non-discrimination and anti-harassment policies, many decisions are by necessity made in the quiet of the entrepreneur's mind because that way there are no minutes, no witnesses, no conspirators involved in these decisions. With that comes loneliness because there is no counsel, no committee, no conference report, but there also is a quiet confidence to that elite group of decision makers. Dictators, some military leaders, a few CEOs may get that feeling, but entrepreneurs know and experience it with regularity as they live out their days as modern royalty.

Few people ever take the plunge and abandon the safety net of a "regular job" to become an entrepreneur. In the beginning rejection is all too frequent, allies too rare, government intervention too common, paperwork too consuming and cash almost always too short. Few realize that while the employees get their payroll check and the government gets the withholding checks, the entrepreneur may be left out of the mix; if cash is short, they receive nothing. While their own payday is missed, vendors and creditors won't miss the opportunity to call about their receivables or cut off services until the invoices are caught up. The developing entrepreneur is always balancing the present with the future, dreaming of what things will be while struggling to make certain the business survives its current challenges.

Many entrepreneurs find themselves perpetually in the development stage; they never emerge from it to join the capitalist royalty. Things don't go quite the way they were supposed to. Chronic cash shortages, unending government entanglements and a swamp of self doubt lead most to break . . . and fold, close, sell or go bankrupt, abandoning what has occupied their thoughts, hopes, dreams, every waking and often non-waking moment since its creation.

A business journalist once asked an entrepreneur whose company had achieved high visibility and great market success, "What's it like to be an overnight success?" The entrepreneur knew full well he had struggled and almost failed numerous times over the previous ten years. He had sacrificed a good marriage, lost most of his old friends, borrowed money he couldn't repay, driven old cars, never bought a home, worked six or seven days a week from 8 a.m. to 8 p.m. He had personally guaranteed every debt of the company and knew that if interest payments weren't made or the financial statements could no longer support the loans, the bank would seize the business, liquidate the assets, pay itself back and leave him

with nothing. Entrepreneurs don't get unemployment insurance; they only get the phone calls, law suits, letters of derision and sometimes the government regulators that come along with business failure. The entrepreneur responded to the reporter, "I've spent ten years becoming this overnight success and it feels pretty damn good!"

Ninety percent of all new businesses fail in their first five years; another five percent fail in the next five years, meaning that only about five percent of start-ups make it ten years or more. Usually what the survivors have found is a market for whatever they do, an ability to deliver it, a method of keeping track of what they do, some sort of financing and an entrepreneur who has been able to plan, lead, organize and control the entire venture. Endemic to the species is risk: risk taking and risk management. Risk and entrepreneurs are joined at the hip, inextricably inter-twined . . . the ice cream and apple pie of capitalism. This natural combination caused Henry Ford to make cars and permanently change the world, Howard Hughes to make airplanes, finance movies, bankroll Las Vegas and make a permanent mark on our culture. Steve Jobs has, on two separate occasions, led Apple to greatness by taking risks, and adventurer Sir Richard Branson made Virgin Airlines a surprising success with risk management as his guide.

With today's business world full of multi-nationals, conglomerates and publicly financed corporations, the space available for the entrepreneur in many industries has greatly shrunk. Corporate giants with vast resources, access to capital, sophisticated management tools and repositioning systems tend to excel at quantitative analy-sis: the ability to gather facts, figures and data, assemble it all, then quantify opportunity with relative certainty.

Qualitative analysis is the more subjective alternative

that entrepreneurs use when they follow their instincts, smell opportunity, swim up the stream. "He has a nose for it" is one of the old expressions for someone who does it naturally, "like falling off a log." Where quantitative analysis requires teams of researchers and analysts to determine feasibility first, implementation second and, of course, profitability, qualitative analysis can be done in the quiet of one's mind and implemented by the sheer force of belief and blind confidence.

After an entrepreneur has had a string of victories, lasted in business for ten years or more and refined their ability to make decisions through qualitative data, that confidence sets in. Some may even call it cockiness, but by whatever name it fuels the entrepreneurial senses. It allows one to take risks, and then even larger risks, and can create in the mind of that risk taker a sense of calm — they've managed those types of problems before, negotiated these difficulties in the past. Where the same facts might terrify the senior manager of a multi-national working with a quantitative analysis, those very facts are met with an energized calm and quiet confidence in a veteran entrepreneur.

As successes add up, real entrepreneurs begin to seek out others like themselves, whether it be from their community or others. They're usually careful to avoid competitors, and seek out rare peers who share qualities like self-sacrifice, commitment and most importantly success. The self-made entrepreneur has little regard for the trust-fund kid who has had his wealth or position bestowed upon him. The self-made types are also dubious of the corporate types — the CEOs and executives of multi-nationals and large public companies who, they generally believe, have ascended from the risk-averse mediocrity for a five- or ten-year term as

CEO to be supported by risk-averse staffs, line groups and directors. So while entrepreneurs serve alongside corporate types and trust-fund kids on boards or for a good cause, they consider themselves separate from them, and from the rest of the world.

Once someone has survived for 10, 15 or 20 years as a self-made business success, a star quality sets in. Professional advisers, attorneys, accountants, financial planners begin to treat the successful businessperson deferentially. The trips and vacations, though not frequent, become more and more exotic and expensive. Clothes become more important, with professional shoppers and wardrobe consultants replacing retail sales clerks. Cars, homes and second homes become key signifiers of one's status in the world.

For many at this stage of their career, they're lured into book deals, public speaking engagements, community service and philanthropy. Inevitably because of their high profiles, successes or self-promotion, they become desired subjects for journalists, writers and reporters. These articles are most often "softball" pieces for magazines hungry to provide details and photographs of the capitalist royalty to their readers. Occasionally, there are serious, thoughtful and thought-provoking pieces about the individual or their business, but virtually always with a positive twist to maintain access to the prince or countess, as the case may be.

For many self-made entrepreneurs a mid-life crisis occurs when it's time for them to sell some or all of their business to the public, to a financier or to a group of partners. While, on the one hand, the sale creates a financial bonanza and a sense of stability perhaps never felt before, the period also begins to move the entrepreneurs from that role that they cherish to that of a CEO or manager of the business, a role for which they may not have the skill set. Suddenly, new voices in the company are calling out for quantitative analysis while the self-made founder has always thrived on qualitative analysis. The converging cultures prepare for collision and conflict.

It's at this stage of business life that this book begins: the confluence for Ron Weinberg and Micheline Charest of a very successful, very private company made public. With high profiles and vast amounts of money, they were already a part of modern royalty. The company they had struggled to build and had devoted their entire lives to was now about 20 years old. For John Xanthoudakis who had started life as the son of Greek immigrants, his business was about ten years old. Self made and well established, he too had committed all of his efforts to his company's success. People often said of John that he "talks nothing but business" and it was true. He had seen the other ninety-five percent of start-ups fail and fall by the wayside while his operation grew in its success. Lino Matteo was the son of Italian immigrants and he had been building his business piece by piece. Not as far along as Weinberg and Charest or his old friend Xanthoudakis, he nevertheless had the traits, characteristics and commitment of the self-made entrepreneur and was enjoying the high that came from the position. Certain of his qualitative analysis skills, he had assembled a string of victories and was already going public.

Weinberg, Charest, Xanthoudakis and Matteo were about to enter into a tightly woven web that would closely bind them for about eight years. In fact, they would never truly be separated from each other again. These four self-made entrepreneurs — capitalist royalty — were about to converge.

Corporations and businesses, like people, have a lifespan. They are conceived, born, have a childhood, adolescence, adulthood, maturity and death. This is the story of three businesses that would go through this cycle and then be caught in a death spiral that would destroy them and many of the people around them.

Small
Beginnings

They would first meet in 1976. She was a film graduate who was attending the New Orleans Film Festival. She was smart, attractive and ambitious. Born in Quebec, she had left Canada and studied in Europe before settling in London. Now, after five years of knocking around, she would meet the film festival's organizer, Ron Weinberg, an American who had more interest in organizing and money than he did in film. From the moment they met he had an interest in Micheline Charest, this film fancier, and in days they were making plans for their future together. They would move to New York and before six months went by they started a business named Cinar Films and began to distribute foreign language films to art cinemas.

The business was run by circumstance more than strategy. They struggled to live in a very expensive city with little or no money. They were forced by market necessity into animation, and they purchased foreign cartoons, dubbing them in English, and selling short animated features. They didn't know or have experience in their newfound field, but it paid the bills. Keeping their heads above water was their main preoccupation. After seven years of struggle, they finally decided to leave New York and move to a place where the expenses could be lower and they might have a chance to survive.

In 1984 they would become parents. They would move to Montreal, back to Charest's native province, where the business climate was waiting to embrace aspiring filmmakers. The Canadian government was subsidizing the country's film industry, which lived in the perpetual shadow of the American film industry that loomed across the border. With tax reductions, grants and subsidies the government intended to help fledgling companies like Cinar survive and thrive. Across the U.S. border in the mid-eighties there was a proliferation of cable television that had no precedent. With new channels and networks surfacing constantly, there was a serious need for programming and a big opportunity for production houses. When market need meets talent and solid capital, magic can be the result.

Some of their first breakthroughs were with Nickelodeon for production deals, then with other cable broadcasters. Working with Japanese and American partners in 1987, Cinar Films would produce *The Wizard of Oz* narrated by Margot Kidder. Cinar in this era would establish itself as a producer of nonviolent children's programming. This position would find huge support with

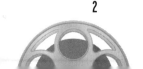

the industry press and critics and serve the company well into the future. While *The Wizard of Oz* venture would be helpful in establishing the company, it didn't make it an industry phenomenon. That would come in the form of an eight-year-old boy aardvark. Back in 1976, while Weinberg and Charest were first meeting in New Orleans, Marc Brown was creating a hugely successful picture book character named Arthur, who, along with his sister D.W., would entertain, teach values, and help kids all over North America to fall asleep at night. Brown resisted all attempts to have Arthur become a television character. "I just knew that in no time they'd have him carry a weapon in his backpack," he offered.

In 1994, eighteen years after Arthur's first appearance, WGBH Boston, a huge Public Broadcasting Services affiliate, persuaded Brown that Arthur could be done respectfully and appropriately. WGBH was PBS' largest programming producer. Carol Greenwald represented the affiliate, and once Brown was on board, the work began in earnest to find a producer who could make good on the claim. A global search began and Greenwald and Brown traveled worldwide visiting production houses. Finally, they would settle on the winner: the Montreal firm headed by Ron Weinberg and Micheline Charest would produce *Arthur*. Their reputation in the industry was now firmly in place.

The show would be an unmitigated success, winning Daytime Emmy awards in 1998 and 1999. *Arthur* would be the most popular preschool series in the United States, and Charest's creative genius and ability to take children's books and transform them into popular, nonviolent television programs would earn her celebrity status. Cinar was now supplying programming in 40 languages to over

150 countries, and they boasted more programming on television in France than any other producer in the world. The productions now included *The Busy World of Richard Scarry, The Adventures of Paddington Bear, Are You Afraid of the Dark?* and *Caillou.* Associated with Viacom, Sony, Time Warner and PolyGram, the company was a true powerhouse. Cinar went public in 1993, and by 1999 Weinberg and Charest's stake in Cinar was worth $151 million and they owned 1.5 billion (CAD) of the children's television market.

Smart
and Flexible

Whenever she arrived at work, Micheline Charest would sweep in and turn heads, never one to quietly find her place. Her outfits, her flamboyance, her confident walk, her loud voice, her vivacious laugh, her fragrances . . . they all got attention. She was Micheline Charest, one of the most powerful women in the entertainment industry; in her early forties, she was bright, energetic, beautiful and clever. *Arthur* was now one of the world's favorite preschool cartoons and more creations like him were on the drawing boards. Cinar was bustling, often referred to as the "Disney of Canada." Charest and her husband, Ron Weinberg, were its founders and primary owners. The offers to take the company public had poured in and the offerings had been very successful. They were now powerful, creative and very, very rich.

Charest was deeply involved in the creation side. She could have strong opinions: "What is this goofy idea? Arthur would never do that! Why would you even show me this? Arthur wouldn't look over the other students' shoulders; he wouldn't cheat, even in jest. That's just not him. We need to know our character as if he were in the room with us, like we grew up with him. Do you know, I have some friends that are so close to me that I can finish their sentences or they can finish mine. Do you follow me? Do you understand?"

Micheline was as direct, as nurturing, but as firm as she could be with the young art director who had developed the newest episode of Arthur.

"The best way to think of it is that while we all have flaws and certainly Arthur does, too, the flaws are flaws in judgment, not flaws of character. So, Arthur would never cheat, steal or lie. His values wouldn't let him. We all make errors in judgment, but those are forgivable. Are we together on this?"

"Yes, Ms. Charest," was the quick response. Arthur was one of the world's leading cartoon characters, appearing in 60 countries throughout the world, and was one more powerful messaging tool for the dynamic and successful Micheline Charest.

They had always wanted to be rich, but hard work, creativity and commitment don't always lead to wealth. The legend was that they worked out of their car in the early days; they sacrificed and scrimped, proud of their work, proud of the recognition, but not proud of their payday . . . not yet. They had always run the business like a private company, having the company pay any expenses that could reasonably be charged to it. The cars were in the company name, the maid was paid by the company and when there was a home improvement project, the company paid the bill. All their entertainment, gasoline, car repairs, clothing, gifts, travel, vacations and donations were paid for by the company. Ron would keep track of all the "smart ways" to do things and even created some ideas of his own.

Ron Weinberg was the co-CEO of Cinar. He kept track of their money carefully and when it came to making deals, he would prove to be smart, shrewd and willing to follow good advice. Many who met him found him to be quiet and somewhat enigmatic, but everyone felt he was smart. He could calculate numbers quickly and accurately; he kept track of things like a librarian. From the first days of his partnership with Micheline, he would defer on creative issues and she would defer on business, but neither of them was incompetent in the other's field.

The Canadian government granted tax credits to companies like Cinar if they used Canadian writers, rather than Americans or people of other nationalities. Ron liked this idea, but Micheline wasn't as impressed with Canadian talent as she was with American talent. No problem, Ron would figure out a "smart way" to get both. He would get advice on financial matters from one of the world's largest accounting firms, Ernst & Young, and they would learn quickly that their client liked to learn "smart ways" to make money, defer money, invest money and hide money.

One of the things Ron was looking for in his world of finance was anyone who knew how to bend the rules of accounting. Ron was looking for a "smart bender." Ernst

& Young was proud to supply Cinar a stream of these talented young people. They would audition by being on the audit staff, where Ron would be in a perfect position to assess and judge how smart and bendable they were. The most flexible would eventually be recruited to move on staff with Cinar, where their talents could be honed and developed in one of the most creative environments in Canada. They were now the "Finance Group" of Cinar and Cinar was one of the most flexible, successful and creative companies in the nation — a nation home to the Cirque du Soleil.

Hasanain Panju would emerge from the Ernst & Young spawning stream and rise to be Weinberg's anointed Chief Financial Officer (CFO). He had that rare combination of traits that tends to elude accounting types. While he was certainly good with numbers, bright and hardworking, he was also charismatic, articulate and morally flexible . . . an especially desirable trait at Cinar. Panju had learned through his audit experience that he and Weinberg could work together, and work together very well. Surrounding Panju in the Finance Group were Henry Rosenhek, Lucy Caterina and Andrew Porporino, all former Ernst & Young auditors, none of them as talented as contortionists as Panju or Weinberg, but they were definitely double jointed.

Ron had called the meeting, and they were seated around the table in the company's boardroom. The room was not typically used for staff meetings, but Ron felt this session was special, not business as usual. Over the previous months Cinar's fortunes had shifted from "up-and-coming" to "we've made it." The cash was rolling in from Operations and the brokerage firms. Up to now it was Micheline who set the tone and ran the staff meet-

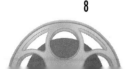

ings for the creative groups. But now Ron actually had a talented, distinguished staff of his own in Finance. They were no longer the accounting department; they would now be known as Finance.

"The rule is simple; we don't pay taxes unless there is absolutely no choice. We apply for every grant, program or incentive there is, and if we don't get them, we figure out how to. Finance departments make money; accounting departments just keep track of it. You're in Finance, and we will make money! When we make a deal, I expect us to win and I don't mean lose or tie, I mean win. I expect discounts from everyone, including those who don't give them; I expect us to make money off of our money and that means we pay when we have to pay . . . that's have to pay! We have moved to the land of multiples where every penny we wrangle is multiplied as earnings per share and finds us more. This is exciting stuff, folks. You're in the right room, at the right time." Weinberg sounded more like a football coach than a senior executive, but he meant every word and the audience now knew what he expected. He expected Finance to make money . . . what a fresh perspective.

Panju was the High Priest of this methodology. In short order he would begin to develop ways for Finance to make money. The terms of the initial public offering (IPO) had come together, and it became increasingly clear that the negotiations had tipped things to Weinberg and Charest's advantage. When the dust settled, they would retain two-thirds of the voting stock of the company, through preferred shares of voting stock. They would remain firmly in control of Cinar even though they owned only twelve percent of the equity through common shares. So now with cash filling the coffers from the IPO, and Operations unable to swallow anything close to the $150 million (IPO) pill, Finance needed to go to work. But the big question remaining was, "Who are we making it for?" After all, since the public was really a minority position just riding along at thirty-five percent of the voting shares, things hadn't really changed much from the days when Cinar was a private company owned by Ron and Micheline. The High Priest had some ideas.

Ron and Hasanain were at lunch in a tony old Montreal restaurant, only a few blocks from their office. As they enjoyed a light appetizer, they began to talk quietly. Weinberg would begin.

"Micheline has a few things she really cares about and I'd like your thoughts on how to get them done. She wants a new house in Magog; it might require some furnishings and a staff. Any thoughts?"

"That one's easy. I'll arrange financing from the company and we'll put the staff on the payroll," Panju enthused.

"There are some car issues."

"No problem. Consider it done. What's next?"

"We need to have some funds available for acquisition," Ron continued.

"Now, that's something we can do and I've got some additional thoughts on that one," Panju said.

"We're going to be sitting on a huge pile of cash. What can we do to get a decent return?" Weinberg asked.

"I'll have a report and some ideas for you. Anything else right now?"

"No thanks, Has."

With those issues on the table, they changed their conversation to food as their entrées arrived.

Mario Ricci was a young chartered accountant on his way to his second interview with Cinar. The day was warm, the kind of humid day in Montreal where the number of pretty girls on Saint-Catherine becomes incalculable. The city with the second largest student population in North America, the city with a legal drinking age of 18, the only city in North America where the women seem to dress for men rather than other women, was blooming. Mario had worked for his current employer for three years; he had endured tantrums, humiliations and chronic headaches. He had resolved to leave, but he still held an odd fascination for his boss, Lino Matteo, a bellowing ogre who displayed streaks of brilliance between bouts of dysfunctional behavior, as he gobbled entrepreneurs and stifled creativity.

Ricci was still single and his head swung like a gate as he passed the pretty girls. This was one of those years when the fashion was short skirts, and nowhere are they shorter than in Montreal on a hot day. Was he ready to accept the position if they offered it today, or was he just running out the door because of Matteo's last round of abuse? "Well," he thought, "everybody there is from Ernst & Young, so they'll probably never offer me the position anyway." Two hotties passed Ricci, smiling and laughing as they walked. He reflexively turned not only his head, but his whole upper torso as they walked by. They noticed his movement and started to giggle, knowing full well their effect on the young accountant. He had been so distracted he had actually walked right by the front door of the 12-story Cinar building.

When he walked into Panju's office for interview number two, he felt confident and sure. Panju offered coffee and Ricci accepted.

"Your references checked out very well, Mario. The only thing that concerns me is that you're an accountant."

Ricci was taken aback. "Isn't that what you wanted?"

"So the ad said. But what we really want are people ready to work in a finance department that makes money. We're not accountants who keep track of what everybody else is doing; we're a profit center for our owners and shareholders — that's Ron and Micheline. Do you think you could be creative? Because we consider our work as creative as what the writers and cartoonists do. Could you fit into that?"

Ricci's mind swept back to his last humiliation, a dressing down because he had released a check at the time it had been promised to a client. The action had taken away his boss's leverage over the client, and Matteo had become furious.

"Mario?" Lino asked. "Did you release that check to Bob?"

"Yeah, this morning," was Mario's response.

"Don't tell me that. Why would you do that?"

"You'd signed it and we had promised it to him, so I released it."

"Well, now you need to un-release it," Lino said emphatically.

"Un-release it! What the hell is that? Un-release it?"

"Get it back. I don't want him to have it yet."

Ricci knew full well that if he stopped payment on the check, it would cause Bob's payroll to bounce and his payments to equipment suppliers to fall through, leaving Bob with a huge mess that he might not be able to clean up. Ricci's mouth went dry as he thought of the consequences.

Suddenly, Lino's patience with the conversation was

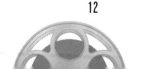

over. "Mario, don't do a fucking thing. I'll do it. It'll make me feel good to stop payment on that check. From now on, just because I've signed the check and you're supposed to release it, doesn't mean you should release it. Do you understand me?"

"Yes."

Ricci had watched his boss march away, knowing that within minutes Lino would issue the stop payment. Bob's books would be in disorder for weeks. His payroll bounced and his employees lost confidence in Bob as their own chequing accounts piled up overdrafts. He lost one supplier and rolled with heartburn in his bed the next two nights, wishing he had never met Lino P. Matteo.

Did Ricci want to get some distance from stuff like that? Sure he did.

"I can be creative and I love to make people money," he offered. Ricci's coffee arrived and they talked for another half hour. The offer was made on the spot and Ricci would now be the new controller of Cinar and the only guy on the block not from Ernst & Young. He would need to tell Lino he was heading out. Easier said than done, but do it he must.

Mario would be leaving his job as controller of Mount Real Corporation, an Alberta Stock Exchange–listed company that was, according to their annual report, a "Financial Management Services Company." Exactly what that meant required a lengthy explanation. What Mario had figured out during his tenure was that it included some loan-sharking, oppression (squeezing owners out) and factoring (high-interest, inventory-type financing). Lino Matteo was a driven entrepreneur who could control groups or individuals with his wile, wit, size, unrelenting verbiage and downright intimidation.

He was hard on employees, tougher on his clients and abusive to professional advisers. He was a demanding husband and father, but faithful and caring. He had built Mount Real into a fast-growing little company whose stock was trading well and whose value was moving up. He had clients in secondhand car sales, telemarketing, telephone equipment, vitamins and nutraceuticals; he was their business adviser, administrator, bookkeeper and lender.

Ricci was very nervous about giving his notice. Lino hadn't known he was looking for another job and he was the kind of guy who couldn't imagine why anyone wouldn't want to work with him for their entire career. There was never any telling how Matteo might react to news of something beyond his control. It could be with a cool rational mind, philosophical chagrin or a maniacal outburst. This time it was philosophical chagrin. Lino wished Mario well, invited him back to work or visit, promised lifelong friendship and said it was the best thing for him. Ricci left the meeting relieved and surprised things had gone so well.

Ricci settled into his new office and position quickly, though the cultural differences would be dramatic. The tantrums seemed far away, and the cash shortages non-existent, but arrogance and elitism were not qualities exclusive to Lino. In no time it became clear that instead of one prima donna, Cinar had several: Weinberg, Charest and Panju. Clearest of all was that there was a lot of money around this new place, and everyone wanted to know what to do with it.

"Mario, do you have any contacts in the Caribbean?" The question Panju asked seemed direct and simple enough.

"Why, yes I do," Ricci answered. "Would you like to meet them?"

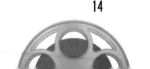

It was that simple. In only a few seconds, one question and one brief answer would put into motion the beginning of a story that would affect tens of thousands of lives and billions of dollars. Ricci and Panju made plans to go to Nassau. They would golf, swim and meet two men.

Enter Norshield

The city is a strange dichotomy of rich meets poor. Nassau is a city of 211,000 where most citizens are educated, well dressed, churchgoing and black. The island is fairly small, only 50 miles long and 20 miles wide, but as long as the Castro regime remains in Cuba, Americans continue to go to Nassau on cruise ships and to gamble; the economy is okay, employment is okay and the place is okay. But if that balance is substantially upset and the cruise ships stop visiting, or Atlantis (the giant casino) loses its allure for gamblers, the island could become a destitute spit of sand in the beautiful Caribbean.

Ricci and Panju would arrive with golf clubs and briefcases; they would schedule only one meeting at 155 Bay

Street, the offices of Norshield International. Norshield International was the location of Tom Muir and Bob Daviault, affiliates of Norshield Financial Group of Montreal. The two expatriates of Canada were now permanent residents of the Bahamas, and through Norshield International they had a couple of small hedge funds named Globe-X Canadiana managed by Norshield Financial Group in Montreal.

The pair were chain-smoking, coffee guzzling and talkative. Tom was likable, Bob clever. They both had the ability to be trustworthy and dishonest at the same time, a difficult thing to accomplish under any circumstances. But that's exactly what someone wants when they are trying to hide money offshore: trustworthy and dishonest. Mario would smell the smoke that unavoidably accompanied the two wherever they went. He would shake Bob's hand first, then Tom's and introduce his new boss, Hasanain Panju, to the pair. The meeting wouldn't last long. A creative, flexible guy like Panju could read this situation very quickly and bend it into a configuration he could understand and explain. Now it was time to play some golf, after which the four of them would never again be in the same room together. Bob and Panju would meet again before they departed for Montreal, just to double check a few things and test out some financial gymnastics.

Back in Montreal Panju gave Ron a demonstration of how flexible he really could be. No CFO of a major public company was more flexible than Panju in the summer of 1998.

"Ron, these guys in the Bahamas are worth testing out. They're up and operating, but not so big or successful that they don't need us or that their creativity is all gone. They're honest enough that I trust 'em, and not so honest that we can't do business. I want to start out doing some transactions that are called 'back-to-back' deals . . ."

"How do they work?" Weinberg interrupted.

"They're basically back-to-back transactions where we send down company money, open an account or a series of accounts, put the money into the account and then these guys loan it back to us. We invest where we want and keep the profits of the investments in the Bahamas where they're tax free. We can pay off the loan, close the account and get our money back whenever we want, but we'll keep the profits offshore. Do you follow?"

"Oh yeah, I got it and I like it. Simple, legal, clever. How much are we starting with?"

"I think $3 million. We can add to it as we want."

"Heads we win, tails we win," Weinberg remarked.

"That's what I think, too," Panju said.

"Good."

"I've got something else," Panju continued. "There's a company in Israel — EduSoft. I have it set up so that we can buy it. We'll buy it ourselves, you, me and Micheline. We can pick it up for less than a million; the sellers have agreed to stay on the board. I think we should partner with them for a while and see if there's a fit. If there is, maybe we should have Cinar buy it. If not, we'll sell it to someone else."

"What business is it in?"

"Children's education."

"Perfect. That's the right business for us. I like the idea of doing these kinds of deals out of the country — Nassau, Tel Aviv — very good. How are you coming with the offshore trust?"

"Very well. The Bermuda trusts are all set, and Micheline's Magog house is purchased."

"I think Finance may make more money than Operations this year!"

Ron and Hasanain had both been under pressure to make acquisitions. After all, part of the reason for going public was to generate capital for such deals. The problem, or better stated the real situation, was that Finance was doing so well with their own operations that they could meet their forecasts without the acquisitions, so it created the perfect opportunity to rationalize the EduSoft deal in Israel. After all, they'd all agreed that if someday the company ever did have trouble, they'd be the first to step up and loan the company money, if it needed it.

Two days later Panju poked his head around the corner of Weinberg's door. "Ron, can I see you a minute?" Weinberg was at his desk studying numbers and lost in thought.

"Sure, come on in. What's up, Has?"

"I've been working on year-end and doing my best to project everything out. If you've got a few minutes, I'd like to take you through my thoughts and processes, to see what you think."

"Fire away," Ron said.

"The analysts are projecting our earnings to end up around $21 million plus for the year. Now, I think we're likely to beat that number."

"That's great. I wasn't sure if we could," Ron said.

"Well, that's part of my point, Ron. I think we'll be north of $25 million, but as I work my way through it, I don't think that will bump the stock meaningfully. It will just be a higher outcome. So, I've been working out some smoothing strategies, and I think I've got an idea that could work very well, if our friends in Nassau cooperate."

"What have you got?"

"Well, think of it like this. We do about $50 million a year in U.S. dollars, maybe even more. So, we're constantly at risk as it applies to currency fluctuations. It would make sense for us to hedge against that risk by taking positions in Canadian/U.S. dollar currency hedges. Do you follow me?"

"I think so."

"Well, let me show you a sheet I've worked out as an example over the last year. This sheet shows you what would have happened if someone had a $50 million hedge position on the currency fluctuations. Do you see how sometimes the account would be up and sometimes it would be down?"

"Yes, I see it," Weinberg answered. "Like in June, the account is up almost $2 million; in August it's down almost $3 million. Oh yeah, okay, here in October, look at that, it's down over $4 million."

"Exactly! That's actually a date I've been working from — October 29th, to be precise. If, on October 29th, whoever was holding the position decided to get out, they would owe $4,464,117.43. Do you see why?"

"Yeah, I see it."

"Okay, so what would happen is the people closing the account would immediately have to pay $4,464,117.43 to the traders they were dealing with. Now, let me tie together the smoothing of our earnings per share with this hedge idea. The analysts expect twenty-one mil in earnings. We can deliver over twenty-five, but there's no great reason to do it. So, we can defer $4 or $5 million to next year, or we could reduce earnings by $4 or $5 million because of costs we've incurred. As I said, it makes sense for us to take hedges on currency. From this example you can see how the currencies worked to our advantage as a business. This year we actually made $4,464,117.43 on currency gains by October 29th, by doing business."

"Are you suggesting that our friends in the Bahamas may have to take a hedge position for us this year?"

"Exactly! They may have been hedging all year for us. We tell them to stop as of October 29th; that would mean Cinar would owe them $4,464,117.43, which we would need to pay right away. Now, my guess is that they'd be more than glad to put some of that money into our 2950995 Canada Inc. account or Killington, or any place else we want it, and let them keep ten percent for their trouble."

Weinberg shook his head. "Wow, this is a tight little idea, very creative! We hit our earnings projections right on the nose. Doing currency hedges makes sense. This year we may not have needed it. We pay for the insurance just like we should, but if our friends down there want to help us, they move the money to our other accounts, no tax effect."

"You've got it," Panju nodded.

"What next?"

"I need to talk to our friends, see if they're game."

It was a short, startling meeting. Panju would call Bob, who immediately caught on to the concept.

"I can generate the paperwork to support the position, no problem. You'll need to send me the letter calling off the position. I'll generate the invoice for settlement. Consider it done."

That night Ron was very cheerful at dinner, so much so that Micheline even asked, "Did you have a special day or something?"

"Hasanain had some really good thoughts and the year end is coming together. You know, I think we'll meet the analysts' earnings projections." He grinned. "So, I'm in a good mood. How was your day?"

As he lay in bed that night Ron realized that not only was this smoothing strategy brilliant, it was something they could do year after year. It wasn't a one-time trick. This was a perfect way to get $4 million tax-free dollars offshore and no one would be the wiser. What made it even better was that the company actually made the $4 million plus on the currency so nobody, in Ron's mind, was out the money. After all, he reasoned, the analysts projected only $21 million in earnings, so let's keep the analysts happy.

When the boys in the Bahamas, Tom Muir and Bob Daviault, got word that there was $20 million on the way to "try out some of the FOREX deals," they both lit up cigarettes and changed from coffee to beer. (The FOREX transactions were a way to hedge currency risk that Cinar might encounter in its normal course of business between the Canadian and U.S. dollars.) This was the biggest day of their lives. After they were finished, they called John Xanthoudakis at Norshield financial in Montreal. John was a self-made rising star in the now emerging Canadian hedge fund business. Arguably one of the most successful innovators and the closest business associate of Muir and Daviault, Xanthoudakis would manage all their funds through Norshield and the success of one would determine the success of the other. On the other hand, if John X sneezed, both Bob and Tom would catch cold. In his early forties, John was movie-star good looking, clean-cut, didn't smoke, rarely drank, worked hard and was a philanthropist at heart.

The boys would tell John about the rapidly developing deal, and his excitement would almost exceed theirs.

Everyone knew this could lead to more and more transactions, because it would work . . . no doubt about it.

There is a tavern in Nassau called Billy Bongs — a must-stop for Australians, New Zealanders and Brits who find their way onto the island. Many arrive by boat, working as crew members on the various sailing ships that wander into Nassau harbor. Mick Jagger is said to frequent the place, as does Rod Stewart if he's in the area. The food is just fine, the bar has character and the beer is cold. There is a sign in Billy Bongs that says simply, "Welcome to Nassau, the home to thieves, smugglers and pirates."

How a
Slugger Feels

The transactions worked just as advertised. While Cinar appeared to lose money, someone would make money, and in this case the winners were the founders of the company, Ron and Micheline, and their High Priest, Hasanain Panju. Throughout this period there was always a good business reason to do the deals because Cinar was exposed to currency fluctuations between the U.S. and Canadian dollars. It was prudent. It's always difficult for corporate directors to keep track of a company's "goings on." At best, being a director is a part-time position in a fast-moving, constantly changing, full-time world. The brightest and best directors can only hope to get an overview and to maintain a sense of the pace in the firms they direct. Cinar was even more complex because, while the company was publicly traded, it was still controlled, managed and owned primarily by Weinberg and Charest. While most public companies are criticized for their senior management having minimal investment, at Cinar the issue was just the opposite. This company had been run as a very private business for 15 years, but now that it had more shareholders and was public, things hadn't changed much. The directors would meet and listen to management presentations, receive their stipends, accept their stock options, smile at the annual meeting and accept accolades on the company's behalf at the country club.

Hasanain and Weinberg willingly accepted the passivity of the board. They rightfully felt their job was to run the business, and run it they would. "Need to know" was the operative phrase; if you didn't "need to know" you weren't told. Matters like brokerage accounts, hedge fund accounts and bank accounts were left to management. The board liked to think of themselves as "strategic big thinkers"; the details were for the management team. As the per-share price moved to over $32 and Cinar's market capitalization expanded to close to a billion dollars, who could doubt that this formula was working? It was obvious that everything was on track.

There may be no charity in Montreal that brings together the city's philanthropic elite like the Children's Hospital. Captains of industry, renowned entrepreneurs and hockey players current and past — the benefactors pour out for this gala. Beautiful women in designer gowns, with capped teeth and breast implants, find their tables as the evening begins. On this evening, Weinberg and Charest would arrive in a limo and Micheline would make one of the entrances she was famous for. She was a real Quebecker, but more than that she was one of the world-wide entertainment industry's most important women, a fact not lost on others in attendance. Also arriving were John and Kathy Xanthoudakis — he in his tux, she in a beautiful gown that reminded everyone why this self-made Greek tycoon had fallen for this mercurial Italian beauty. In the crowded room, John would see Weinberg, excuse himself and make his way across the room to introduce himself. While they didn't really know each other, they were certainly doing business together, and both of them were pleased with the relationship thus far.

"Ron, nice to see you," John said with a smile and held out his hand.

"John! I was hoping to see you tonight," Weinberg said as he shook his hand. They moved quickly, the way powerful people do, to a quiet spot against the wall where it would be hard for any well-wishers to invade, and began to talk.

"John, we're pleased with the transactions that we've been doing in the Bahamas, and we could be interested in expanding. Any thoughts?"

"I'm happy you like what you're up to. I definitely have ideas about other funds and things that could be done. I'll talk to Tom and Bob about how we could do more. What range were you thinking?" Weinberg was silent for a moment, and John hoped his question wasn't too pushy.

Then Ron said, "I think we'll start with another $20 million, but it could become five or six times that."

John's mind raced as he realized he was talking to the single largest client he'd ever had. The numbers bounced in his mind as he said, "I've definitely got ideas and I'll get back to you. We're ready to handle those amounts or

more. Should I follow up with you or Has?"

"Either way, we'll do this together," Weinberg responded.

When some people get good news, they prefer to savor it like a good wine: breathe deeply, sip it, roll it over their tongue and swallow slowly. There are others who pop the cork, watch the bottle overflow — like ballplayers in a locker room, they drink straight from the bottle, not caring if they spill some as they drink. With news like this, John was like the ballplayer. Leaving Kathy to fend for herself, he moved into the entryway of the hall and made a cell call to the Bahamas. "Boys, I'm at the Children's Hospital event. Weinberg's here and he's happy. I think he's ready to come in heavy . . . really heavy."

Tom and Bob were listening intently. "What does that mean, John?" Tom asked.

"Guys, it means we might have the biggest customer of our lives! I'm talking about $20 million, maybe $40, $60, $80 million or more! They like what we're doing, and I've got some ideas they'll like even more. I better get back to the event, but I wanted you to know that things are on track. Talk to you soon."

The boys looked at each other in amazement and smiled. Then Bob broke the silence and said, "This could be big . . . real big."

The rest of the night John Xanthoudakis had a special energy; he was more outgoing than usual and he actually tried to tell a few jokes at the table, something he never did. As the evening went on, he even asked Kathy to dance, something he never, ever did, and he seemed to enjoy it. John always liked fundraisers and really cared about helping people, but on this particular night it may have been more than philanthropic zeal that brought him his special energy.

Panju called the Norshield International office in Nassau and asked to check three account balances. He offered all the security codes to the voice on the Nassau end, which was slow and deliberate, with the distinct British clip that Bahamians have. Finally satisfied, the voice confirmed that Account A (Weinberg) had $3,980,000, Account B (Charest) had $3,980,000 and Account C (Panju) had $3,980,000. The FOREX back-to-backs were finished and the funds were to the benefit of Weinberg, Charest and the High Priest. Now was the time to fund the new deal tied to the Discretionary Management Agreement; the new strategy was the Enhanced Bond Yield Formula — the perfect way to park some money, get a better yield than certificates of deposit and get some juice to freshen the throat.

Panju grabbed the phone, and when Ricci picked up he said, "Mario, I need a wire transfer prepared."

"Okay, who to, how much and when?"

"Globe-X Management, $20 million USD, now."

"Got it . . . right away." Ricci sounded almost military in the way he responded.

When the wire arrived in Nassau it was almost a surprise; Globe-X, a struggling little survivor, had just landed its biggest deposit ever. To put it into perspective, the industry standard on these funds is a one percent fee to the manager (John), plus incentive of twenty percent of growth and one percent to the administrator, or in this case $200,000 to Tom and Bob. This deposit, by contrast, was equal to all their operating expenses in the previous year, and there might be more on the way. They both lit up cigarettes and made a tee time for that afternoon.

John was already successful and he had made some big deals before, but this was the biggest ever, by a wide margin. When he got the confirmation, a smile spread across his face and warmth surged through his body. This must be what a slugger feels as the ball is leaving the stadium. John had now cranked one out of the park: a $20 million account had been opened, and it could get a lot bigger. His view was from the tallest and most prestigious building in Montreal. He walked to the windows and looked out over the river and the city as if he owned it.

A Little
Help from Lino

Martin Wardman was a Brit now living in Canada, a former sprinter who, these days, liked to run with the stylish and the beautiful. He was publishing a magazine called Ocean Drive, the Canadian version of the successful fashion and lifestyle mag out of Miami, Florida. The magazine had a clean look, a European approach to fashion and was an art director's dream. Despite its success in the field, its dirty little secret was that it lost money every month and Wardman's pockets weren't deep enough to keep the ink flowing. Genteel and proper, Wardman was waiting in Lino's reception area for their first meeting. He had arrived in his Jaguar, wore a well-tailored suit and a bow tie. As he waited, he chatted with Lino's longtime receptionist, Paulina, a Portuguese immigrant who was now a real Montrealer. Then she said with a smile, "Mr. Matteo will see you now."

Wardman walked up the flight of stairs to Lino's office. He knocked and entered. Lino sat behind a large leather-covered desk; to his left was his computer table with two flat screens next to each other. Behind him was his book-case filled with books and magazines. In the other half of the office was a conference table, which he never used, a punching bag (that many people wished he would use to release his constant aggression), a wet bar and a refrigerator, which he never used either. Across from his desk were two swivel office chairs; it was his style to direct people to whichever of the two chairs he preferred them to sit in.

When you looked out the windows of this office, you saw a middle-class Italian neighborhood and all its trappings: a Couche-Tard convenience store with the east wall covered in graffiti, the Métro (subway) station and small retail stores. The building itself was a small apartment building that Lino had converted into the worldwide headquarters.

The only time Lino would not dominate a conversation was during the first ten minutes or so of a first meeting, when he really wanted to judge someone or something. This was Martin Wardman's ten minutes in the sun. He proceeded to show Lino the newest edition of his very attractive magazine; he talked about his advertisers, his budget, his promotions and his success. The problem was that no one meets with Lino unless they have a problem. And Wardman didn't seem to have any. So finally Lino broke his silence.

"Martin, I don't believe someone as successful as you has the time to come and meet me, only to tell me how successful you are. Now, my guess is that something is fucked up in this pretty little world of yours, or you'd be having tea somewhere and not be here bullshitting me. Am I right?"

Wardman nodded.

"So, what's fucked up?"

"I'm losing about fifty thousand a month and I don't know how to fund it anymore. I've been using my money, my wife's money, my investors' money. We're so close, but we're not there yet."

"Let me see your income statement," Lino said and Wardman handed it over. With a highlighter he began to mark up the pages and in less than five minutes, Lino looked up and said, "You should only be losing about twenty grand a month, not fifty. If you agree to the changes I've marked, that's all you will lose, and I'll fund the losses."

Wardman reached for the marked-up sheet. "Can I see it?" he asked.

"Are you going to do what I'm saying or not?" Lino countered.

"Well, I don't know what that is, do I?" Wardman said in a very British way.

"Look. You want money, I've got money; you need help, I'm offering help. If you want to debate it, or you think this is a consulting session where you review my plan, then get out your checkbook and pay me for my advice, before I show it to you." There was silence for a moment. "Now what do you want, help or no help?"

"I want help," Wardman whispered.

"Then do you agree to follow my plan?" Lino asked directly.

"I guess I do," Wardman responded.

"Good. Here's where you're at. Cut two of the sales-

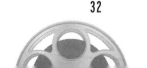

people, can the editor's assistant, throw out the reception-ist, tell the editor he's going to pay half of the next two issues, chop the writing budget, stop buying all these lunches and tell the other salespeople they've got three months or they're all fired, too. By the way, your own salary is cut in half; that will make it easier for you to cut the editor's salary. Now, you can also fire the bookkeeper and the accounting firm because from now on we'll be doing all of that work here. I'll be signing the checks and I'll cover the shortfalls. Everything understood?"

Wardman wiggled in the swivel chair. He could feel his ass getting tighter and tighter; it was like there was a big screw in the chair and the screw was going right up his butt. "I understand," Wardman said. He had his elbow on Lino's desk, his head resting on the palm of his hand. He looked like he had a headache, a butt ache and indigestion all at once. But this deal would save his magazine.

"Can I see the sheet?" Martin asked.

"Sure," was the reply.

When Wardman told his wife and investors about the deal, they were all relieved. The magazine would survive. Implementing the other changes would be harder; he'd do them one at a time — the cuts, the layoffs, the threats — but he'd do them all. He had to because he had just agreed to be in business with the most consuming person he had ever met, and he had just been consumed.

Looking Pretty
Good Around Here

As the Cinar treasury swelled, placing money where it would have maximum effect and multipurpose flexibility became the priority. Frequent wires would arrive in Nassau. Some of the money would go into investments; some would pay redemptions; while other amounts would pay expenses, fees and commissions. The boys were riding a big wave and they knew it. They had never had so much, they had never been so liquid. At this point, the amount had exceeded $80 million, a sum of money beyond their wildest dreams.

With their newfound success came new social responsibilities, like a new country club membership and the requisite golf schedule that comes with it. The handicaps move down, the bar tabs move up, the visibility in the community increases and the time in the office decreases.

It was 10:30 on a Tuesday morning. Nassau traffic is unusually bad for a small island because all the roads are single lane, and all the traffic runs in one direction. While Tom would usually arrive at 9:00 a.m. sharp and then smoke cigarettes and drink coffee, Bob would normally arrive after the rush hour. In the summer, the Bahamian heat never lets up. The heat and humidity hover around 29°C and eighty-five percent humidity. When it gets too hot, it usually rains, which might knock the temperature down a little, but increases the humidity. By 10:30, the cruise ships are usually in and the cycle begins as tourists pour off the ship to shop, lunch, haggle and visit. The economy needs these daily transfusions from up to five cruise ships per day.

Paradise Island had evolved over the years from a hard-to-reach little island within sight of downtown, with one Holiday Inn, to a resort complex of immense size and stature. Atlantis, the hotel-casino resort, is now the prominent architectural feature on the Nassau skyline. From the water, the city or the hilltop, Atlantis beckons to every eye and pocket. It is the largest employer in the Bahamas. Being an employee is the only way a local can visit the place: it's off limits to residents. Many of the cruise ship gang rush to Atlantis to see the Caribbean's largest casino.

Bob strolled into the office, said "Morning, Tom," and sat down. They both lit up. "What a night last night. I should've quit that game at nine, and didn't get out till one," Bob whined.

"Oh, I knew you were in trouble when you started raising those bets. I just smiled and snuck out the back door," Tom said.

"Wow, I look around at all the things we've got to do here and I realize we need some help. Accounting-wise I'm running behind, and there are some audits to catch up on, but mostly I'm worried about some of the new requirements they're laying in down here in the Bahamas. Have you talked to John about personnel needs?"

"No, I haven't," Tom said.

"I wonder if we shouldn't give him a call and go through it."

Within minutes John Xanthoudakis was on the phone.

"John, we're falling behind down here on some of the administration and accounting. We really need some help, and we might need as many as five or six more people," Bob said.

"Guys, how are you going to manage all those people?" John asked. Good question. Tom pressed the mute button.

"Hell if I know, Bob. I don't have the time to manage all those people," Tom blurted. He released the mute button and Bob spoke up.

"John, we need an administrator to do that, someone who can back office this place."

"I thought that's what *you* went down there to do, Bob," John responded.

Bob grabbed a smoke and lit up. "That was the idea a long time ago, John, but things have changed. This place is now handling a lot more money and we need some heavy duty administration."

"Let me think about it, guys. But for now, keep up to date and I'll work on it."

"Oh, don't worry, John, we'll keep up, but let's move on it 'cause we're getting busy." Bob hung up the phone.

"What time do you tee off today, Bob?"

"Noon. I've got to get going. See you at the club."

A few days later John let the boys know that he had an idea. His sister-in-law, Maria Castrechini, had been working in the Norshield office in Montreal. She was a buttoned-up ball buster who could run things and keep the boys in their comfort zones. Maria was willing to move south, but not without some incentive. She got better money than in Montreal, a bonus, a wardrobe allowance, moving costs, a new sports car, a private office and she could pick the staff she wanted. With Maria on the way, the boys' worries were over. They could do what they did best: entertain clients, entertain their friends and entertain themselves. Maria would do the rest.

A couple of weeks later, Bob returned to the office from a lunch at the city's largest hotel, the British Colonial. One of the city's oldest and best, this place had hosted presidents and pirates, executives and scoundrels. What had caught Bob's attention was that they were now about to build an office tower next to the hotel; in no time it would become the most prestigious address in the city. The views would be of the bay where the cruise ships turn around as they move into their mooring posts in the Nassau harbor. The beaches below were beautiful, and there had never been a building this tall in Nassau.

"Tom, I've got an idea." They both lit up.

"What's up, man?"

"Do you know that they're building a new office tower next to the British Colonial?"

"I heard something about it," Tom responded.

"Well, they're doing it, Tom. They've got a construction crane landed from the mainland. This thing is a go!" Bob said. He sounded excited about it.

"Do we care? What's so important?" Tom asked.

"This will be *the* address in this town for business.

Anyway, I think we should go and take a look. And I've got a special tour set up for you, Tom. As soon as the crane is up, they're willing to give you a ride up to what your office view would be if we decided to move!"

"Really? Hey, Bob, I don't know that I want to move, but I'm willing to go look, that's for sure." They put out their cigarettes and went their separate ways.

The crane was up and functional. The construction "supe" wasn't used to having his tools used for sales promotions, but Nassau had never had a project like this one before, so what the hell. The British Colonial was a business hotel and resort complex combined, the kind of hotel where a businessman or a money smuggler would stay and bring his wife or girlfriend for a few days while he worked or played, or both. The property enjoyed a big swimming pool and easy access to the beach for swimming and water sports. The views from the hotel were beautiful. They included the view of the bay, the view of the harbored cruise ships, views around the swimming pool where the wives and girlfriends gathered, and views of the beach, where at the north end the European guests would set up to sunbathe topless.

As the supervisor loaded Tom into the crane, the ever-curious executive packed his binoculars in one pocket and his camera in the other. As he rose into the air, he lit his cigarette and began to enjoy the view. Nassau's tallest building was five stories. He had now risen far above that threshold and was nearing the tenth story. As they reached the spot where the new Norshield International headquarters would be, the crane halted and Tom began to take pictures. He photographed the bay . . . it was beautiful! He photographed the cruise ships in the harbor . . . very impressive! He photographed the swimming pool with its

LOOKING PRETTY GOOD AROUND HERE

iridescent blue water and he photographed the beach below. As he did, he almost dropped his camera. He slowly raised the binoculars to his eyes and there in a line, lying on beach chairs, were two rows of topless European sunbathers. He studied the group slowly and carefully. Reality was now setting in. This could be the view from his office window every day . . . every single day!

Within days, the leases were prepared. It would be a while before they could move; after all, the building wasn't even built yet. It would be built on "Bahamas time," so there was no certainty of schedule. The boys signed anyway. When the building was ready, they'd be ready. That day another wire arrived: about $8 million more. That was a good reason to play golf, so they did.

When you first see Maria Castrechini, you feel her more than see her. You feel her energy, her intensity. What you see is a fortyish, sharp-featured woman with blond hair and black roots. Men notice her breasts right away and that's not an accident. Very little with Maria is an accident. She chooses her outfits carefully, her shoes thoughtfully, her accessories impeccably. She chose her furnishings lavishly and she would pick her staff selectively. She was demanding, loyal, hardworking and fun-loving. Maria dove into the backlog unflinchingly.

She seemed to understand that since people had now sent down almost $200 million they would probably want someone to keep track of who was owed what and when. She was having a sudden glimpse of the obvious: a financial firm should have books and records, and account for the money that was received. She knew that even in the Bahamas, there might be some regulations about how you did it. Maria could smoke with the boys, joke with the boys, swear with the boys, but she wasn't "one of the boys" because if she was "one of the boys," she couldn't control them, and that's what she was there to do.

There Are Two
Sides to Every Story

When Lino Matteo got angry, there was rarely a definitive sign or sequence to indicate it was happening or about to happen. Something would just snap, and at that moment anyone in the same building could hear, feel or sense that Lino had popped his cork, blown his lid, hit the ceiling and that the full fury of his wrath was being delivered on the unfortunate soul seated in front of him.

"Are you stupid?" he would shout rhetorically. "No, you're not stupid, you're playing with me. You think I'm stupid! Well, I'm not stupid and you're going to learn not to treat me like I'm stupid. You want to play with me? Great, I like to play."

Reaching into his desk drawer he would grab the carpenter's hammer he kept there.

"Now, put your hand on my desk," and whether the hand was there or not, he would begin to pound on the desk with the hammer — with his full strength, all 250 pounds of him. "Put your hand on this desk, you coward, put it on the desk! You don't like to play games? You don't like games anymore? Get out while you can still walk! Get out, get out of my sight. Forget about your payroll, it's not going out. Forget about your payables, I'm holding them. Forget about your tax payments because nothing is getting paid until we sort this out!" All the while he's pounding for emphasis. Now he slowly stands and, toning it down one notch, says, "I told you to get out while you can, now move, move, move!" Invariably, the recipient would move, move, move.

The office staff couldn't feign ignorance. No doors are made to contain the sounds or the fury that was just put forth. The reception area on the floor below wouldn't be spared; it was right below his office. The pounding would reverberate through the desk and into the joints and trusses holding the building together.

The awkwardness following one of these incidents was complete. Most adults hadn't seen such a tantrum since their childhood and then it wasn't delivered by a 6'2" 250-pound, thirty-something multimillionaire. For most, it would take days to shake off the tension. Some never would; they would just pretend it didn't happen or else plot how to escape Lino. For some people, neither alternative was open to them because they were just too far in. Their business and its future were hopelessly intertwined with this curious character, a genius at times, a controlling megalomaniac at others. Lino never met a strong person

he didn't want to control or a weak person he didn't want to demean.

His favorite targets were people who had advanced degrees; he regarded them as intellectually inferior.

To his attorney, Michael Maloney, he would say over the speakerphone, "Michael, now don't talk, don't think, don't waste my time, just listen to me. Just ignore Smirnio's deposition, just ignore it."

"But, but, I can't," Michael would respond.

"Oh, yes you can, Michael. I've told you not to talk, think or waste my time and now you're doing all three. So, shut up and throw the deposition away. Let me hear you throw it away." The decibel level was rising. "Put the phone by the wastepaper basket, Michael, and throw it away so I can hear it fall in. Do it!" he yelled.

Over the phone, the thud of the deposition hitting the basket resounded on the speakerphone.

"Now, get back to some work that matters."

"That's my attorney," Matteo continued, "he can be such a dick sometimes. I wonder why I put up with him. Now, how can I help you?" And so began a meeting with one of his clients — me, Bill Urseth, an American businessman who had done some financing deals with Mount Real. I had just seen another glimpse of Lino Matteo.

There would be no doubt as to who was in charge. He was Lino P. Matteo, president and CEO of Mount Real Corporation. In 1999, it was little more than a public company cover-up for a big telemarketing scam that sold magazine subscriptions to Americans over the phone and a loan-sharking operation that had a couple of unique twists to it, but even its closest observers didn't know that.

One day I sat alone in Lino's office, waiting for him to finish a meeting in the conference room across the hallway. This was the office with the huge impressive leather desk, the private bar, refrigerator, and the four assistants waiting in attendance outside the door. Near the window was a huge globe of the world in a beautiful wooden floor stand. I had seen it hundreds of times before, but this time I studied it carefully. It was a globe of the world from the 16th century. As I studied it I realized that the continents were in the wrong place; while Europe was approximately correct in placement, the countries were unrecognizable. North America was a mere fraction of its actual size and even the continent's greatest rivers were not in place, yet to be discovered or correctly charted. New Zealand didn't exist at all and much of Asia squeezed together like a tired, used orange. If one was to navigate using this globe, one would always be approximate, but never correct. One might think they knew where they were, but never be certain of their locale. It was then that I realized this was the paradigm of Lino's life . . . a world where only he knew what was certain and others would struggle to navigate. Forget about GPS or even a compass; it was a place where longitude and latitude were yet to be discovered. He would navigate by the stars, instinct, tradition and his own rules. Others would all be uncertain, but they could witness his success and then choose to live with the ambiguity. The globe so prominent by his desk would ultimately teach me more about him than anything else.

If you became a Mount Real client, you could gain access to financing and reduce your expenses at the same time. Part of the loan contract included a financial management services agreement: Mount Real would take over

your firm's accounting, administration, accounts payable, accounts receivable and treasury functions. Why, from that day forward you'd never have to sign a check again. You could eliminate your CFO, your bookkeeping and accounting staff. You were now "outsourced" and your only concern would become "Will they do what I ask them to do, when I ask them to do it?" He was Lino Matteo and when he was around there was only one boss in the room.

Over the next ten years, I never saw one company survive this arrangement with their business intact, but it would take ten years for me to realize it. Lino's presence was always felt in any room, any building, any public park, airplane, train, car or meeting.

Our Records
Indicate . . .

Two issues of *Ocean Drive* had gone to the printer since Martin Wardman had made his deal with Lino. In line with the deal, the accounting staff was gone, two sales-people and the receptionist had been canned and Wardman and the editor had taken fifty percent pay cuts. Everyone knew the pressure was on to produce, and eyes were watching carefully. Monday mornings always seem like the day when people make their collection calls. Perhaps it's because they put it off and don't call on Friday, or maybe they check their receivables over the weekend and realize they need to get on top of things. On this Monday morning, the calls started right away.

"Mr. Wardman?"

"Yes," he responded in his special British way.

"Monique LeCavalier from Trans America Printing calling about your invoice, sir," and in that instant Wardman would realize that his printing bills were unpaid. And other calls would come.

"This is Gianni from Ace Photography. In checking our records we see your bill is now over sixty days."

"This is Monica from the building office. Mr. Wardman, your rent hasn't been paid now for two months. Could you please check into this situation?"

The telephone company would call and threaten to cut the phone service; the trucking company would call, the guy who did the promotional T-shirts and coffee cups and the modeling agency would call. It was becoming very clear that something was wrong. But Wardman attempted to stay calm.

"Sasha, could you set up a meeting for me with Lino? I need to catch up with him a little bit, today if possible."

As Martin drove to the meeting at 2:00 p.m., his Jaguar swerved as a soccer ball flew across the street in front of him. It brought his focus back to the road. He had been distracted by his worries . . . why weren't the bills paid? How could they be so far behind? Maybe the system just wasn't up and operating yet? All these thoughts shot through his mind.

He arrived at 2:00 p.m. sharp and sat down in the reception area at Mount Real. He grabbed one of his own magazines and flipped through it. At first one would have thought that there was some moving going on upstairs; there was a distinct thud and then a series of thuds. One might almost think it was a party taking place. Loud voices, yelling, then more thuds. It was indiscernible to Wardman what was happening until his eyes went to

Paulina, the receptionist, and he got his first clue. She was flushing red with embarrassment.

The level of the shouting had now gone up and Wardman could vaguely make out the words "Are you trying to cheat me? If you are, I should pound you into the ground. You lying fuck!" More pounding followed. "Don't you ever look at me that way! Never! Do you hear me?" The sound of books hitting the wall resounded through the building. "I'm so tired of your lies and whimpering. If you have even one ball, you'll get up right now and say something . . . say something!"

There was total silence for almost a minute. By now, there was also a small group of Mount Real employees gathered in the reception area, speculating on who was the victim of this barrage. Wardman watched the speculation and now he knew for certain that it was his partner putting on this demonstration upstairs . . . it was Lino P. Matteo.

"Get out, get out, you make me sick!" The door to the president's office opened, but the shouting didn't stop. Now it was loud and clear. "If you ever come around here again saying my people made a mistake or didn't do a good job, you had better come with clean feet and no skeletons of your own, you lying scam artist. Now go before I throw you down the stairs."

Rushing down the stairs was a young man in his late twenties, thin and wearing black wire-rim glasses, a sporty shirt, brown trousers and a leather jacket. He looked shaken. Eric Robichaud ran a telemarketing room that had gotten into some trouble. Some of the trouble was with the law; some of the trouble was with his processing through the bank that ran his credit card charges, without which a telemarketer cannot survive. Robichaud had gone to Lino for financing when his processing dried up. At the

bottom of the stairs, all of the speculation as to who was the recipient of this dressing-down ended. One of the speculators said audibly, "Robichaud." The others nodded. To no one in particular, Eric said, "What a day!"

He continued, "Paulina, can you make me an appointment for Thursday with him because I've got a payroll on Friday and I can't have that go bad." With that, he walked out.

It was now about 2:45 p.m. and Wardman had been sitting and waiting in the reception area for almost an hour. He knew that Lino was aware of his presence, but a part of him wanted some time to go by before he went upstairs.

Then Paulina turned and said, "Mr. Wardman, he'll see you now." Martin walked up the flight of wooden stairs, turned left and knocked on Matteo's door, not certain what he would see when he opened the door. He heard the words "come in." Matteo would instruct him to sit in the chair closest to the window, which he did.

"What's up?" Lino said casually.

"Lino, I've been getting calls that have been rather disturbing. The printer, studios, photographer, landlord and many others all say they haven't been getting paid," Martin said in a very formal way. "I assume there's just a glitch of some type in the setup phase of our agreement, so I thought we should have a session on that," Wardman continued.

With a sneer, Lino responded, "Martin, from now on when you get collection calls, send them here so you don't need to worry about these things."

"Who should I refer them to? Is there one person?" Wardman said.

"Send them to Phil. All I want you to do is focus on creative output and sales. You don't need to worry about the small stuff," Matteo offered.

"But isn't Phil the guy who is supposed to be paying the bills, and obviously isn't?" Wardman countered.

The room became completely silent. Martin realized that a nerve had been hit. Lino just looked at him; not a word was said. Thirty seconds went by, forty-five, a minute and Wardman became more uncomfortable by the second. Finally, he couldn't take it anymore and blurted out, "I'll have them call Phil."

Quietly, Lino began. "Martin, you've gotten yourself in this mess, so don't show up trying to blame Phil or anyone else for your problems. You were spending too much money for too long. You've been selling too little; you've been printing too big a magazine. It's not Phil!" Now the decibel level moved up. "Now listen good, Martin. There are setup fees that need to be paid to Mount Real before your payables get paid. They're probably pretty well paid out of your receivables at this point, but that's the way things are. Now, don't you ever come in here again and talk critically about one of my employees. Do you understand me, Martin?"

Wardman took a breath and tried again. "When do you think those bills will get paid?"

Quickly, Lino said, "Maybe never, if you don't get out of here and leave me alone. Now I'm going back to work. This meeting is over." With that he turned to his twin screens and started answering emails. After a couple of moments, Wardman realized the meeting really was over. He had learned nothing, except that he was now even further from controlling his own fate than he had been that morning when he woke up. He got up and left.

Jeff Klein was a software engineer, bright and creative. He could find solutions where others could find only confusion and ambiguity. He and his team had developed software that allowed an ad agency or creative department to more effectively manage their time and business than anyone else had ever developed. Lino was the financier, and while the business was doing okay, it seemed like it should ultimately do better. There were two key issues before it: how to continue financing, and whether the program should be available only to Macintosh users. These two issues were the agenda items for the Honeybee board meeting. In attendance were Jeff, Lino, Mark Jourdenais (Lino's lifelong friend and also a software guy) and Eric Clement, an accountant turned business type whom Lino found loyal. This 5'2" Scottish immigrant with a wrestler's build would usually sit quietly and when the meeting was over execute whatever was decided.

As always, Lino would begin the meeting. "I know Jeff has reservations about going public, but I feel it's the best way to attract new capital and finance this business. Jeff seems to be afraid of the public idea and I don't know why. It's obviously the best alternative; by accessing public markets, we can get the funding we need for growth. We have a good story, and the market wants high-tech deals. There's no reason not to do it. As far as this fear of being too narrow by having Apple software only, it's obvious that graphics people and agencies are Mac-only users and that's the way it is and the way it will stay. It makes no sense to develop a Microsoft alternative. It's just a waste of time and money."

Klein spoke up slowly with a slight stutter. "In-in-in the field, I'm seeing more Microsoft and PC equipment. I-I-I don't know why, but it's there, and lots of it. May-maybe it doesn't make sense, but people are buying it."

Matteo interrupts Jeff. "Do you want stupid clients?"

"No, ah no," Klein stammers.

"Well, I think you can agree that if someone brings a PC situation into a creative environment, they're stupid, right? So, who wants stupid clients? Eric, do you want stupid clients? Mark, do you want stupid clients? See, Jeff, no one wants stupid clients. If you want stupid clients then that means you're stupid, and this company doesn't need stupid people, do you follow?"

The meeting was over, but the meeting is never over until Lino decides it's over. "On the public thing, I'm going to get things started so we can be ready by spring. Any objections? Okay, then, we'll get it going." He got up and left . . . *now* the meeting was over.

The

Israeli Deal

EduSoft was the kind of acquisition that analysts would praise. The Israeli company was purported to have software that was developed as English as a Second Language (ESL) instruction. The addition gave Cinar the ability to publish multimedia software that incorporated its television characters and showed off the synergy between the company's two divisions — entertainment and education. Industry experts applauded the diversification and went out of their way to demonstrate the high profit margins in the educational materials market.

In March 1999, mere months after Weinberg, Charest and Hasanain had made their deal with its former owners, the new board of EduSoft would agree to a selling price of

$56 million; EduSoft was now the property of Cinar.

Ron and Hasanain had pulled something brilliant since software is so difficult to judge and value. They had not only engineered the self-enriching EduSoft deal, but were actually being praised for it by the pundits. What they'd paid for the acquisition wasn't important; what the synergy could do for earnings was. The world believed EduSoft was going to make Cinar a lot of money. In fact, it would never make the company one red cent.

As Ron and Hasanain worked through their monthly review and status reports, they made their way to the "Israel deal" as they referred to it. The transaction was complete now and they had stashed the money away in one of their offshore accounts. Then they circled back to Killington, the foreign exchange transactions with the back-to-backs. Finally, they focused on the Globe-X deals and how much they had actually placed there.

"Over $80 million," Panju offered, "and so far everything has worked just like they said it would. We carry it on our balance sheet as short-term investments. They leverage the funds and we get an above-market rate of return, along with a little juice. I think it's working for everyone. We have a tax issue coming up, though, and I was thinking we should test the relationship a little bit and ask for a loan — maybe a million or two — and see if we can't sweeten things a little more."

"Why not? Give it a try before we send any more money down there. Let's take their temperature and see if they understand quid pro quo," Ron reasoned. "How much more are you thinking about sending down there?"

"Thirty or forty million more. Nobody else can give us a return like that," Panju responded. "But let's test out the loan idea first and see how flexible our southern partners

really are." Weinberg nodded and moved on to the subject of the house in Magog.

Down in Nassau, when the phone rang, Bob realized right away that this call was different from most of their conversations. Panju was direct and very authoritative.

"Bob," he began, "we've got a tax issue coming up. Ron and I were talking and we realized that we need a couple of mil. We were wondering if you could loan us the money."

Daviault paused only briefly. "Sure, Has, I don't see any problem with it. How long do you need it?"

"It might only be months, but it could be longer. Does it matter much?"

"No, not really," Daviault answered.

When the call was finished, Bob wandered into Tom's office, lit up a cigarette and told Tom what had happened.

"Sounds okay to me," Tom said.

The loan would be used to clear up a brokerage account with a firm called Progenesis, an account that Weinberg, Charest and Panju used to trade stocks, including Cinar stock. They would repay this first loan in a few months as promised; interest was not charged and no collateral was asked for or received. The way this transaction went made Tom and Bob comfortable when, a year later, a much larger loan would be requested — $12 million.

Maria was asked to prepare the wire. She had made a lot of progress on the administrative front, but the accounting was still way behind and the audits were excruciatingly slow. As the boys continued to be active at the country club, Maria was beginning to find a life for herself in Nassau as well. Exercise classes and parties began to creep into her lifestyle. She wasn't the type of woman to go unnoticed in a small city on a small island. A blond in a sports car does not go unnoticed for long in any city, but definitely stands out more in Nassau. Most of the Cinar funds were now spent; some had gone to fund redemptions, some for fees, some of the money was paid out in interest to other Globe-X investors, and about half of the $80 million had found its way into leverage deals and private placements that John had found in Montreal and throughout the world.

Private placements are usually development phase companies looking to capitalize themselves so they can demonstrate their real value in the market. John Xanthoudakis and his staff were becoming active venture capitalists and merchant bankers by putting a million or two here, a million or two there. In return, they'd usually get a minority interest in a privately held company that would, hopefully, prove itself in the world. These types of deals are very illiquid, but when they work, they can be very lucrative. John had also become very active in philanthropy. He loved to help people and now that he had the money, he was more than glad to pitch in. He developed a foundation and it was funding projects to help schools computerize, hospitals find cancer cures and police handle juvenile delinquency issues. His heart was in the right place and his pocketbook was open.

The Bahamian sun rose out of the sea; there were no clouds to obscure it. This sun would make for another hot day, but it didn't matter anymore to Bob; he was used to the heat and had grown to like it. He wondered how he could have survived those cold Canadian winters. He was up earlier than usual today because he wanted to get some work done early and then hit the golf course. He puffed his cigarette as he sped his way to work ahead of the rush hour traffic. When he entered the office, he checked his emails and found the note from Panju.

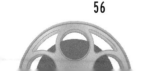

It read: "Bob, have forwarded $30 million more to Globe-X Management. Please confirm receipt and current balance. Have a good day. Hasanain."

"Yes," was Bob's thought, a smile consuming his face as he lit up another smoke. He printed out the email and left the copy on Tom's desk.

Mario Ricci at Cinar was asked to prepare the wire, which he dutifully did. His promotions had come rapidly and without contest from Panju and Weinberg. He was doing very well, but there was something bothering him. Despite having done well in his young career, he had never worked for a boss he was proud of. Matteo had been an ogre, Panju and Weinberg crooked and he seemed to be tutored by bullies and schemers. He was ready for a change.

Mario's conversation with John Xanthoudakis began innocently enough. They were talking about Globe-X and how the funds were doing and, suddenly, the tone changed and Mario spoke about what he'd like to do with his life. Things spoken can rarely be unsaid, and now John realized that Mario would like to do something else, and that Cinar might not be in his future. John needed talent in his growing and thriving business, and Norshield and Mario Ricci might be a perfect fit. Over the next several weeks, the deal was struck. Mario would let Weinberg and Panju know, and give them plenty of time to find a replacement, but Ricci was going to Norshield.

"Flaws are beginning to show"

At their country home in Magog, the Weinbergs could escape the pressures of the business and the pace of the city. It gave them a chance to be a family and enjoy their children. This was a long way from roughing it. The estate was large and impressive, the kind of place a power couple would choose to impress their friends and guests. There are few places more beautiful in October than Quebec. Its maple trees produce sugar and syrup in the spring and in the fall those same trees produce colors that captivate the eye and invigorate the senses. Lac Memphramagog would reflect the glorious colors and mirror the shoreline. The newspapers from Montreal would arrive by 8:00 a.m. While Ron and Micheline would go to Magog to escape the city, they never wanted to escape too much.

"Why those bastards! What a bunch of cocksuckers!" Charest would say out loud. "What the hell kind of story is this? They haven't talked to us, they haven't called. What is this shit?"

Weinberg wandered in. "What are you talking about?" he asked.

"Look at this! Look what a bunch of shit this is. This story says that we're under investigation for improperly receiving federal tax credits. They're accusing us of cheating and using American writers instead of Canadian writers for the *Arthur* series. Why those bastards! How dare they run this shit without our comments?" her tirade continued.

"We've been out of touch, maybe they did call and we don't know it."

"Whose fucking side are you on?" she fumed. "This could be really serious, do you realize that? Because what they're saying is exactly what we do. This isn't some wild goose chase; we do use American writers. How could we have such a great show if we used Canadian talent? Those idiots don't know how hard it is to get a show that good. Do they realize how much we pay in taxes because we're good? If we weren't good, we wouldn't be paying all these taxes. This is a bunch of shit!" She threw the paper down and stormed out.

Weinberg picked up the newspaper and read the story. As Weinberg mulled over their predicament he realized how many documents and how much evidence existed throughout their offices on this matter. He would begin the process of "sanitizing" the file by pulling document after document and stuffing them into a gym bag to be given to Panju. He thought it would be best if these documents ceased to exist. The other side of him thought that this was serious, but at worst it was a $10 or $15 million slap on the wrist. They could afford it, they would survive.

When the story broke, Lino was in his office. He had three newspapers delivered every morning and he read or, at least, scanned them all. Lino was a news junkie, and he read magazines and newspapers voraciously. He loved information and he absorbed it like a sponge. The Cinar story jumped off the pages because he knew that Cinar had become a major client of John's. He had no idea how much money Cinar had sent south, but suspected it was sizable. He had stayed close to Mario and knew that Weinberg and Panju's ethics were flawed. He had actually done business with them himself and had gotten a couple of million dollars from them for his own business. Lino was smart enough to see where this might go — broader scrutiny and review. He pushed his intercom and asked one of his four personal assistants to come into his office.

"Make copies of this story and forward the copies to Mario, John and Bill. Include this note: *'This might be the beginning, flaws are starting to show. Lino.'*" Within minutes, all three would receive their copy of the story and the cryptic message.

The Cinar board included a senator, the CEO of one of the nation's largest retail firms, the president of a grocery chain and some very successful lawyers and businessmen. Up till now, these jobs had been easy and their tour of duty a snap. But this was a full-blown public relations problem and a business issue. As far as they were concerned, it was a problem, yes, but as Weinberg had estimated, it had a price tag Cinar could afford. The key

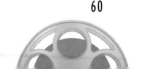

was to contain the problem and not let it grow. When lawyers and businesspeople handle a problem, they have a tendency to deal with the problem like one might deal with a flat tire. The tire is flat, so let's change it. They don't overhaul the car. When the press sees a problem, however, especially a problem that clearly demonstrates an ethics issue, they start digging, because people rarely have ethical lapses just once.

CHAPTER 11

DATE   OCTOBER 1999

SCENE   Cinar – Montreal

Let It Blow Over

The board didn't know that the company that created illusions for the children of the world was itself just that. There were many who had bought it hook, line and sinker: the market cap of the stock was over $1 billion, some of Wall Street's most prominent firms had under-written the offerings and in the process "approved" the way Cinar was managed. Major banks solicited their business. Ernst & Young were signing their audits and, in the process, furthering their legend. Now, for the first time, a crack was forming; the accusation was clear — Revenue Canada believed that they had been hood-winked by Cinar and cheated out of $12 million.

As the board meeting began and before it could reach

a fever pitch, Weinberg calmly stood in front of the board and analytically summed up the situation.

"It appears that the government feels we are out of line on these tax credits, in that the writers we used don't qualify. They may be right, they may be wrong, and just like all contentious situations, you can decide to fight or you can negotiate a solution. In this case, I recommend we do the latter. If we have to refund the money, we'll refund it. We're having a great year and it won't hurt us much to settle. I think we have a great case if we want to fight it, but it may not be worth the effort. Any thoughts?"

Heads nodded in agreement. "Let's get it behind us." "It doesn't pay to fight the government." "It's an unnecessary distraction." "There're better ways to spend our energy." These were all recitations heard from the board. With that, Weinberg swung into his usual upbeat explanations about the business of the day.

When Panju and Weinberg left the boardroom at the end of the meeting, Panju made a simple gesture; he took his left index finger and gently rubbed the palm of his right hand. Weinberg smiled as he said, "In the palm of my hand," and they shut off the lights.

The next morning, Micheline swept into the office. Her outfit was striking, a lime green suit — the skirt short, the jacket impeccable — the kind of outfit that men notice and women admire. As the office door closed, she demanded the presence of her cohorts, Ron and Hasanain, over the intercom. They appeared quickly. There was no chitchat, no conversation about the weather. Micheline stated bluntly, "We can't let them get away with this. We need to fight. We need to let them know that they can't push us around. If we have to, we'll threaten to move the business, but we cannot knuckle under. Those clock-punching bureaucrats have got to learn Cinar is not to be trifled with. The bastards will be checking our wastebaskets and watching our fuel gauges if we let them."

"Micheline," Panju interrupted, "Ron really got the board on our side last night and everybody agrees we should . . ."

"Let it die," Weinberg said, finishing Panju's sentence.

"You two haven't got a good fight in you. Between you, you haven't got two nuts. You don't get it. If you don't fight, they'll keep on coming. Now it's tax credits, next it's payroll audits, then it's sales tax, then it's something else. We can't budge. I will bust their balls! You two go hide with your stuffed animals and video games."

Ron interrupted. "That's enough! The board is solidly on our side. They never asked how or why this happened. Who made the decision? Are there other problems we should be concerned about?"

"Micheline, Ron did a great job last night. This problem could have gotten ugly if they started digging because this garden is full of buried money and we don't need anyone digging, hoeing or weeding."

"You putzes haven't got shit figured out. When the government comes in here, they'll come with a fuckin' Rototiller, and then we'll really have headaches!"

The phone rang and Micheline answered. "Oui, hello?" Ron and Has used the opportunity to sneak out. As they closed the door, Weinberg said with confidence, "She'll come around. Have you got the write-up on the Israel deal? I'll show her how well that's going and she'll realize we can afford to pay the government and get on with things."

The newspapers weren't kind to Cinar, but as Ron

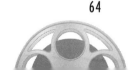

predicted, things quieted down. Micheline was right as well. The investigations would broaden. Soon it would be found that her maids were on the payroll. The triumvirate was running this public company like it was still private. But, overall, with some good spin control and success in the field, things promised to return to normal — a new normal, perhaps, but normal.

Friends
from Way Back

Lino's antennae went up when the Cinar stories broke. He had done some business with Panju and Weinberg and knew enough to know he didn't trust them. He suspected that they were doing business in the Bahamas, probably with his old friend, Tom Muir, and his longtime nemesis, Bob Daviault, but he had no idea how much business they really had done.

Lino's instincts were that his best friend, John Xanthoudakis, was involved in it all, but everyone was mysteriously quiet on this subject. It killed Lino to suspect something and not to know, so he'd use all kinds of tricks to get information; it was part of his personality. He'd ask one person a question, then ask another person the same question, and he'd probe any little differences between the answers, always keeping each party unaware of the other. He'd use "grey ops" to gather information and encourage others to help him. His memory was excellent, so he'd absorb information faster and longer than most people and he kept a staff of four personal assistants who would research, catalogue and organize paper and electronic data for his recall. A prolific reader, he would cut, sort and paste seemingly disparate information in his own cryptic way. Amazingly, it would sometimes make the difference in solving a problem. As much as he was an egomaniacal bully, he could also be intellectual, contemplative and engaging.

Probing and using his tricks, he was now certain that Cinar's situation would get worse and that this wouldn't be good for John. Despite their relationship going back over 15 years, and his usual openness, John just wouldn't give Lino much on Cinar. He knew that Lino had done a couple of million dollars of financing with Panju and wanted to do more. He was concerned that if Lino realized how much business John had actually done with Weinberg and Panju, he'd come unglued, especially if he thought that Daviault was the one leading the account. The two had never gotten along.

In 1982, Daviault, Matteo and Xanthoudakis were all orderlies at the Montreal Children's Hospital, working as students and paying their own way through school. These were not the noblesse; there were no silver spoons. John and Lino's parents were all hardworking immigrants from Greece and Italy. These power brokers of the late 1990s had been emptying bedpans and running errands just 17 years earlier.

From the start, Lino didn't like Bob. In the old days,

Bob and Lino would work closely together and perform the same job. That allowed them to change shifts to accommodate each other's study schedules and social lives, a relationship that worked pretty well for both of them.

One day, Lino shouted down the hall, "Bob! Can I catch up with you at break time?"

"Sure," was Daviault's response.

When they met up Bob asked, "What's up, big guy?"

"Listen, I really need a favor. As you know, I've got my wedding coming up and the hospital has got me scheduled to work the night before my wedding, which is when the rehearsal and groom's dinner are supposed to be taking place. So, I was wondering if we could switch shifts. I'll cover for you earlier in the week, if you could cover the Friday. How about it?"

"Man, Lino, you know how I hate those Friday night shifts, but I know this is special so what do you say I cover Friday night for you and you work the last half of my shift Tuesday and my whole shift Wednesday? Deal?"

"Yeah, it's a deal, Bob. I need to be at that rehearsal, so that'll work."

Lino relieved Bob Tuesday for the last half of his shift and then worked all Wednesday for him. But at school on Friday Lino got an envelope from Bob at his locker. It said simply, "Lino, something has come up and I can't work tonight. I checked with a couple of other guys and they can't either. Good luck, Bob."

Lino would miss his rehearsal and the party that followed. He worked until midnight and then cleaned up to join the small group of revelers that remained. There are things you forget in life and there are things you don't. Lino has never forgotten that Bob stiffed him.

Years later they would work together at Norshield,

Lino as controller, Bob eventually as CFO. The closer together they worked, the more the sparks would fly. When Lino finally realized that Daviault now had over $100 million of Cinar's money, and he had only $2 million, sparks would fly for sure. But a good trader must learn when to talk and when to shut up, and John was a good trader. So, for now, it was a standoff; Lino would probe, John just kept quiet.

The Glitter of
Ocean Drive

The winters in Montreal can be long, dark, snowy and cold. The sun sets around 4:30 or 5:00 in the afternoon; the temperatures range from 0°C to -20°C. The snow starts in December and can continue into March. No city on earth does a better job of dealing with snow, and no city spends more money in the process. In Montreal, the city even shovels the sidewalks in front of people's homes, and the snow on the street is plowed to the side of the road. Then it is blown into trucks that haul it off to get dumped elsewhere. All this effort makes one feel the snow only for days at a time, rather than months, unlike in most cold weather cities, where what falls in December stays where it is until it melts.

Most people in the city rent, and the rents are quite reasonable. The Métro system connects the city very effectively underground, so that most people don't need cars. When you combine reasonable rents with no car payments, no fuel costs and no insurance payments, the outcome is a lot more discretionary spending. Montrealers spend money on clothes, fragrances, food and, most importantly, partying. The winter is party time, and cold, snow and darkness don't affect the lifeblood of the city. The parties don't even start until 10:30 or later, and they go on and on until early morning. Some of the hottest parties in the 1990s were tied to magazines and other media. Others are tied to the film industry that in those days was booming in the city, in part because of available talent, in part because of the currency differentiation of the U.S. and Canadian dollars.

Ocean Drive might have been losing money, but no one except Wardman and Lino knew it. To the chic world, it was a monthly testament to fashion, lifestyle, beauty and wealth. The party had started at 11:00 p.m. At 12:30, the music was rolling, the shots were going down and the hotties continued to line up to get into this party of parties. The fashion show would start in a half hour — swimwear — always a hot draw even on a night of -10°C. This is one of those rare parties where the audience is as good looking and fashionable as the models on the runway. Suddenly, one of the bartenders clears a space on the bar where she's serving, about 20 feet long. She's a striking redhead in a short black leather skirt with a very small *Ocean Drive* T-shirt that could barely hold her breasts in check. She extended her arm and sprayed something onto the open space. Within seconds her intent became clear and she lit the liquid spray on fire.

For 20 seconds, the bartop burned like a torch and everyone cheered.

Wardman knew that Lino would never come to a party that started at 11:00 p.m.; he might not even show at a party that started at 9:00 because he just isn't a night guy. As the father of three and married only once, he was certain to be at Mass on Sunday morning, at his mother's for pasta at noon, and taking a nap from 1:30 to 3:30 on the only day of the week he didn't work. Despite his mercurial behavior and dominating presence, he was a family man, didn't run around, didn't cheat, didn't even pinch or look. Wardman knew this would be a long night; the party would go for three or four hours after the fashion show. He had asked his assistant to buy him a newspaper as soon as they hit the streets, so he could sneak off and read as the party roared.

As if on cue, the audience began to form itself around the runway that would suddenly be lit up and the focus of attention. The music would rise; the announcer's voice would welcome everyone in French and announce the show. Swimwear is a language of its own. Montreal may be the most bilingual city on earth, and on this evening there would be French, English and fashion as the languages "du jour." There were ten female and ten male models. They would each make nine changes over the next half hour. The music blared, the flashes and strobes glared and the audience appreciated with applause, hoots and bravos. Wardman knew he had just staged another hit and that *Ocean Drive* was on the lips of every advertiser and agency executive.

The show had just ended and Martin's assistant handed Martin his newspaper. He put it under his arm and slowly moved toward a quiet office where he could sit

THE GLITTER OF *OCEAN DRIVE*

down and read, shaking hands and waving to people as he went. When he arrived at the office, he sat down and opened the paper. The headline read "Cinar Claims $122,000,000 Missing!" He dove into the story, as readers all over the country did that morning.

CHAPTER 14

DATE MARCH 2000

SCENE Nassau, Bahamas

Foul Wind
in the Caribbean

Bob Daviault grabbed the phone by his kitchen table. "Hello?"

The voice on the other end was subdued. "Bob, I need to come down and see you."

"Has? Is that you?" Bob responded.

"Yes, it's me."

"When do you want to come down?"

"Tomorrow."

"That's kind of short notice, but I guess it will be okay. I'll let Tom know. Look forward to seeing you." Daviault thought it was odd, but what do you say when someone who has sent you $108 million says he'd like to come visit?

Bob and Tom were smoking and drinking coffee when the receptionist said, "There's a group of people here to see you."

"How many?" Tom asked.

"Four," she responded.

"I don't know, Tom. He made it sound like he'd be alone. Well, let's go say hello — we may make some new friends today!"

As the introductions began, Bob and Tom were looking at three familiar and one unfamiliar face. Hasanain Panju was there, but subdued. Ron Weinberg was there, but there was no smile or sense of familiarity. Michael Barnet was holding out his hand, but why? Barnet was one of Nassau's most prominent and most expensive attorneys, a litigator who was famous for tough cases and victories. The unfamiliar face was a smallish, lean man of 5'5", not over 130 pounds, with a shaved head and full of kinetic energy. He immediately took charge and introduced himself as Bill Brock, a Montreal attorney representing Cinar's board. They all went into the boardroom and sat down. Tom has always been a small-talker, a chit-chatter; his amiable nature makes him good at it.

"How was your flight?" he began.

"We're not here to talk about flights," Brock responded.

"What are you here to talk about?" Bob asked.

"Guys, we're here at the direction of our board, to get back the money we've sent down here. There seems to be a question as to whether we were authorized to open the account and invest it here in the Bahamas. So it will be best if we just get the money and leave," Weinberg stated concisely.

"Ron, that money is all invested, just like we told you it would be. We can't just grab it and give it to you."

"Well, that's what you had better do," Brock said, "or your lives are going to be so miserable you'll wish you'd never heard the name Cinar."

"Has, what's up?" Tom said, turning. "What's going on? You know the terms; you know that the money can't be returned until the end of November. This is all under the Discretionary Management Agreement. We all signed the contract. Why aren't you saying anything?"

Brock interrupted. "Mr. Panju has been fired, gentlemen; he's out. Now you're dealing with me, and I want the money!"

"Is it true, Has? Is it true?" Daviault asked. Panju nodded his head without saying a word.

"Ron, you know the terms, you know the deal."

"I believed that we could get the money back whenever we needed it. We told you that these were funds that might be needed for acquisitions," Weinberg offered.

"Just sell your positions and get us the money!" Brock insisted.

"The positions and the accounts are all leveraged. None of them can be liquidated, and you guys know that. The premise of the enhanced yield fund is that everything is leveraged. You guys knew that!" Bob countered.

Brock turned to Weinberg. "Did you know that these accounts are leveraged? You told the board that these funds are in a high-interest savings account. You made it sound like we were walking to the teller's window at RBC. I have no choice but to report back to the board about what's going on here. Mr. Barnet, we've got some work to do because we're going to be seeing these boys in court. The Supreme Court of the Bahamas."

Weinberg said nothing and the silence was deafening. Suddenly, Tom spoke for the first time. "Maybe we could

get you guys some money, just so you know we're committed to working things out."

Brock rose like a trout to a fly. "How much?" he snapped.

"Maybe $15 million. That should show you we're serious."

The room relaxed. Still, Weinberg knew the issue for him wasn't getting $15 million. The issue that would cook his goose was that he knew all along that the funds were encumbered, and that he had said otherwise. All his life he'd been able to slide by with little half-truths . . . not lies, just not quite the whole truth. That habit had never hurt him before. He had amassed a fortune, he had attracted a dynamic wife, he had built a phenomenal company, he had hidden away millions in accounts and deals all over the world . . . never by lying, just a little twisting.

He had told the audit committee that he hadn't known, that Hasanain Panju had done this deal, and that certainly he should be fired. Ron fired his friend Hasanain knowing it was the best chance to save himself, but now maybe he couldn't be saved. It was just too obvious that he knew. Suddenly, he realized that this could get worse if the talk turned to the FOREX transactions . . . or Killington . . . or the numbered accounts that he, Panju and Charest had at Globe-X Management. The best way out was to acknowledge Tom's offer. He would try to maintain this weakened alliance. Oddly enough, his own company might now be his biggest enemy. The world had flown off its axis in just 48 hours.

When Tom and Bob retreated to Tom's office for a smoke and to call John X, they left their four visitors in the conference room.

"Can you believe this shit?" Bob began. "Can you believe it? Panju is fired; it looks like Weinberg is on his way out . . . out of his own company . . . and suddenly nobody remembers the terms of the deals we made. They want all their money back! These were supposed to be long-term deals. This is going to kill us! We can't redeem over $100 million. I've never seen such crap as this!"

"Do you think $15 million will keep them quiet for a while? Buy us some time, show this Brock prick we mean well?" Tom said.

"Hell if I know, but I don't have a better idea. Let's call John."

They took John through the situation blow by blow, sequence by sequence. He had just seen the papers and knew that the press had no idea where the money was, but that Cinar was declaring it missing.

"Holy shit!" was John's first comment. "What a mess. Who are we really dealing with? If Panju is out and Weinberg is crippled or gone, is it lawyers?" he asked.

"That's what it looks like," Bob responded. "There's a little prick here named Bill Brock who is throwing his weight around and acting like he's in charge. I don't get it. Weinberg owns two-thirds of the voting shares of this company and some goofball attorney is acting like it's his business where Ron puts his money . . . this is nuts!"

"I think where things went wrong is that Ron told the audit committee to get their own attorney on this matter. He probably thought they never would and the whole thing would just blow over."

"Well, it's blowin', all right, and every foul wind in the Caribbean seems to be blowing right into this office. Can you get us $15 million fast?"

"Yeah. Will it buy time?" asked John.

"We hope so."

When they returned to the conference room, it was clear that Weinberg was out. In one cell phone conversation with the audit committee over 5,000 miles away, his 18-year career would end. He would be fired from the company he had founded and built. He would need to explain to his wife that she was fired, too. Two of the highest paid executives in Canada had been turfed out, even though they had all the votes.

"Sit down, gentlemen," Brock barked. "It may not be necessary for Mr. Panju or Mr. Weinberg to stay on." He turned to them. "Would you guys rather leave?" Panju and Weinberg nodded in unison and left. "How long have you guys been running this little scam?" Brock asked derisively.

"What are you talking about?" Bob responded.

"I know enough now that I have a decision to make. Do I treat you like businessmen, or like criminals? You have $122 million that doesn't belong to you."

CHAPTER   15

DATE   MARCH 2000

SCENE   Norshield International –

Nassau, Bahamas

"How did we get into this mess?"

Bob and Tom were waiting for the knock on the door. Maria entered, grabbed the cigarettes off Tom's desk, said, "This is the wrong month to quit smoking," and lit up. In minutes they were dialing John in Montreal and the conference began. Tom spoke.

"This guy is a little prick, John. He's treating us like criminals and con men. I don't get it. They sent the money here, Weinberg controls sixty-six percent of the company, they were the authorized officers, and now they claim they didn't have board approval! These people have opened accounts all over the world without board approval, the board never gave a shit, and now it's a big deal!"

Tom was rolling now. "John, we offered $15 million just now and they actually said they want to think about it. Unbelievable! They don't know anything about the money business."

John interrupted. "What condition are the books in, you guys? They could bring a court action and the court decision will lead to releasing the books."

Silence filled the room. Bob walked to the window looking out over the Nassau harbor where cruise ships powered to port. Tom took a long drag and Maria stared at the floor. "Hello? Are you guys there?" The room was still silent.

Then Maria spoke up and said, "I've made a lot of progress, John, but when I arrived the books were in shambles. Some progress has been made, but now this explosion. So even some of the basic bookkeeping isn't done. Forget about audits or anything of that type." The implications stunned them all, though they were hearing what they already knew.

"That means they could make you look like crooks. We might have two weeks before everything blows up. In Montreal, people don't even know where the money is, much less all the other things going on. You've got to dig in on the accounting. I'll start selling some positions and get that $15 million together," John offered.

The call ended and Bob said, "I don't think I'll see the golf course for a while."

Maria smiled.

Within days it was obvious to Maria that they were in bigger trouble than even she thought. The records were scant and the bookkeeping little more than entries in the checkbook. To make matters worse, the checkbook made things look like the money that came from Cinar had been used to pay redemptions and fees, and wasn't even invested on Cinar's behalf. The credits that should have been issued to prove the indebtedness had never been issued. Then she would learn that a new rule was coming down in the Bahamas that would require an issuer like Globe-X to have audited statements in place before they could legally accept investor funds. With that news, she called John.

"Things are really fucked up, John," his sister-in-law sighed. "We're going to need help fast to clean things up, get into compliance with the new laws and to have Cinar think we're not half-assed. Any ideas? 'Cause this boat has a big hole in it."

"Yeah, I'll send Mario Ricci down, and I think Lino Matteo might have an accountant available who can help. Book flights for all of you to Miami and bring along whatever you've got. I'll get you help from up here. And Maria? Tell those guys to stay calm."

"Yeah, I will, but I don't think they can. They're both wrecks, John. Don't forget that Bob and Lino hate each other. This could be a big mistake."

"They'll work together. This isn't business as usual."

In March 2000 John Xanthoudakis went to Lino's office in Montreal, sat on the other side of his big desk and brought Lino up to date. When Lino learned that these guys had gotten $108 million of Weinberg's money, while he had gotten only $2 million, he was incredulous.

"You two-timing fucks!" was his response. When he learned that Brock was "down south" and treating Daviault and Muir like kids in a school yard, he said, "It's just what they deserve, the bastards." When he learned

that the books were a shambles, a total mess, he said, "With that dipshit Daviault, what do you expect. Lazy son of a bitch." Then he learned the reason for the visit.

"Lino, I need you to help clean this mess up. The court is likely to subpoena the records and there basically aren't any records. The fact is, if there were, it would be clear that the investments have all been handled properly, but the books aren't in place." After hearing this, Lino realized he was going to have to straighten out another Daviault mess, something he'd done plenty of. Going all the way back to the Children's Hospital, then at Norshield and now, the biggest mess yet . . . a $108 million mess. Maybe this time his friend John would realize what Daviault was really all about. Lino finally said, "I'll do it, but that means I'm in charge."

"Okay," John sighed.

Tom and Bob knew Brian Murree from the country club. He had been educated in England and was considered one of the island's top lawyers, a gifted litigator and a good match for Michael Barnet. Brian listened carefully as they described their situation. The story seemed incredible even in the land of thieves, smugglers and pirates. He agreed to take the case and calmly asked for a retainer.

"How much?" Tom asked.

"One hundred thousand," he replied. He needed to leave for court so they shook hands and parted. As he walked toward court, this middle-aged portly black man had a trim mid-forties black man in a suit walking right behind him, carrying his briefcase.

In Ottawa, Jo-Anne Polak was reading her briefing paper. Senior Vice President of Crisis Communications at Hill & Knowlton Canada, Polak was one of Canada's leading crisis spin masters. Usually working on big clients' messes or political flash points, she was fascinated by the complexity of this Globe-X debacle. At one time in history, she had been the only female general manager of a pro football team. I had gone to Jo-Anne after Lino and John had asked me to find a PR heavyweight who wasn't afraid of controversy and crisis. I had met with her at length and prepared the briefing papers myself. As the crisis brewed I awaited her response. Smart and tough, she emailed me saying, "This is right up my alley. Yes, I will do it. My retainer will be one hundred thousand — Jo-Anne."

Bill Brock, attorney for the Cinar board, and Michael Barnet were in Barnet's downtown Nassau office. They were drafting their legal actions, which would be filed shortly in the Bahamian supreme court, the court in the Bahamas that handles all cases over $5,000. The suit would basically seize all the assets of Globe-X, associated companies, the officers and directors, and would do so without trial or right of defence, based on the premise that there was a probability of flight by the defendants. Even Barnet and Brock thought their suit rather groping, but now was no time to be shy, and Barnet was certain the case would come before a judge who would accept the rationale. Most importantly to Brock, when this suit broke it would catch the attention of the Canadian press in such a way that the focus of the stories would be on who had the $122 million, and how they had gotten it from the dethroned trio. Nowhere would the press focus on the sloppiness of the Cinar board. These people had let their own management pillage the treasury, file for false tax credits, open accounts all over the world and commit acquisition chicanery like the Israel deal. (This was the deal where they had

"HOW DID WE GET INTO THIS MESS?"

connived with the sellers, gained control of the company, then sold it to Cinar for $56 million.) Brock's boss, Robert Vineberg of Davies Ward Phillips & Vineberg LLP, was, after all, a member of that board, and the last thing the law firm needed was a corporate governance scandal with one of their partners right in the middle of it. They smiled as they read their suit.

"Groping, perhaps, but it will do," Brock said.

Lino had demanded that Mario sit down with him before Mario flew to Florida to meet Bob and Maria. He had prepared a strategy sheet and outline. The work was detailed, no nonsense and offered insight and direction no one else on the file could have provided. Mario was at this point working for John Xanthoudakis, but Lino never altered his attitude toward his former employees. When he is reunited with them he acts as if they never left his guiding hand, or his employ. And Lino was helping his friend John out of the biggest mess of his life.

"Whatever you do, don't listen to that moron Daviault. This plan will get you through this, but if Daviault knows it's my work, he'll fight it. So, don't let him know. Most of the accounting can be done up here in Montreal. If you do it down there, it will be slow and sloppy. Whatever Bob says he'll do or get done, cut it in half. Whatever Maria says she'll do, she'll do. This is all way over Tom's head; just keep him out of the way." The directions were simple, the play clear. "If there are questions, call me, not John. I'm in charge." Lino nodded and Mario got up. The meeting was over.

Basil Angelopoulos wasn't yet 40. He had his own law firm and a reputation for litigation. Good looking and trilingual (French, English and Greek), he was a father of three and a city councilman in a large suburb of Montreal. He was the kind of guy who can do anything well and always does it with charm. Lino briefed Basil on the situation. He, like others, found the whole situation surreal and beyond belief, even for an experienced attorney.

"You might be all the good things people say you are, or you might be one more bag of shit attorney, I don't know. What I do know is that you and Bill Brock used to be friends, and I need you down in Nassau because of that," Lino said.

"How soon?" Basil asked.

"Now."

"I'll need a retainer."

"How much?"

"One hundred thousand dollars," Basil responded.

Lino laughed a deep, menacing laugh. "There is no way you're getting a hundred grand, but I'll give you twenty-five. And I need you to leave right away." Basil considered this. Lino Matteo was a piece of work. That much was clear. And the job was intriguing. So, he agreed, and soon was on his way to the Bahamas.

Weinberg had flown from Nassau to Montreal. When he left the airport in Montreal, he jumped into his car and drove to his home in Westmount, the posh suburb of Montreal near downtown. This enclave has a separate municipal government, with its own services, parks and schools . . . all for the benefit of its affluent citizens. The parks and pools require resident cards, and non-residents

of Westmount without cards are ordered to leave. Ron didn't know how much his wife knew about the situation, and he consciously decided not to call and discuss this over the phone. He pulled into the garage and went into the house. The voice boomed.

"Well, you conniving bastards have gotten *me* fired! Yeah, me! After eighteen years of work, commitment and fucking genius, two sneaky accountants have gotten me fired . . . fired from the company I own. I've got two-thirds of the voting shares and I'm thrown out on my ass. They've locked my office, disconnected my phone." She began to soften and tears appeared on the iron woman's face.

"I'm sorry," he stuttered. "I never thought they could get us."

A junior from Barnet's Nassau office would be given the suit. He would walk from the firm to the Supreme Court of the Bahamas to file it, as he was instructed. The lawyers had now taken over. The "Disney of Canada" had a cease trade order on it on the NASDAQ. With a $1 billion market capitalization, the company was in free fall. While no one had protected Cinar's treasury from management during the previous three years, there was now no one to protect the treasury from hostile lawyers and consultants. The faces had changed . . . the game stayed the same.

CHAPTER 16

DATE   MARCH 2000

SCENE   Nassau, Bahamas

In Search
of a Deal

The judge had been born in Nigeria and had migrated to the Bahamas. He had become a judge despite his unusual accent, and once named to the supreme court, he found himself very much in love with his own voice. He would willingly deliver speeches from the bench, offer advice to the attorneys before him, and in his monologues would telegraph to all observers where he was leaning in his rulings. This was no "Poker Alice." He wouldn't hint, rather he would deliver clear signals as to where he was headed. Basil Angelopoulos had never seen a judge behave like this before. Despite years in Canadian courts, he was completely unprepared for this situation. Bill Brock had been briefed by Barnet about the judge's likely behavior, but even with preparation he was pleasantly surprised. On the other side of the court, the relationship between Bahamian Brian Murree and Canadian Basil Angelopoulos was strange. Murree felt vastly superior to Basil, but understood that the client's decisions weren't being made by Bob and Tom in the Bahamas, and so he assumed that Basil spoke for the real clients in Montreal. In fact, Lino was now running the show, even though John was the most affected party. Basil's checks would come from Lino's accounts, but that money would be from John's coffers.

At the lunch break, Basil and Murree spoke — I was with them.

"Can you object to his behavior?" Basil asked. "My God, he's coaching Barnet and treating us like we're convicted criminals. What's going on?"

"I could object, but it will do nothing for our case, and it'll make him my enemy for life. We'll lose here, that's obvious, but we will win the appeal. Just stay calm."

Later, the two lawyers wound their way through the streets of Nassau, Basil and Brian walking together, and right behind Brian was the man who carried his briefcase. When they arrived at the legal office, Tom and I were waiting.

Murree said, "You guys can head into the conference room. I'll have some lunch brought to you." With that he left and went to the Partner's Dining Room, where he would dine on a four-course meal while Basil, Tom and I had sandwiches and Coke.

After lunch they called Lino to brief him. "We have to make a deal," Basil said. "This is going against us; we're getting our asses kicked. I think we can get a deal with Brock that stays their action, if we give them access to the books and records and show them where the money is." Basil was pleading.

After a shocked moment, Lino responded, "How much time can you buy us? We need as much time as possible."

"By tomorrow afternoon this judge will rule, or adjourn and then rule. Once the ruling is made, they'll have all the leverage."

"Understood. Have Maria call me." And with that, Lino hung up.

Maria called Lino right away.

"Maria, you need to build out some due diligence books on each of the private equity deals. You should have brochures, annual statements and financial information around there. I'll get all the junk in Montreal shipped down to you. Put the books together; make them look as important as possible. They need to buy us a couple of weeks while we finish the accounting."

"You're not going to let them in here, are you? If they get access to this place right now, or access to Bob and Tom, we're finished. They'll make this whole thing look like a scam in a New York minute. It'll be game over."

"I hear you, now build the books." Lino hung up.

Weinberg had met with J. Vincent O'Donnell, QC, for about an hour. He was known to be one of Montreal's top attorneys, with the firm of Lavery, de Billy. He had read a lot in the newspapers, but hearing the story live from one of the main participants caught even his jaundiced interest. As the meeting was wrapping up, O'Donnell looked at Weinberg and said, "I'll need a retainer."

"Of course," Weinberg responded. "How much?"

"One hundred thousand," was the response.

Barry Usher had been named the new CEO of Cinar and he was a new board member. He was a former insurance executive from Toronto who had lived in Montreal at one time and loved to play golf. Why he would come out of retirement to do this job was a subject of speculation for many people, until they realized how much he was being paid. Usher had no previous experience in film, animation or the creative arts. He was taking over a cease-traded company with a sullied reputation, one that was under investigation by Revenue Canada, the RCMP, the Quebec Securities Commission, the Ontario Securities Commission and Revenu Québec. The board of his company had presided over the country's most astounding corporate collapse and had thus far managed to avoid all blame and liability. Usher viewed getting money from Globe-X as a priority because Cinar needed cash to stay afloat. The expenses had soared and the income line was getting tight. His first action would be to fire the company's auditors.

Ernst & Young had been enablers to Weinberg, Charest and Panju. They had audited the statements, designed and endorsed the tax strategies, supplied the company with a flow of young talent who would be "flexible and ambidextrous" in their accounting practices. Usher sacked them unceremoniously. He had a previous relationship with PricewaterhouseCoopers and so he hired them quickly. At the end of his briefing the PWC account executive said, "We'll need a retainer."

"Of course," Usher responded. "How much?"

"One hundred thousand dollars," was the answer.

Then Usher flew to meet Brock and catch up on the situation in Nassau. Brock would brief him quickly and the president of Cinar understood clearly they were winning and that the judge was in their corner. He knew if the judge ruled in their favor, they might gain access to monies Globe-X had left, but that might not be much. It was dependent on the condition of the records and he knew that things would be stretched out while appeals were surging through the court. The newspapers were having a field day with the whole Cinar story. There were leaks to the press from inside his new company, and the stories were pointing to the probability of not just a cease trade, but a delisting. Shareholder lawsuits were now a probability, and Cinar had many battles to fight, not just with its founders and ransackers. To Usher, they didn't need an unnecessary battle with Globe-X, if it could be avoided.

Usher would meet chartered accountant Clifford Johnson at his pwc office in Nassau. Clifford was a successful partner in the firm and a social acquaintance of Muir, Daviault and Maria. He was intellectually capable and tough. But he needed a big file that would offer him and his firm a shot in the arm. The file that Usher and Brock had was a good fit for Clifford. In his early forties, he was athletic looking and had a Sidney Poitier aura about him. As the briefing ended Johnson said, "You understand I'll need a retainer."

"Of course," Usher answered. "How much?"

"One hundred thousand," was the response. This was not the kind of modest retainer one normally sees in Nassau. And yet, like everyone else, Usher threw money at the problem.

The press had begun to link Bob and Tom at Globe-X to Norshield International and, in turn, to John Xanthoudakis and Norshield Financial Group. John was getting phone calls from institutional investors asking what was going on.

"What's this mess in the Bahamas, John?" The questions would flow in. Money runs from problems and doesn't dilly dally. Money flows to strength and confidence and flees weakness and doubt. John feared a confidence crisis; he, Jo-Anne Polak and Dale Smith, John's chief financial officer, were trying to create as much distance from Globe-X as they could.

"There is no relationship between Norshield International and Norshield Financial Group," was what CFO Dale Smith tried to tell the press. Finally, he would acknowledge only that there was a licensing relationship involving the Norshield name. John began to realize that this could get out of hand and that it could lead to lawsuits or worse. He had met Robert Torralbo previously, but didn't know him. He understood him to be a good attorney and scrappy. He briefed Torralbo and indicated he'd like to work with him. At the end of the meeting Robert said, "You understand that I will need a retainer?"

"Of course. How much?" John countered.

"One hundred thousand," was Torralbo's response.

Realizing from every report he'd gotten from me, Maria and Basil that the judge was about to rule severely against the Globe-X positions, Lino called Basil.

Lino was short and terse. "Basil?"

"Yes?"

"Make a deal."

"Listen, I'm not so sure . . ."

"Don't argue. Just make a deal."

It was 8:00 a.m. in Nassau. Basil Angelopoulos was in his room at the British Colonial Hotel, overlooking the harbor. His direction from Lino was clear. His old friend

Bill Brock, who was representing the Cinar board, was staying in the same hotel. He called Brock, who was just back from his morning run.

"Can we have breakfast?"

"Great. Twenty minutes. See you at the patio restaurant."

They met outside where the view included the harbor and the pool. They both ordered light, just juice, coffee and toast. Basil offered, "Let's strike a deal." Brock's eyebrows went up. Basil started counting out on his fingers.

"We'll give you access to whatever you want. No copies, notes or photos leave the Globe-X offices. No press, everything is confidential. You don't have to drop your action, just stop it. No access to Tom or Bob. I'll work with you and your representatives myself."

"I'll float the offer by Usher. I think he'll do it."

Within two hours it was done; a deal was struck. Usher, Brock and Clifford Johnson would be welcomed into the conference room of Globe-X, something unthinkable at any time in the previous two weeks. I was there to welcome them. Bob and Tom would never see or meet with them at any point or time.

When the time came, Maria had dressed for the occasion: spike heels and a sundress with a low-cut front. She could be charming, and today she would be. Once they were all seated, not surprisingly, you could cut the tension with a knife. Always needing to be in control of the room, Brock began.

"Well, it's good to be inside the sacred walls. Hey, have you heard this one? This guy gets on the airplane and he's in his seat and down the aisle of the plane comes this absolutely gorgeous gal. Every head in the plane turns as she walks by. She sits down next to this guy and he can't

believe it. He could barely talk, but finally says, 'Good morning.' She turns, smiles and says 'Good morning. How are you?' He says, 'Fine.' 'Well,' she says, 'I'm on my way to Vegas to give a speech to the North American Association of Nymphomaniacs about my life of sexual experimentation. In my extensive analysis, I've found that the largest penises are not found among black men like many people think, but among Native Americans. While most people think the greatest lovers are Italians, I actually have found Jewish men to be the best, and for good old-fashioned frolicking and rolling in the hay, I think plain old American rednecks are the best. Oh, listen to me rattling on. Tell me about yourself.' The man responded with a small stutter. 'My name is Tonto Goldstein, but my friends call me Bubba.'"

Usher couldn't help but laugh, wishing Maria wasn't in the room. Johnson and Basil laughed out loud. Maria smiled and then laughed politely. Brock laughed loudly at his own joke and then said, "Jewish guys have always been the best lovers, everybody knows that. Okay, Basil, it's your turn."

After about an hour Brock said, "Barry here is really tired. He flew all night from Toronto. What do you say we get back together tomorrow about ten o'clock and get started with the records?" They all said their goodbyes and left.

Maria sat down, her head in her hands. She looked up at Basil in amazement. "Wow, they never asked to see one damn thing. Unbelievable! Now, I've got the whole night to build the file."

CHAPTER 17

DATE MARCH 2000

SCENE Norshield International –
Nassau, Bahamas

"They'll use your own money to destroy you"

Throughout the night Maria built books . . . big, fat, three-ring binders filled with brochures, annual reports, financial statements, news articles, anything she could find that would beef up the file. There were 19 binders. Each binder held all the information on the 19 private equity investments that had been made by Norshield on Globe-X's behalf. Nineteen separate equity investments each were minority positions in various businesses throughout the world, including software, timber, developmental businesses and second-stage equities. But none of the 19 binders contained any proprietary information or, for that matter, anything that couldn't be found at the library. Perhaps that wasn't the point right now. Globe-X had made investments in each of these firms, so Cinar would be interested in what these businesses were all about.

Brock and Basil met early for breakfast. Clifford started the day at his office. Usher fielded phone calls. At 10:15 a.m. they all arrived at the Globe-X office. It took 20 minutes to bring coffee and soon it was 11:00. Maria brought the books in; they were so fat she could carry only three at a time. After seven trips there were over eight feet of books stacked on the table. There was a barely audible groan as the boys realized what the task in front of them entailed. "Have a nice day, boys," Maria said with a smile as she left the room.

Bob and Tom were in Tom's office when Maria knocked. They all started laughing when she said, "You should have seen their eyes. There must be four hundred pounds of shit in there for them to read, and that Brock is so ADD, he'll be yapping the whole time the rest of them are trying to read." They all lit up another cigarette and quietly smiled.

They knew that back in Montreal Mario Ricci, Lino Matteo and four accountants were painstakingly doing the Globe-X Management and Globe-X Canadiana accounting that should have been done over the previous two years. The debits and credits were being made, the debentures were being created, and the basis of an audit was being established. They would need two weeks. Could Maria's ruse possibly buy that much time?

In the Nassau conference room, as Clifford began reading, Brock remembered he had to make a phone call, which he loudly made on his cell phone while the other three tried to concentrate. After the call, Brock said, "Let's break for lunch, it's almost noon." They all agreed immediately.

"Maria, we'll be back at two-thirty. We're taking a break for lunch," Brock called as they filed out.

"Have a nice lunch, boys. See you soon!" Maria called back. "This just may work," she thought.

She went into her office to look at the calendar. This was Thursday and they'd already wasted most of the day. They'd probably work until 4:30. Tomorrow was Friday; they'd quit early for sure and head for the airport. Monday will be a half day because of flights; next Friday is Good Friday. Good God, Easter is next week! Son of a bitch, it's Easter! They'll leave on Thursday and won't start until Tuesday, she thought. Luck was buying her time.

It was the first time that Lino and Bob were on the same call. The Globe-X books were making good progress and Lino was updating everyone on the status. Bob, Maria and Tom were in Nassau. Mario, John and Lino were in Lino's office in Montreal. Lino was presiding.

"We're about two-thirds finished. We seem to have the things we need. We're basically working from eight in the morning to nine at night; we'll work all weekend, and with Easter, we'll pick up four days when the others won't work at all. By the time those guys get back from their holiday break, we should have financials for them."

"Can you hold them off that long, Maria?" John jumped in.

"They're so lazy, John, and I've given them a truckload of stuff to read. It shouldn't be that hard."

"Maria," Lino said, "they all get paid by the hour, and Brock is five hundred per hour. Clifford must be three hundred. Let's just hope they don't bring in a bunch of juniors who may actually want to work the file."

"Fingers crossed," she said.

Tom asked, "John, how are you coming on that $15 million?"

"It's just about ready. We should be able to wire it tomorrow."

With a low resonance that only Lino could muster, he spoke up. "What $15 million are you talking about?"

Suddenly, everyone realized that the peace offering they all knew was in place was something Lino was unaware of. No one spoke.

"What $15 million are you talking about? John, what is he talking about?" The silence remained. "Do I gather that you sniveling morons have offered these fucking extortionists $15 million?" His tone was rising and his anger building. "Why in the world would you pay them anything? Once they've got that money, they'll just demand more and more. Once you've paid them, it shows that they are right and you're wrong."

Lino's hands curled into fists. He pounded hard in the center of his leather desk. "No way! No fucking way! You can't pay them, it will never stop. It won't be long before they'll have all the money and they'll be using it to chase you down. You don't feed your enemy! Keep them starving or they'll use your money to destroy you!" He kept shouting and pounding . . . and no one said a word. "I'm in charge. I'm in charge, and no money gets paid. Is this one of Daviault's brainless ideas?" The civility the two had demonstrated up to now was broken and Lino realized it. Calming down he said, "This meeting is over. No money!" He punched a button on the conference phone and Nassau went dead. John and Mario didn't dawdle on their way to the door.

In Nassau, Tom spoke first. "He doesn't get it. If we don't pay they'll go right back to court and seize everything."

"But Tom, he's right that they'll use our own money to chase us," Bob followed. "We're damned if we do, damned if we don't. If we think we have a future as a business, we *should* pay them. If all we want to do is defend ourselves and the money, then we *shouldn't* pay them. One hundred and eight million dollars is a lot of defence, but $15 million buys a lot of offence."

Tom was insistent. "They may be acting like a bunch of clowns right now, but don't forget how mean Brock was when he first arrived. And the judge is clearly on their side. Lino can shout all he wants. We need to pay."

 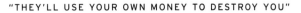

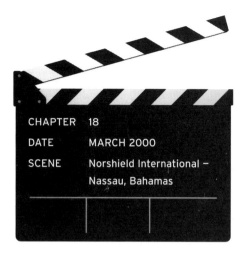

CHAPTER 18

DATE MARCH 2000

SCENE Norshield International –
Nassau, Bahamas

Buying Time

With the boys in Montreal working day and night, the accounting was getting done. When work resumed the week before Easter, both Brock and Usher would beg off; Clifford Johnson and an assistant were left with the job and the books. As the week ground on, he began to sense he was being snowed and eventually he would confront Maria.

"Maria, when will I get something of substance? I want the records, the books, the accounting materials and the swap agreement."

"What?" she yelled. "What? How do you know there is a swap agreement? How would you know? Why, Clifford Johnson, you duplicitous, sanctimonious son of a bitch, have you been sneaking around these offices spying and peeking? Are you a Peeping Tom, Mr. Johnson? Do I have to plug the keyhole when I go to the washroom? How would you even know there *is* a swap agreement? How?"

Johnson was speechless. The mere mention of it suggested he'd indeed been snooping around. Slowly he said, "Well, there has to be."

"I'll tell you that you've violated our agreement. You have no basis of knowing if there is or there isn't, so you can consider today's session over, and you can leave right now!"

"Maria, come on, I have a job to do. You can't throw me out."

With that she grabbed his briefcase and marched it out into the hall. "Get! Get!" With no other choice, Johnson left. Another day was gained, and now with the Easter holiday coming, there was no doubt the books would be done.

When the accounting was complete the story was actually pretty good. The investments were doing well and except for the liquidity crisis due to Cinar's unscheduled redemption, things were good.

As Bob and Tom smoked and crunched numbers, trying to figure out how much money they could pay to Cinar and how soon, they began to worry that unless a realistic payback schedule could be arranged, this might be game over. The funds that they needed to find would have to come from a combination of principal and appreciation of the invested assets. The fund was producing at a rate of twelve to fifteen percent prior to the conflagration and the returns seemed to be holding steady, but the principal was declining. Conversations with RBC had been going very well about introducing a leverage concept into the portfolio by borrowing money from RBC so the prin-

cipal withdrawals for Cinar wouldn't reduce the net return to the fund, due to principal reduction. But after hours of conferences and review, they realized that they could pay Cinar in the short term over $50 million plus a payment stream of $6 million per month from July to November. So, that was $80 of the $108 million back in Cinar's hands.

"This is an astounding amount of money, Tom. Do you think we can actually do it?" Bob asked.

"I think so. I just don't know if this will keep them happy or not. My God, how did we get into this mess?"

In the end, John Xanthoudakis would tacitly agree to the proposal; two months had gone by since the first meeting and the boys had delivered on their promises to date. Usher and Cinar still had a lot of other wars to fight; maybe they wouldn't see the point of another one if Usher could get what he wanted, or almost get what he wanted, without a fight. Bob and Tom wanted their lawyer Basil to make the proposal. So of course, Lino learned of it.

"Have you guys lost your minds? You're going to hand over $50 million and promise another $30 million, and break yourselves and your fund to make the problem go away? Don't you realize that they'll use the money to chase you for more money? There is no way out of this. Keep the money and fight because you'll never satisfy them. They've got everybody after them . . . RCMP, tax people, newspapers and securities people. They're delisted; there will be class action suits, and shareholders going nuts. If you give them money, they'll survive and you won't. Don't be stupid, Bob. You've always been stupid. Is this your idea? I will not be a party to this idiocy. No deal, no deal, no deal!"

When the conference call was over, Tom and Bob lit up and Tom shook his head sadly.

"I can't take a lot more of this pressure, Bob, and the pressure won't go away if we don't pay. Lino has helped us, but it's not his life here, it's not his business. We've got to pay or this will never go away."

"I agree, Tom. We need to do this."

They decided they would proceed with Usher themselves.

Once he realized what was being offered, Usher instructed Brock to get a deal done. This would mean that Cinar would get about $80 of the $108 million over the next eight months and, hopefully, recover the rest over the next year. Cinar's liquidity problems would be over and now they could focus on other things. The Dot-Com era was ending, the bull market of the late nineties was over and how Globe-X was going to be able to become liquid and stay alive wasn't Usher's problem. He was worried only about how Cinar would stay alive and nothing else.

In this way, the deal between the businessmen came together quite easily. But a lawyer can't bill much if a deal is easy and uncontested; this had a chance to be the biggest billing file in Canada that year. So Brock and Basil would log long hours and fight tooth and nail for every point.

As Lino's influence weighed heavily on them and Cinar was now a liability rather than an asset, the relationship between Bob and Tom began to fray. Despite Tom's easygoing way, they both knew their world had changed forever. When self-made entrepreneurs lose their money or suffer a setback, they may be sad or regretful, but they know how they made their money. They usually know that if they apply the same skill sets, tools, energy or ideas, they can do it again. Frequently, it may be in a different field, but the talent is the same. When heirs, lottery

winners or businesspeople who are just plain lucky lose their money, it's gone because they never knew how they made it in the first place; they have no map, no compass to find their way back to it. Bob and Tom could try to hold on to what was left, but they knew that what they had had just months ago was lost forever. They intuitively knew they couldn't find their way back.

Rules Are
for Other People

Golf tournaments serve as a summer rite to Montreal businessmen in a city where the warm days of summer are few and cherished. The charity fundraiser golf tournament is a networking mixer. The way the formula usually works is that a cause finds celebrities, each celebrity finds a sponsor, the sponsors find the attendees who, typically, find their wallets and buy tickets, greens fees, raffle tickets, drinks, dinners, side bets, more drinks, live auction items and, sometimes, cab rides home. The protocol is simple: if you invite someone to your fundraiser, they can invite you to theirs. Most executives try to limit their golf tournaments to four or so, but there are the serious golfers who may work in 10 or 12 tournaments, due in part to their social consciousness and in part to the fact that they've figured out this is the best corporate perk left, one the company cost-cutters haven't yet chopped out.

Lino preferred to limit his charity golf tournaments to four per year, one of which was the Mike Bossy Tournament, which he would help to sponsor himself. Mike Bossy, the former National Hockey League great who really did outscore Wayne Gretzky (if you calculate the games played and acknowledge his shortened career due to injuries), is a likable four-time Stanley Cup winner who cares about his community. These days, he pushes potato chips. In one of Lino's intermittent and infrequent attacks of charm, he persuaded Bossy to serve on the board of one of his companies, which made them kind of "business cousins" and gave people unlimited name-dropping opportunities. The Bossy Tournament was a business and social obligation for most of the people who traveled in Lino's orbit, whether they golfed or not. If they didn't golf, they could caddy, ride along, come for drinks or dinner, but they would show up. As for Lino himself he would enter the tournament, grab his clubs and, for five hours, remind everyone in his foursome that they weren't the worst golfer on the course . . . he was.

He played golf with as cavalier an attitude as ever hit the dimpled ball, and he had a slice that could terrorize the unwitting. He would literally tee up facing way off target in the hopes that the ball would curve around and eventually find the intended fairway. The reality was that, on mature courses with tall trees, the ball would frequently find other things before it found the fairway: trees, traps, water hazards, birds, even other golfers. And while his partners would vigorously shout "fore!", Lino rarely did. Given his distinctive voice, it's likely that his silence might have, in part, been due to modesty. While his driving was unguided by any standard, his short game was typified by deep divots, missed balls and shots flying vigorously over the green. Episodes in sand traps were easily resolved with his "foot wedge," as were obstructed lies and impaired views of the green. He had no touch with a putter and whenever his score reached 11 or 12, he'd pick up the ball, declare a "gimme" and mark his score a ten.

Golf is one of those games where scoring is sacrosanct, a thing of honor, where everyone knows that to be in the club you must follow the established ethic. Lino never had a partner who questioned his accounting, his arithmetic or his outcome. It is said that President Bill Clinton miscounted, moved his lies and even had secret service agents improve his position when he played golf. Most people chalked it up to his extreme competitiveness, the fact he was president or just that he thought he was getting away with it. Whatever the case, he was never called on it. It took the ethical lapses with Gennifer Flowers, Monica Lewinsky and Paula Jones for the media to realize he had character flaws; the golf course was just a symptom.

In Lino's case, he never regarded himself as being competitive at golf. He never seemed to collect on bets or prizes with false scores; he just had no regard for the rules of golf, or any rules, for that matter, that weren't his own.

Most serious golfers will tell their own version of this simple story. Golf is a character test. You learn more about a person by watching them on the golf course than you will ever learn in church, at a PTA meeting, on a business call or playing cards. You can see when or if they're tempted to improve their lie. You can see when or if they pretend they found their ball when it is really lost. You

RULES ARE FOR OTHER PEOPLE

can see if they add numbers incorrectly or forget the penalty stroke from the out-of-bounds.

If you have a partner who sneaks on the rule, he's likely to sneak in other parts of his life, so if you're his wife, look out. If your partner openly miscounts his score without remorse or regard, look out if he's your vendor. If he "finds" golf balls that are hopelessly lost, look out if he's your business partner. If he's constantly improving his lie, watch out if he's your banker.

Lino could make a 184 look like a 120 on the scorecard; sometimes he would even leave a hole or two out completely and still add the scored holes to a total. This practice made complete sense to him. They just weren't rules he intended to follow. All his life, Lino Matteo had made his own rules.

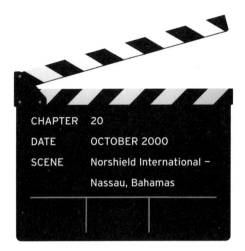

CHAPTER   20

DATE   OCTOBER 2000

SCENE   Norshield International –

Nassau, Bahamas

The Post-Crisis . . .
Pre-Crisis

Ironically, they found themselves moving up in the world just as things were falling apart around them. Tom, Bob and Maria discovered that their new offices had been built and were ready for occupancy. As the move was completed, the boxes unpacked and the finishing touches applied, the boys now had the finest offices in all of Nassau. Tom and Bob were hanging the paintings on their walls and putting up their most valued plaques and mementoes. Maria's office was perfect . . . the view, the paintings, the furniture, the flat screen television (the first to find its way onto the island). When the delivery-man arrived at the posh reception area he said, "Mr. Muir, please." As the first visitor, on the first day, at the new offices of Norshield International, he was even offered coffee, even though he was only a deliveryman. Tom walked quickly to the front, hoping this was the delivery he was waiting for.

"Good morning," he said. "Are you from Baron?"

"Yes, sir," the man said, blowing on his coffee. "Perhaps I can help you with the assembly, sir?"

"That would be great."

Tom grabbed the box. The deliveryman sipped his coffee and they headed back to Tom's corner office with a view of the bay, a view of the port and a view of the hotel below.

The two of them opened the box and began to assemble the tripod, the mounting assembly and, most important, the telescope. Tom was minutes from having the best mechanism for scanning the best view in the Caribbean. As the final assembly was completed, he forgot his melancholy of the previous months, he forgot his worries about how to make the next Cinar payment, and he forgot the mortal feeling that had dogged him the last six months. He focused his new toy on a small pier directly below his office. When his focus was perfect, he shifted the angle of his telescope closer and steeper. There below him on this sunny Nassau October day were 12 topless European sunbathers. The deliveryman took a peek. "Success has its privileges," he murmured, "and this is certainly one of them." Tom nodded. He now had the best view in all of Nassau and the best way to enjoy it.

While the move had brought Bob Daviault some renewed energy, he knew that he just wasn't getting revved up the way he usually did about work or future prospects. Golf was fun, work was not. The highs were missing; the surprise $15 million checks were gone. The island is only

50 miles long and 20 miles wide, about 1,000 square miles. Sounds big when you say it that way, but in reality it's very small. For Bob, it was feeling smaller all the time.

Despite the publicity that had accompanied the Cinar mess, John's business was thriving. The bull market was over and contrarian theories like his hedge funds were prospering . . . earning returns of twenty percent and more. John and his type were the new wonder boys of finance. While most brokers were afraid to answer the telephone or respond to their emails, John was opening new accounts and getting stronger and stronger financing. He had entered into a unique banking arrangement with the Royal Bank of Canada, something none of his competitors had, and that gave him a sizable advantage. The agreement was with Canada's largest bank; it gave him access to a credit line supported by a hedge fund basket. The leverage ratio was 6 : 1; so for every $15 million Norshield held, RBC would advance $85 million. And the bank would hire Norshield Financial to manage the funds.

The bank would contract with John's own managers to manage the fund; the bank would share fees and incentives with him and, suddenly, boom! He was bigger and more leveraged than anyone could imagine. The funds under management would grow, thanks to this arrangement, from $125 million to $1 billion. John was doing just fine . . . Norshield was prospering, his philanthropic work flourishing. Magazine profiles proclaimed his genius. The only annoyance was the recurring liquidity problem he needed to solve for Tom and Bob because of Cinar. The dust from the Cinar mess was leaving a grimy film on what was otherwise a perfect life.

Lino, too, was prospering. Mount Real was being recognized for growth, profitability and solidity. The business magazines wrote glowing tributes to the entrepreneurship and genius of Lino Matteo. The company's worth grew to $100 million and its profits were running at nine to eleven percent. While the market never seemed to give him the multiple he thought he deserved, the stock did well and investors were pleased.

While Mount Real was growing nicely, other aspects of growth also emerged. A media business was forming thanks to the *Ocean Drive* investment. Magazine sales were done by Honeybee, magazine production by Red Chili Media. There was a radio company, too — part of *Menz* magazine, which was a Red Chili Media production. It included outdoor adventure magazines and radio shows, new high-profile websites and e-zines. I was editing the outdoor magazines for the operation and doing the weekly radio show, which was gaining good popularity. On its own, Honeybee Technologies was growing, evolving from a software development company to a business Lino really knew: telemarketing.

For decades Montreal had been a telemarketing Mecca. Separatism had left a well-educated, "English only–speaking labor force that was unemployable post-1980. To work for large companies or the government, you needed to speak French; if you didn't, you were out. This shift pushed hundreds of thousands of people down Highway 401 to Toronto and away to other locales throughout Canada and the world. The Quiet Revolution of Quebec displaced much of an entire generation of "Anglos," and created opportunities for Francophones that were previously unavailable to them. One sector in which unilingual Anglos could work and prosper was telemarketing. The sales were in the United States where everyone wanted to speak English anyway, and the laws governing sales practices were Quebec or Canadian laws, which were quite lax, as long as you were calling out of the country. The ability of the various governments stateside to enforce their laws in Canada was highly variable, depending on the will of the federal administration and their relationship with the Canadian government at the time. As a rule, only the worst offenders would occasionally be slapped by enforcement.

Lino liked to run a "clean operation." It was good business and he was a businessman. Scammers and con men are, by their nature and practice, liars. If you lie to one person, you'll lie to another, maybe even your boss, so Lino avoided scammers — anyone who might try to run side scams on people they were telemarketing to. The problem with the industry is that if you get rid of all the scammers, you end up with no sales force, no sales managers, no trainers, and finally, no sales. He would try to solve this problem by visiting the sales office once a week — not often enough to catch the scammers, and anyway, everyone knew to expect him on Wednesday afternoons. In a way, he turned a blind eye to what he could not stand seeing. His force sold magazine subscriptions, multiple magazines for multiple years. Before the consumer knew it, he or she had bought six to eight magazines for up to four years and owed $800 to $1,500, which was charged to a credit card. With a good infrastructure, good publishers, good financing and a clever sales force, this business would be the fuel that was putting the Mount Real/Honeybee rocket into orbit. None of the annual reports ever seemed to say this, none of the press releases ever touted the fact, but the good old Montreal

specialty of telemarketing was the grease in the Mount Real wheel.

It was Wednesday, Lino's half day at the sales office. He was working quietly in his office when he decided to take one of his walk-arounds. As he moved slowly and decisively through the bull pen, he noticed that one of his salespeople was wearing a cap with the visor reversed. Lino approached him and removed the cap, saying, "No caps." He set it down and moved on. The young man grabbed the cap and stuck it on his head just the way it had been, never missing a note while he pitched the client on a $950 order. Lino reversed his course and went back to the cubicle where the pitch was taking place. He removed the cap a second time and said, "No caps." The young man responded identically and kept on pitching. At this point Lino grabbed the phone line just as the young man was getting the credit card number for the order. He stood next to the young man until the order was complete and then pulled the line out of the wall.

"You're fired," he said.

"Why?" the young man asked.

"Because of your cap. You know we have a 'no cap' rule."

"I think better with a cap on."

"Well, then put your cap on and think about why you got fired," Lino shot back.

The unit manager said, "Mr. Matteo, Darin is our leading salesman this week and I've been waiving the cap rule. Can't we settle this somehow?"

"It has been settled," Lino responded. "Now get back to work."

The Dilemma

Clifford Johnson was standing in the silent conference room, gazing at all the paper. So much paper, so little information. On top of that, his fights with Maria were becoming chronic. The phone rang, Clifford jumped. It was Bill Brock. He told Clifford that it wasn't certain yet, but it looked like Globe-X might miss a payment.

"That would open the door," Brock said brightly. "If Usher would just agree to drop the hammer, we could be in complete control of the assets and prove that these goat ropers are the dipshits we know they are. If we could gain control of the liquidation that would allow us to pursue suits in at least three countries, Canada, Bahamas and the U.S., and have sound funding for years."

"Bill, what do you think the chances are?" Johnson asked.

"High. The market is eroding; Tom and John have got a fund that's going south and they don't dare stop the payments. But if they don't stop the payments, it'll all turn upside down. How fast can you move if we give you the nod?" Brock said.

"Same day," was Johnson's response. He put the phone down gently and nodded to himself.

Increasingly, Clifford felt that with time the Globe-X situation would worsen. He would bide his time, hoping that when Globe-X defaulted, he would be named the liquidator of the Globe-X estate. Clifford had been successful in his rise as a chartered accountant, and then his employment and partnership at Pricewaterhouse-Coopers. At no time had Clifford ever had the chance to control a file as visible, as lucrative or as multinational as the Globe-X file would be. For that matter, there weren't many bankruptcy trustees in all the Caribbean who had ever worked a file as big as this one. There were only two problems: one, Globe-X hadn't defaulted on their payments yet, and two, Clifford had signed a confidentiality agreement that would make him ineligible for the assignment, if he was awarded it. He was confident that Tom and Bob would solve problem one for him, by defaulting, and problem two he would just ignore; hopefully, no one would ever realize it.

CHAPTER 22

DATE   JUNE 2001

SCENE   Norshield International –
            Nassau, Bahamas

A Darkness
in the Sky

Small signals are virtually always more important in life than big alarms. Prior to a heart attack, which seems so sudden, comes shortness of breath, chest pains, angina pains in the left arm, sometimes for years in advance. If someone listens to the small signals, they might alter or change things before the arteries fill up, become plugged and a coronary occurs. Before melanoma becomes fatal, it reveals a change in the color or texture of a mole. As diabetes begins to take over a body, thirst and tiredness set in to signal the body's chemical imbalances. Animals perceive a coming earthquake before it arrives, the barometer falls before the weather changes and, of course, the skies shift before the rain.

Despite the swanky address and assembled demonstrations of wealth, the new offices of Norshield International had a hollowness about them. Bob was on the golf course again and Tom was sucking up to Barry Usher, using his telescope and golfing as well. The heart was full of blockages, the spirit gone. There was no plan to rebuild, just a desperate hope. The payments were becoming more difficult to make and liquidity tougher to squeeze from the managers. How do you maintain high returns when your capital base is dwindling? "Thank goodness redemptions are low and most of the investors are rolling their returns back into the fund," Bob said out loud.

"We have to increase risk, John, we have to increase risk," Tom lamented.

"That may get you more cash now, but what about your non-Cinar related clients? Their risk moves up, but their returns may not. You have to think about them, too."

"John, I know that, but our focus needs to be Cinar payouts or our clients' fate is sealed anyway. We'll be done." John reluctantly agreed. "There is something else you need to know. Bob is thinking about leaving. We don't need him anymore now that the fund is dwindling, there's no Cinar to service and besides all that, he's fried," Tom continued.

"What's he going to do?" John asked.

"I'm not sure if he knows, but I think he'll move to Canada. He's gotten much more involved in his church and maybe he'll just do things differently."

"Are you okay with this, Tom?" John said.

"Oh yeah, things have been strained. Things change and it's time." They said goodbye and Tom hung up. He lit a cigarette and looked out his window.

When Lino heard that Bob might be leaving, he said, "It's about fucking time! Listen John, whatever you do, don't let Tom give him a big severance or settlement. Better yet, have me do his severance, because by the time I'm done with that son of a bitch, he'll owe money."

"Oh, settle down. We need to treat him fairly," John retorted.

"Mark my words, John, his last victim will be you. He gets a severance, and he'll undress you bastards. Don't give him one cent!"

The conversation was over before John could tell Lino anything else. For instance, that he was about to increase the risk ratio and leverage of the funds to accommodate and continue Cinar funding. Lino wouldn't feel the chest pain, the shortness of breath or the tingle in the left arm.

Martin Wardman didn't get his warning signal either; the news came out of the Montreal sky. The person on the other end of the line was very clear and very deliberate. "The licence will be revoked in thirty days if the payments aren't caught up to date. There have been no royalty payments made for twelve months, and this is not acceptable. The amount owed is $120,000, and it's due immediately."

Wardman physically slumped as he heard the words. He knew cognitively and intuitively that this was the end. His stomach began to ache as if he had been hit. His knees were weak, purely because of nerves. This meant that Mount Real hadn't made any of the licensing payments that allowed him to use the name and logo of the magazine he'd nurtured and built. The equity of the business was now in play, the trademark gone. He didn't call Lino for an appointment, he just went. His Jaguar sped through the Italian neighborhood of Ville-Émard. He parked and jumped out of his car, heading into Lino's

worldwide headquarters. As he drove, as he climbed the stairs, as he waited for his nod, he turned over in his mind what he wanted to say.

"Mr. Matteo will see you now," Paulina interrupted his thoughts.

He was in no mood for a lecture, chitchat or condescension. He was out of business and he knew it, unless Lino coughed up $120,000 to keep the deal alive.

"Lino, I've just talked to the Miami office. They say that no royalty payments have been made for a year, and that if —"

Lino interrupted. "If all the payments aren't made now, they'll pull the licence. Well, Martin, I guess you're out of business." He looked Martin directly in the eye and waited. Wardman was frozen. Then Lino said, "Is there anything else to talk about, Martin?"

"How is this possible?" Wardman whispered.

"It's possible, *Martin*, because you never made enough money. It's possible because you paid too much in salaries. It's possible because your print costs were too high. It's possible because you're a shitty manager, Martin. How many more reasons do you need?"

"It happened because you didn't make the royalty payments," Wardman countered.

With a roar Lino screamed and pounded his desk with both fists. "Don't go there, Martin: *you* are the fuckup here, not me. I don't make mistakes. You can't walk in here as the big shot publisher and play 'duh' with me. Duh, I didn't know we were short of cash. Duh, I didn't know my payments were tight. Duh, I never saw a payables list."

"But I didn't," Martin said.

"Then you should have! Now go cry somewhere else.

Get the hell out of here!"

Wardman left, and he never went back.

When a business fails, it's amazing what's kept, what's stolen and what's thrown away. When *Ocean Drive* closed, they boxed up all the old issues because no one could comprehend that the world wouldn't want to see them again. Old photo shoots and submissions would be carefully archived, while advertiser lists and information would be discarded, along with financial statements. Wardman and his investors would lose every cent, the licensor would receive nothing, the employees would get their last paycheck and the creditors would get nothing. Wardman would leave the country and move to Chicago where there was a population of expatriate Brits to melt into, a big city to get lost in, and start over fresh.

In his Montreal law offices, Michael Maloney's phone rang; it was his client.

"Yeah, Lino." The voice on the other end was unmistakably Matteo.

"Michael, I want you to check out the availability of the name *O.D. Lifestyles*. I'm thinking about a new magazine. If that doesn't work, check *Overture*. Michael, we're in the publishing business now."

The market had dropped precipitously that day. It had nothing to do with *Ocean Drive*'s demise or Matteo; it was just an off day. John Xanthoudakis' traders were having a harder and harder time getting liquid without jackknifing their investment models. As he sat quietly in his huge office, which overlooked the St. Lawrence River on one side and downtown Montreal on the other, he reviewed the report from the trade and Tom's requests. As the sun was setting behind Mont Royal, it created an unusual light reflection through his windows. At first it

frightened him and then he realized it was just the errant light. Once the mystery was solved, he wrote orders to his traders. "Stop liquidating positions. The fund cannot take the pressure in this downward market." Then he wrote a memo to Tom. As the fund manager he had fiduciary responsibility to protect all the investors in the fund, not just Cinar.

"Dear Tom: I have ceased liquidation of the Globe-X funds in a falling market. The requests cannot be met without serious risk to the total net asset value. I would suggest you tell Cinar that $86 million is all they're going to get for a while. Given that most portfolios have lost over twenty-seven percent of their value in the last 12 months, their recovery is pretty darn good. You can't afford to pay them, you must renegotiate. — John"

The Quebec
Securities
Investigation

The Quebec Securities Commission (QSC) had landed on Norshield International's doorstep because their investigation of Panju, Weinberg and Charest was gaining steam and they were convinced that they needed to pin the three firmly to the mat. This was the largest case of impropriety in their docket and the press' appetite for Cinar stories seemed insatiable. Worst of all, though, it appeared that Revenu Québec and Revenue Canada were winding down their investigations and the RCMP wasn't pursuing criminal charges. So that made the QSC the lead agency responsible for bringing the trio to justice. Only 18 months earlier, Cinar had had a market capitalization of $1.5 billion, virtually all of which had been erased now, and the stock price had been over $30 per share. These are not the kinds of failures a securities watchdog can afford.

The investigation meetings were to take place at the new Norshield International headquarters in Nassau. Tom was to give his deposition first and Bob would go second. The QSC sent down Laurent Lemieux and Reginald Michiels; before they arrived, it had been agreed that both Bob and Tom would receive immunity from the QSC because it was Weinberg and Charest they were after. To anyone reading the subsequent transcripts, the questions ranged from routine to intriguing.

I had spent the first 20 years of my career in a variety of businesses, but primarily marketing, sales and advertising. I found myself drawn into the Mount Real/ Norshield orbit due to a combination of factors, including a non-compete that kept me out of the United States, and some joint ventures with John Xanthoudakis and Lino Matteo. I'd worked on a variety of distressed deals as a consultant and had been involved in this situation since March 2000. I was one of the first hands to step in and help Bob and Tom.

In fact, I'd gone down to help Bob and Tom prepare, at Lino's suggestion and John's insistence. The preparation was complete and now was the time for the boys to perform. Tom gleefully showed the visitors his new office, including the telescope. It would be impossible for anyone to not be impressed with the view and the quarters. Tom's deposition was over by noon and upon completion he raced out of the room to have a cigarette.

Bob's deposition was certainly going to be the meatier of the two. Tom had always accurately maintained that he was distanced from the transactions and Cinar itself. Bob was the contact man and he knew the deal best. The meeting began:

Question: First of all, what is Norshield International?

Bob Daviault: That's a service company, sort of a catchall for the fund managers or for the funds to report, to provide different types of services for clients, banking transactions if they have bank accounts and so forth. The relationship that Norshield has with Globe-X and all of the funds and companies we're involved with –

Q: Do you remember when was the first contact with Mr. Panju? Your next contact was with Mr. Panju?

BD: Right.

Q: Do you remember when and how and where?

BD: Not specifically. My first contact, I think, with Hasanain, was in 1997, I think.

Q: You remember what part of the year?

BD: September, October, November, the later part. And it was in Montreal.

Q: You came up to Montreal?

BD: Right.

Q: Do you remember what were the services and investments that you could provide at the time

BD: At the time, as I said, the issue was the understanding that they had some foreign exchange needs. They also were looking to invest a lot of those proceeds, not just a question of hedging them. I think it's a simple strategy. They are looking against currency risks that would exist when you are having American dollars and reporting Canadian dollars; and looking, maybe, to make acquisitions in Canadian dollars, which they would be looking to hedge the value on upswings or downswings – of the Canadian dollar.

Q: Was it the only strategy discussed then?

BD: After that there were also discussions about, as I was saying, the need to invest these proceeds until they were subsequently needed for use, and the initial intention was a bond portfolio.

Q: Could you explain something else; why this transfer of $12 million [back up to Canada]? Do I gather some commercial paper had matured or is it something else?

BD: Something else.

Q: Could you explain?

BD: In my opinion, it was intended to be a short-term loan to the directors, or specifically the numbered company, Ron's numbered company.

Q: When did you become aware of those holding companies, those numbered companies? First of all, were those holding companies in business with you as far as investment is concerned?

BD: Those numbered companies were a client of mine prior to this $12 million being sent. So when I sent the $12 million to Cinar, I understood it was for a short-term loan for those numbered companies that I knew to belong to Ron and Micheline.

Q: Who was answering for those? First of all, who were you dealing with when those companies were investing through your companies?

BD: Hasanain.

Q: Mr. Panju?

BD: Right.

Q: Who told you that those two companies were holding companies that belonged to Mr. Weinberg and Ms. Charest?

BD: Certainly Hasanain would have.

Q: Did they have the same kind of investment strategy that Cinar had?

BD: They did, except for the enhanced bond strategy. I am not sure if one or both had a currency strategy as did Cinar, and they also had a debt instrument, fixed term debt instrument similar to the commercial paper exclusively. That was it.

Q: Who initiated those transactions? Was it Mr. Panju?

BD: Yes, it was.

Q: Have you ever spoken to Charest or Weinberg about those investments specifically?

BD: Again, when you say the two of them, Micheline or Ron, again, it would have been in passing. They are not sophisticated-type products we would have gone at length to discuss. It's either a fixed product or currency hedge.

Q: To your knowledge, did they know they had investments through those numbered companies over here?

BD: I couldn't say with one hundred percent certainty, but if I were to guess, I'd say yes.

Q: If I understand, at a certain point in time you transferred $12 million to those two numbered companies −

BD: No, to Cinar.

Q: Who told you to transfer the money?

BD: Hasanain, I believe, provided the instructions for us to wire the money.

Q: As far as you know or understand, at that time who asked that the money should be transferred to Cinar instead of . . . not instead, but to Cinar?

BD: That would have been Hasanain, I believe. And he would have asked us to wire the $12 million to Cinar.

Q: And did you know, then, that this $12 million was tied up with the two numbered companies?

BD: I knew the intention was that the proceeds of the $12 million were going to be used by the numbered companies. How and where, that wasn't disclosed.

Q: And you said that it would be a loan?

BD: Right.

Q: A loan from who to who?

BD: From CIS to the numbered companies.

[CIS was Comprehensive Investment Services, a Bahamian corporation owned by Tom and Bob and used as a holding entity, conduit and investment fund for Canadians trying to do tax deals in the Bahamas.]

Q: Okay, it was a loan. Was there a contract between CIS and Cinar or the numbered companies?

BD: Embarrassingly not.

Q: And who gave the order to Globe-X Management to put the money in CIS?

BD: I did.

Q: You did?

BD: I did.

Q: And did you receive an order from somebody to give this order?

BD: No.

Q: But why did you do that? Why did you put – how much money did you put in CIS coming from Cinar?

[break in transcript]

Q: Do you know Mr. Xanthoudakis?

BD: I do.

Q: According to you, what's the job of Mr. Xanthoudakis?

BD: He is the President of Norshield Financial Group.

Q: He is the . . . has he any authority on your company Norshield International?

BD: None whatsoever.

Q: And on Globe-X Management?

BD: None whatsoever.

Q: Do you see him very often?

BD: Not since I moved down here. As I said, I was part of Norshield Financial Group and we worked closely together. But now, I think we're too busy – certainly, our dealings here kept us very, very busy. I typically get off the island four, five, six times a year, a lot of that being personal. I haven't been to Canada since October of last year.

Q: Do you know if Mr. Xanthoudakis has anything to do with the investment of Cinar or Globe-X Management?

BD: Not directly. As I said, the Norshield Financial Group does provide services that encapsulate the assets that are, in part, involved with the Cinar portfolio, but other than that, no.

Q: Do you know if Mr. Xanthoudakis did something to put Cinar, Weinberg, Charest and Norshield International in touch?

BD: Not in touch. I wouldn't be surprised if any one of the Cinar people would have looked as a reference and said, "What do you think of these guys?"

The meeting would take about two hours, and in that period of time the QSC would be the first to learn under sworn affidavit that Bob clearly believed that he had loaned Weinberg and Charest $6 million each in November 1999. (But had they probed further they would have discovered that a year earlier in November 1998, he had loaned them a further $1.8 million, which they repaid several months later.) Bob knew little if anything of what would happen to the millions after they went north. But the QSC was discovering that the money would flow from Globe-X to CIS, which sent the money on to Cinar. Cinar would then debit Weinberg's and Charest's Directors' Loans Accounts. They would then use the money to buy more investments with a firm called Progenesis, where personal accounts held by the married couple would rise in value. In addition there was a margin on the Progenesis accounts and they tried to zero it out every November. (In previous years the vari-

ous investment accounts that Weinberg, Charest and Panju had established went unnoticed and unexamined by Ernst & Young, but by the fall of 1999, the climate had changed due to the tax scandal, so Ernst & Young was chasing down those accounts. The Progenesis account was one of several personal investment accounts being funded by Cinar leverage.)

Bob had also established that Weinberg knew and understood that the investments with Globe-X were leveraged. Weinberg's continued assertion that he "knew nothing" didn't jibe with Daviault's statements. Lastly, Bob acted like, and insisted he was, the CFO of Norshield International and Globe-X. He said that John Xanthoudakis had no authority over them in the Bahamas and that it wasn't John who introduced Cinar to Globe-X. It was, in fact, he and Mario Ricci (now VP of Norshield Financial) who had put the deal together.

At the top of their new headquarters, Bob Daviault seemed to be very much in control and confident in his role. He would open the conversation of the "twelve million" which would be a recurring locus of rancor in courtrooms in various countries and jurisdictions for the next eight years. He didn't mention that in his desk he held stock certificates for over 500,000 shares of Cinar stock (which went as high as $32 per share, or about $16 million), including some of the Weinberg/Charest super voting shares that gave them two-thirds of the votes, while owning only twelve percent of the equity. When the loan to Ron and Micheline's numbered companies hadn't been repaid in January 2000, Daviault shrewdly asked for collateral. Weinberg had sent the shares, which now secretly sat in Bob's desk drawer.

Shortly after the deposition Bob accelerated his

conversations with Tom about leaving the company and the island. "It's time for something new, the thrill is gone," he would say. He would, as Lino had predicted, try to get a severance or separation package. Both Tom and John were afraid to have Lino negotiate the package, so they did it themselves. Bob was looking for $1.5 million. Where the number came from or how the value would be supported isn't known; it was just a number. Eventually they agreed on $900,000 with $600,000 to be paid right away and the last third in three years. Neither John nor Tom would dare tell Lino the terms. Within weeks, Bob Daviault and his family would move to Calgary to start a new life and distance themselves from the mess that had become Globe-X and the nightmare that was Cinar's death spiral.

CHAPTER   24
DATE   AUGUST 2001
SCENE   Montreal

Same Problem,
New Faces

Clifford Johnson's cell phone rang. Bill Brock sounded exuberant. "They're going to default. Tom has called Barry Usher; there is no doubt that they're in trouble and they're going to miss a payment, Clifford. We should be very close now," Brock said.

"That's great, Bill, but is Usher going to let us drop the hammer if they do default?"

"I'll be all over him. I'm sure I can get him to do it," Brock said.

Back at Cinar in Montreal, Barry Usher was waffling, just as Clifford had worried he would. "Bill, these guys have paid us a lot of money . . . $86 million. I honestly don't know how they even did it with the markets going to hell like they have been. I'm going to renegotiate with them and give them some time," Usher said firmly.

"Barry, they still owe us almost $40 million. That's a lot of money, and you have a fiduciary responsibility to collect it. You can't go soft now; the liability will fall right on your head."

"Are you threatening me, Mr. Brock? This is no public relations platform, so let's speak bluntly. I don't know how you've convinced the press to keep printing those numbers, but we never had $122 million with Globe-X; it was $108 million, and when you do the math that leaves $22 million, not $40 million. The only way you get $40 million is with a currency conversion to Canadian dollars, which is another clever trick you seem to keep pulling on the press. Bill, I'm not the press and I'm not going to be intimidated or hoodwinked. I will think about what you have said, but I don't need another unnecessary fight with Globe-X, and I don't know that we'll get more money if we change course anyway."

"If you let me and PricewaterhouseCoopers loose on these guys, we'll get the money and we'll tear them down. These guys are bad actors and con men. They deserve to be torn down and we can do it. They continue to take money from people and pretend they're legitimate. It's our duty to bring them down. We have the power to do it and the ability to do it." Brock subsided into his chair.

"Bill, do you realize these guys have done everything they've said they would do up till now, and that they might just be good guys caught in a bad situation? It was Weinberg who sent them the money; they didn't take it from him." Usher shook his head. "Why don't you get

some rest, it's late." When they parted Barry Usher sat for a long time, thinking.

"Be ready to move, Clifford," Brock said. "Any day now you'll be ready to throw them into bankruptcy, and as soon as it happens, you need to become the receiver," Brock urged. Johnson never mentioned how that step would be in violation of his confidentiality agreement; he would just hope that no one would ever notice.

"I'll be ready, Bill," he said.

After three months of resistance, Usher finally relented and the bankruptcy filings were put into motion. Bob was already gone and Tom was no longer the amiable, carefree guy who had moved to the Bahamas 11 years earlier. He was drinking more, not sleeping at night and, as always, chain-smoking. He had done something that he had never done before that worried him hugely. He had yelled and raised his arm toward his daughter. Now 12 years old and the love of his life, she hadn't deserved the vocal or physical reaction that Tom had shown. He knew he was wrong, and he, too, was exhausted. The day after the episode with his daughter, Tom responded to an email he had left unanswered. At Lino's urging, Lowell Holden, a Minnesota businessman, had approached Tom with a proposal that included him taking over the non-Globe-X portion of Tom's business, cis and Silicon Isle.

Along with cis, Holden had proposed buying these businesses from Tom and moving him out of the fire. Just two days earlier Tom had had no interest, but after the incident at home, he knew he was not holding up to the pressure, so he responded to Holden.

It didn't take long for the willing seller and the willing

buyer to come to terms, and with documentation waiting, the two of them met to close the transaction that
would move Tom out of the front lines and put Holden
into the trenches. But as Tom would learn, there were to
be no safe rear areas in the new war that the lawyers and
accountants would launch. With quasi-judicial status,
bankruptcy trustees can do pretty much what they like.
They can summon, subpoena, seize and cast innuendo
wherever they like. When they seize assets they can use
the assets to pay themselves and fund their continuing
projects. They are not required to declare a windup date
or distribute the seized assets to creditors or debtors until
they choose to. They can distribute meanness and retribution more completely than any other agents in the
cultures of the first world.

As Usher called Tom to tell him what was about to
happen, Tom told him about the event with his daughter.
The two of them had talked at least monthly for the previous year and had come to a point of mutual respect. Usher
wasn't completely comfortable with the pending action, but
was going to acquiesce. He was relieved when he learned
Tom was bowing out. Usher hoped that would keep him
out of the storm, but doubted that anything could.

"I'd always hoped we could play that golf game we've
been promising each other," Tom said with a tone of
sadness.

"Me, too, Tom. My putting has been getting better and
better, and I'd have liked to play. Who knows, if you're
retiring now, maybe it will be easier to get together."

"Yeah, maybe." It would be the last time the two of
them would ever talk.

Clifford Johnson and his attorneys strode to the
Bankruptcy Courts of the Bahamas to file their petitions

as soon as they could. This would give them complete control of the Globe-X entities. They would now represent and become synonymous with the companies they had fought to destroy for the previous two years. While there were assets, they weren't liquid and, as a result, the funding for their work needed to come from Cinar. Over the next year alone, they would bill Cinar over $750,000.

Now, Bob would pack up his family and leave quietly for Calgary, a city where there was a Christian community of his church members to meld into, a place to start over and begin a new life.

Tom would choose to stay on in Nassau to try to continue the life he was living . . . something very hard to do when your position is lost, your resources low and you're in the visible eye of a storm. Maria would stay and wouldn't even change offices. The new administrator of the funds would be called Cardinal. Maria and a guy named Steven Hancock would run the company — in fact, almost the entire staff came from Tom's former empire.

Bill Brock had set the stage for another record year of billings. The Cinar fee trough had just gone from big to enormous, and now even more lawyers, accountants and public relations types could climb onboard.

CHAPTER   25

DATE   MARCH 15, 2002

SCENE   Montreal

Get It Over With

Hasanain Panju knew his life would never be the same. Remaining in Montreal was pointless and painful. He and his family had immigrated before, and now was the time to immigrate again. A clean slate where people don't know you, haven't seen your picture in the wrong part of the newspaper, where the conversations don't always start on one subject and then circle back to the old days. Panju would move to London where there was an Indian community to melt into and a big city in which to vanish. "Out of sight, out of mind" might be a trite old expression, but that doesn't make it incorrect. With Panju gone and only his lawyer to talk to, regulators put all their focus on Weinberg and Charest. The charges began to fly and, while Hasanain was living a normal new life with his accumulated millions, Ron and Micheline were dealing with the accusations, anger, retribution and depositions of their old lives.

"Is there any way to shorten this? To get it behind us?" Micheline asked. "I was at the hairdresser and it's like I'm invisible. No one talks to me. They wash my hair, they cut my hair, they charge me, they take my tips, but no one chats anymore, no one gossips, no one wants to be around me. The other women that I've talked to for years, their eyes are empty now. Even if they say hello, you wish they hadn't because it feels so hollow."

"I understand. I feel it, too, the lack of recognition. They see you, but look past you or right through you . . . the way you'd pass a beggar on the street . . . or a hitchhiker. It might get easier if they'd just decide whether to charge us or not. What I know right now is that no one wants to be seen or identified with us, whatever their reason."

"Oh, well, fuck 'em! I never really liked chitchat anyway, and if making this go away means losing our money, I'll keep the money," Micheline shot back.

"Well, our accounts are safe, but Brock and those Phillips & Vineberg bastards are building out suits and actions that could be a problem. As long as they're not getting money from Norshield, they're going to try to get money from us. For that matter, they may try to get money from us anyway. But for now, we're okay. Maybe we should sit down with the government to speed things up . . . that might work."

The Chairman of the Quebec Securities Commission slammed his gavel to the table. Suddenly, the hearing room packed with reporters, photographers, lawyers and onlookers fell silent. The verdict was read. The QSC had just levied the largest fine in Quebec's history on Ron Weinberg and Micheline Charest — $1 million each. They had negotiated and agreed to the fine. As well, the couple was barred from acting as directors on any publicly traded Canadian company for five years. There was no admission of wrongdoing; it was only money and maybe, just maybe, a new beginning.

The press was brutal, the stories cold, convicting and unsympathetic. Some opined they had gotten off too light because the shareholders had lost virtually everything . . . almost *$1 billion!* How could $2 million be enough? While it didn't seem like a victory for one side, for the other it might be the end of a string of defeats. The defeats had started with the writers' controversy and the tax credits, and then they just kept coming. The photographers clicked and ran with Weinberg and Charest as they raced to their car. They jumped in and sped off, showing anyone watching that their Mercedes wasn't the model with the small engine.

"Fucking vultures." Micheline was the first to speak. "They're just loving this. We put this town on the entertainment map. We made this town a force in entertainment. This was nothing but a broken-down secessionist ghost town without us. There were more empty buildings in this city than there were full ones. The only thing this place was famous for were whores and crappy schools, and now these ingrates treat us like shit after we paid $1 million each," she fumed. Weinberg sat silently and drove.

Lino put down his newspaper. It lay in front of him with the photos of Weinberg and Charest staring back at him. Lino and I were reviewing the events. Attorney Michael Maloney was waiting outside Lino's door. Sometimes Lino would let him stand there for 10 or 15 minutes waiting to be let in. Maloney was 5'5" with a non-threatening face, a graying mustache and a big belly. It made his pants slouch low in the front and his neckties fall strangely. As an attorney, Maloney had at this point in his career just one client: Lino Matteo.

"Come in," Lino ordered. Maloney sat in the chair Lino pointed to. "Michael, did you see this?" Lino asked, gesturing to the article.

"Yeah, I did."

"Did you read it?"

"Yeah."

"Did you really read it?"

"I think so."

"Well let me tell you what it says. What this story says is that the QSC is happy because they've just gotten the biggest fine in their history. Ron and Micheline are happy because they just paid $2 million and still have about $50 million left that they snuck out of Cinar and nobody has ever found. The board of Cinar is happy because this whole mess has never touched them. But, do you know who isn't happy?"

"No, who?"

"That little worm Bill Brock 'cause he doesn't have their money yet. He has billed over $6 million and he hasn't gotten one cent from those two, so he's not happy. Since Usher got his $86 million, they haven't collected one more cent."

"How did they get into this mess, Lino?" Michael asked.

"Greed and stupidity, Michael. Let me tell you something. Do you know that I'm right ninety-three percent of the time? Well, I am. Now, that's pretty good since most people aren't right fifty percent of the time. Yeah, they'd actually be better off flipping a coin every time they make a decision, and letting the coin decide for them. I've actually calculated it out and I'm nearly always right. The way I do it is I include all the decisions that I make in a day . . . should I brush my teeth or not, should I watch television, play video games, walk or drive to work. Then I include business decisions . . . should I hire someone, should I fire someone, should I invest or not, should I bring on a new broker, get rid of an old broker and so on. I'm tracking all of this with a little ledger and, sure enough, I'm at ninety-three percent. I might get even higher, but that's pretty good, isn't it? Do you know how many traders would like to be at ninety-three percent? How many baseball players would like to hit .930? Most businessmen aren't much over fifty percent, but that's the big advantage I've got . . . I don't make mistakes. Ron and Micheline were greedy and stupid. They were fifty percenters. And I'm telling you something: it's not over for them. Not by a long shot."

CHAPTER 26

DATE MAY 2003

SCENE Mount Real –
Montreal

Lino's World

He sat behind his big black desk as the young men from his media division filed into his office for the weekly meeting. As Johnny and Marty took their usual seats, Lino looked up from his computer to realize that someone else had entered the room.

"What is he doing here?" he said directly to Johnny.

"I thought you wanted Matthew here for the meeting."

"I never said that," was Lino's response.

Awkwardly, Matthew Ross, radio personality and assistant editor on one of the magazines, stood there waiting for some relief from his discomfort. Suddenly, Lino broke the silence.

"Go sit in the corner, don't talk, don't disrupt, don't

even breathe." The meeting then went forward.

After about a half hour of quiet listening, Matthew picked up a magazine and reviewed a previous issue. As he turned the pages, he made some noise.

"I told you to sit in the corner, don't talk, don't disrupt, don't even breathe, and now you're breathing and disrupting. Now put the magazine away and be quiet!" Lino said firmly. A few minutes later when neither Johnny nor Marty could answer a question, Lino said, "You know, it might not be a bad idea to have Matthew in this meeting. If you guys see him you might want to invite him. If he were here, I'd ask him what the page count of the next issue is and what the paper stock weight will be."

Everyone was so intimidated that Matthew sat speechless and Marty and Johnny were afraid to invite their colleague in the corner into the session. When the meeting was over, Lino would say, "When you get to the office, ask Matthew if he could join us for a meeting this afternoon about some of those questions and we can work on that then." The three of them filed out quietly and said nothing for the six-block walk back to the media office. Finally Johnny started chuckling and invited Matthew to join them for an afternoon session with Lino. Matthew accepted.

As Matthew walked back, he remembered his first meeting with Mr. Matteo, their interview. When he sat down, Lino said, "Matthew, right?"

"Yes, sir, that's right," came the response.

"What's the last name?"

"Ross," was the reply.

At that point Lino reached for a big, old dictionary and looked up the word "ross." "It says here that 'ross' is like tree bark. How do you like to be called Matthew

Bark? Is that what you are, a barker?" Speechless, Ross said nothing. Matteo responded, "Okay, Mr. Bark, tell me about yourself."

Months had gone by since Matthew's original interview. His job, as well as all positions in the company, had been filled, but ads for openings continued to run. So a constant flow of CVs and résumés streamed into the office, filling boxes and boxes with 8½" x 11" descriptive sheets of all types of talent. It would take Matthew months to finally figure out that when a CV arrived, the email address would be lifted from it and added to a database called "subscribers." These out-of-work job seekers would become the subscribers to the various e-zines and electronic newsletters. They would be described to advertisers as "upwardly mobile writers, artists and designers with high discretionary income and a proven propensity to purchase high-end clothing, fragrances, brand name liquors and sports cars."

Matthew Ross was getting a glimpse into Lino Matteo's peculiar nature. The man got into everything, had opinions about everything, and the fact was, most people simply took it from him.

We See
Things Differently

"Bill, this has to be a completely memorable event. It needs to be the city's best party. Budget doesn't matter. I want to show the investment world that Norshield has not just arrived, but that it leads the Canadian invest-ment world." John couldn't contain his excitement as he briefed me and Mario on his vision. "We've reached the billion dollar mark! That puts us in rare company and it makes us the largest hedge fund in Canada. We need to invite people throughout the world and really make a big statement."

"We'll make it big, John. You'll get big if that's what you want," I said.

"That's what I want!" The direction was set.

I've worked with all these people and more, in many different capacities. This time, I was working on John's vision. Things were set in full motion. I would commission the famous Toronto artist René Milot to create a series of eight paintings that would tell the Norshield story. Striking visuals that would be foreign to the eye and set the mood for what a unique and forward-thinking company this really is. The visuals would be incorporated into a film that would be shown to the attendees and tell the Norshield story. Dates would be tossed around, calendars checked and cleared. The guest list was international, so the holidays of over 20 countries had to be checked. The date was chosen: November 13, 2003.

When people received their invitation, it was accompanied by a fresh blue rose, the first blue rose most people would ever see. Each invite was personally delivered. The RSVPs rolled in and people from 15 different countries would attend. The venue would be a distinguished building in Old Montreal, with a beautiful view of the Old Port, in the most romantic part of the city, where the streets are cobblestone, the buildings 18th and 19th century and the scent of fine cooking of the restaurants wafted out onto the streets. This is the area where carriages outnumber taxis and one feels the history of the great city.

As the day grew near, the original paintings were ready for the framer, the film was tightened and edited, and the music track was being laid down. The choreographer was hard at work for the live entertainment that would bring the evening alive, and the speeches were polished. The menu was eclectic, ranging from sushi to foie gras, vegan to French desserts.

John was double-checking every detail himself, feeling

strongly that this was his victory party. Despite the Globe-X setbacks, the Cinar missile had missed its Norshield mark, and while it had seemed to damage most of the people it touched, Norshield Financial Group was standing strong and had survived the assault. They had more than doubled their size in three years, and were delivering phenomenal results: twelve to twenty percent returns, year after year. There was a lot to celebrate and no reason not to believe the future would provide even more reason to celebrate as things moved forward.

When John X heard the music for the film, he was emphatic, "It has to go, it's just not us." When I explained to him that "at this point we'd have to go to Hollywood to get the music right and done on time," John said, "Go to Hollywood." He would scratch items from the menu. "Yuck," he'd say and add some that he was certain would please, like chocolate-covered strawberries.

The theme was built around Milot's artwork, and the theme was "We See Things Differently."

The artwork would have an "otherworldliness" to it. One painting would depict a placid lake, surrounded by mountains with a lighthouse, which would illuminate a huge circular hole in the lake that would lead anyone unawares into the void. Another painting would show a breathtaking mountain view with snow-covered peaks, streams and falls descending to a beautiful lake, but behind the mountain was scaffolding that propped up the mountain set. Norshield held out that they "take nothing at face value and search behind the strength to make sure it's really there." One of the paintings showed a dozen or so tall barrier islands in the sea with ominous clouds and a highway that ran over each of them, but the highway was without connecting bridges. The copy would say

hauntingly, "We all know that life can be a great ride. However, we at Norshield know that it rarely stays that way and that change is constant; we know that good times don't last forever."

The conclusion would bring a boardwalk view of the ocean and the startling vision of two suns descending into the sea. It simply said, "At Norshield, we see things differently."

In fact, on this, the night of the grand event, John did see things differently from others. His world was full, he was self-made and rich, had a wonderful wife, three healthy sons, a thriving business, his foundation was making a difference in the community, and it was Norshield that was running the largest volunteer recognition program in the province. As the guests arrived at the ancient hall, they discovered the room was segmented, not by walls, but by light and non-toxic smoke that created a sense of comfortable mystery. People largely arrived on time and were astounded by the food, ambience, jesters and actors who roved the room busking. When it came time to present the CEO of Norshield Financial Group, it was Montreal Canadiens Hockey Hall of Famer Steve Shutt who would introduce John. He was received warmly and the ovation was genuine. He spoke briefly and then the film was shown. It amazed viewers because the images were startling and the concept very simple. As people saw the two suns setting, they realized this company "saw things differently" and that was exactly why they had succeeded while others were failing in this contrarian market.

The dancers used torches as batons, beautiful young women at close quarters to the audience. They brought a life and vibrancy to the room and caused even the skeptical investor to note that this was a very special company at a very special time in its business life. As people left, they actively sought the books and souvenirs that would help them describe to others what they had seen that night. When John left he knew that the impression had been made. The people he had hoped would be there had attended. The impression he wanted to make was made. He didn't want his firm confused with any others . . . after this night, it wouldn't be. John was at the top of his game.

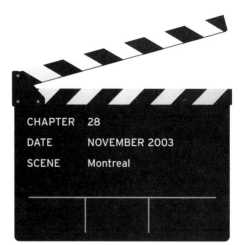

The Showman
and the Raider

Stuart Snyder came from a different world, a world of bluster and bluff, show business at its rawest. He had worked for Vince McMahon of the WWE. They dispensed generous doses of mind-numbing programming to young and old alike. Live events, television and, of course, the combination almost unique to wrestling . . . cross-promotion to drive ratings and boost live audiences. While Snyder was a smallish, bookish Jewish boy from the East Coast, he was a good offset to the boisterous, self-promoting McMahon, bringing business discipline and skills to the wacky world of wrestling. Now Snyder was ready to crawl into another ring, the circus known as Cinar.

Since he'd been named its new president, Snyder would be briefed by various parties, including the outgoing Barry Usher, Bill Brock, board members like Robert Vineberg and a few of the creative types. Many hoped Snyder would provide the creative spark that would bring Cinar back to life. The wrestling world and the USFX represented demented creativity, but at least it was gutsy, and Cinar needed guts again. It had been a long time since the hallways had seen the courage of Micheline Charest or felt her charismatic leadership, as they developed new products to teach, guide and entertain children throughout the world. While the company didn't know for sure what it was getting, Snyder meant change, and change was good. There were still class action suits to defend, Globe-X to chase, creative malaise to stave off, regulators to contend with, financial statements to set right and the stock of the company to get re-listed. There was no shortage of sizable projects for the new president.

Corporate observers never miss one important assessment tool when it comes to new CEOs from out of town: are they moving to the new city *with* their wife and kids? Usher never did; he commuted from Toronto. Now it looked like Snyder would commute from Connecticut.

His energy was exciting, his work ethic strong. He picked things up fast and wasn't afraid to make decisions. All of these things were good. Better yet, within weeks it became apparent that this new president was a problem solver, and heaven knew there were plenty of problems to solve. If Cinar were to be a going concern, it could live with problems, but not without vision. Stuart Snyder was there to solve problems so the company could be sold. There was no burning desire to build it, grow it or inspire it . . . only to sell it. The sooner his board could walk away

from this train wreck, brush off their hands and congratulate each other, the better off they were. How this group of self-congratulatory, glad-handing corporate leaders had managed to avoid legal and regulatory problems for themselves was as amazing as one of Vince McMahon's most brazen plotlines. Selling Cinar was the goal. The shareholders were long forgotten.

An unofficial market in Cinar stock had developed, a kind of a pink sheet bid/ask system. The thousands of shareholders who had bought the stock as a NASDAQ success story could now trade it only in this jerry-rigged system, but it did create some liquidity. With the Internet and a telephone as his primary tools, Robert Chapman, a "greenmail" financier out of California, began to buy up blocks of Cinar stock on the market. (Greenmailers will purchase enough of a given company's stock that the board fears a hostile takeover, and then sell the stocks back to the company at above market value.) He would criticize management and taunt them daily. In a world of chat rooms and innuendos, Chapman thrived. Lino became more and more intrigued by Chapman.

"Do you think Chapman needs an ally? Do you think he needs someone to help with his effort to take over Cinar?" Lino asked.

"You know, it's possible," John replied. "Should we approach him and feel him out?"

"Definitely," was Lino's reply. (I'll never know how serious they were at the time, but in retrospect it might have been a brilliant idea.)

I was chosen for the job. Experienced in deals and mergers, I seemed to be a logical choice as a stalking horse. I'm American, but I have a lot of Canadian experience. The approach would be by phone.

"Hello?"

"Robert Chapman, please."

"This is Robert."

"My name is Bill Urseth and I represent a group of investors who are interested in making a move on Cinar. I know that you're involved in some kind of an effort and we thought you might be open for some allies."

"How much stock do you have right now?"

"Voting rights on about six million shares."

"How much cash do you have available?"

"About half a million dollars."

"How experienced are your people?"

"They range from very experienced in mergers and acquisitions to experienced in sophisticated investing. We'd like to do something."

"How did you get the shares you've got?"

"They were collateral on a loan." (The loan was the $12 million loan from CIS to Weinberg and Charest.)

"Okay, I'll call you tomorrow and we can talk more." With that the call was over.

The next day Chapman called, just as he said he would. I recognized his voice — but I was taken aback when he began to talk.

"Mr. Urseth?"

"Yes, this is he."

"Robert Chapman here."

"Yes, how are you?"

"Don't small talk me. I'm way too busy to waste my time with some blind mouse that's jacking with me. Now, I'm doing this takeover, not you and your amateur buddies. Yes, Mr. Bill Urseth of 1524 Abbott Avenue, Minneapolis, Minnesota, married to Kathy. You have a credit rating score of 669. I would have thought it would

be higher. Actually, Bill, you really should get your mortgage paid down some. At your age, a hundred and twenty grand is a little high. Which car do you prefer to drive, Bill? The Mercedes or the Suburban? Bill, those shares you told me you have are stolen, and if you try to vote them against me, I'll have Kathy wishing you never called me with your phony story line. Now where is the five hundred thousand and tell me the truth about those shares!"

I was speechless, but I'd got what I was after. I knew what Chapman was. He was a raider who didn't want help.

"Bill, if you're not going to talk, then I will. Tell your playmates to go home and not come back to Chapman Park ever again because we play hardball. We do our research, count our votes and step on our enemies with big cleats. Goodbye."

I hung up the phone. It had been many years since I'd felt afraid, really afraid. What started as a little recon mission had ended in a humbling silence. Chapman had repelled Lino's search for intelligence.

A Merry
Little Christmas

Despite his gruffness, rudeness and moodiness, Lino remained a softy for Christmas. He could be truly generous, and while all the festivities would be planned around his schedule and whims, designed to elevate his majesty among the minions, he really did catch the spirit. The season would begin with the company Christmas party. While John's parties were opulent and at a cost of $200 per guest, plus hotel rooms and travel, Lino's parties would be tasteful but budgeted, punctuated by Italian dishes, Italian wines and absolutely "no shots." Lino would pay for beer and wine, but "no shots" would be the standing rule. While the younger employees never understood the rule, Lino knew that shots can lead to casualties because as jaws loosened, people say things that can never be taken back and do things that are irrevocable. Since Lino was always in control, he didn't like rapid-fire Sambuca or rounds of tequila.

The party would always include the mandatory brief speech delivered by Joe Pettinicchio, Mount Real's President. "Joe should give the speech," Lino would always say, "to demonstrate to everyone that he's now the president and 'Big Boss.'" At some point in every speech, Lino would say something, usually a wisecrack, to remind everyone what they already knew, which was that Lino was really the "Big Boss" and there was never room for two.

The second part of the ritual was the Boxing Day party at Lino's house. The food was almost all prepared by his wife, Joanne. It was distinctly Italian and always good. The guest list included his family, his longtime friend Mark Jourdenais, and key partners, associates and occasionally employees. It was a select group that he invited to his home.

Across the board, Lino's lifestyle was relatively modest, almost frugal. Most rising young executives who have built a public company to the $100 million level indulge themselves along the way. Nice cars, a beautiful home, a summer home, frequent trips, expensive hobbies, extensive wardrobes and servants. Lino did none of that. He rarely drove anyway, and if he did it was usually in a mini-van or an aged SUV. His home was clean but modest, a row house in an ethnic neighborhood where the neighbors are likely to carry their lunch to work and never aspire to anything beyond a better hourly wage. He had no summer home, took infrequent trips (usually just to visit family or on business), indulged in no expensive hobbies, dressed casually with rare exception and, despite his father-in-law being a suit maker, he bought off the rack. He was uncomfortable around servants and never considered employing one. He spent money on his children's educations, and beyond that, he simply worked.

Most business contacts, as a result, were surprised when they saw Lino's home because they had experienced the nouveau riche before in other places and expected Matteo to be one of them. Quietly they would speculate how they could be living in a bigger or better home than this visibly successful executive. Most were comforted by the simplicity, however, not put off by it. Lino had plenty of ways to put people off, but his domestic simplicity wasn't one of them. And yet, leaving their families on the holiday night for a mandatory appearance at his home was one of the things to set many spouses off.

The third event of the holiday season was the Pizza Hut kids' party held every year at noon on New Year's Eve. Lino's rationale was that people didn't work hard on New Year's Eve anyway, so why not make it a ceremonious event with a purpose. Everyone with a kid under 18 was expected to be at Pizza Hut with spouse and children in tow. There would be pizza, soda, beer aplenty and kids . . . shouting kids, crying kids, laughing kids and excited kids. The highlight of this two-hour celebration came when Lino would personally give, in ceremonial fashion, a wrapped, personally selected, expensive gift to every single child. Joanne would shop invisibly and thanklessly to make sure every gift was perfect and well received. She virtually never failed.

Lino wouldn't dress like Santa, but he would use his deep voice to beckon the youngsters to his chair at the front of the room and occasionally a HO! HO! HO! would

resonate. Adults would converse and admire the show as 40 or 50 kids would march to the front and sit on Lino's lap to receive their gifts. There was never a suggestion or thought that Joe should give out the gifts "to show everybody that he's in charge now . . . the Big Boss." No, the Big Boss was using the vinyl chair in a Pizza Hut as his throne.

New Year's Eve was also the last day of trading on the various stock exchanges that Lino's various companies were listed on. The price that they closed at on New Year's Day is the price that would linger into the New Year on the various print materials and websites. As a result Lino would do what he could to get a "spike" on New Year's Eve and have his stocks close the year as high as possible. The instructions would go out by cell phone to his various allies, agents and brokers as to what to bid, what to buy and what to do. Between his commands he would shake hands, greet well-wishers and hand out gifts to the kids.

CHAPTER 30
DATE   MARCH 2004
SCENE   Montreal

Sooo Close!

The rumors began to circulate, the whispers became louder, the story on the street began to gain credence . . . Cinar was about to be sold. The efforts of greenmailers like Robert Chapman and other speculators urging management to find value for shareholders had taken hold and Snyder knew he needed a deal. Many suitors had paraded through, numerous due diligence packages had been shipped and reviewed, but now, for the first time, a buyer was acting like something was really up. Cinar was now about half the size it had been in the halcyon days, precrisis. The company continued to sort out its problems, and remained unlisted. Its legal and accounting costs were enormous. Primarily, Cinar was looking to be sold.

The buyer was Michael Hirsch, a businessman out of Toronto with a background in children's entertainment. His company was called Cookie Jar. The fit seemed absolutely right. By mid-February there seemed to be a term sheet and Hirsch was arranging his financing. At this point, Clifford Johnson was firmly in control of Globe-X. As the joint liquidator (with colleague Wayne Aranha of PricewaterhouseCoopers), he was working the file and trying to assess what there was and what it was worth. There were no efforts to settle the many disputes, suits and counterclaims that were flying around in four different countries, dozens of different actions in all.

As Lino was reading his normal ensemble of newspapers, the news of a certain other sale caught his special attention. Lino had introduced Lowell Holden to Tom Muir, and now Lowell had taken over CIS, Silicon Isle and other companies, entities that Tom had formerly headed, the ones the liquidators hadn't taken over. Holden would become the plaintiff *and* the defendant in some of the large Cinar-related lawsuits. Believing he could generate some fee income and potentially save these troubled entities, Lowell had his hands full. Born in Iowa, but having spent most of his business life in Minnesota, Holden was a tall, good-looking former athlete who came across well and was generally likable. Lino had first met him through me, as one of my business associates.

"Lowell, you need to get in to see Snyder. Now is the time to try for a settlement; it's really now or never." Matteo's deep bass voice was even lower and more gravelly than usual, as he hugged the telephone.

"What are you thinking, Lino? How do we start it?" Holden responded.

"Call him and tell him you want to talk."

"Should I approach Brock?"

"No, go straight to Snyder."

At this point $86 of the $108 million that Cinar had invested in Globe-X had been repaid. While the press continued to report that Cinar had invested $122 million and therefore nearly $40 million was still owed, the fact was that Snyder knew full well that only $22 million was still due and there was no reasonable way for him to get it.

I was the only person who had been on the Globe-X/Cinar/Norshield file from the start. I had found and briefed Jo-Anne Polak before the crisis broke. I was on site when Basil made the deal with Brock. It was me who worked things through with Usher and Brock when they arrived at Globe-X, and I was the one who worked Bob and Tom's way through the Quebec Securities Commission. So far, I was the only person who had actually met every key player in the complex mess, and now Holden called me to help with Snyder. I'm very experienced in handling deals, but most importantly I'm a communicator.

"Are you in town, Bill?" Holden began.

"It depends on what town you mean." I'm always traveling.

"Montreal," was the retort.

"Yeah, if that's the town, I'm in it," I shot back.

"I need your help in negotiations. Now is the time to try to strike a deal with Cinar."

"I've been reading the papers and following the rumors. I agree, now's the time. Do you understand this CCE concept that seems to be coming?" I asked.

"No. What are you talking about?"

"As near as I can tell, if the sale goes through and there is no settlement, there will be a fund of $5 million set up

to be administered by this CCE — the Contingent Cash Entitlement Committee. It's basically a litigation committee made up of three lawyers who are authorized to chase down Norshield, John X, and anything or anybody else that they choose to, for the purpose of recovering money. The proceeds would be split with a little going to the exiting shareholders and the rest to the new owners."

"That's quite a fee trough!"

"That is quite a war chest and there are a lot of lawyers, accountants and even some PR types who can put their kids through college on this one. My point is simply this: once this regime is gone, there will be no one to settle with until all the money in the fund is spent," I responded.

"When can we meet, Bill?" asked Holden.

The meeting was set for the next morning. I said, "The research people put this together; you might want to take a look. It's a breakdown on Snyder as a person . . . résumé, articles, other info. He seems to be a showboat, but a decent guy. Here's the background and breakdown on the board of directors who need to approve the deal, so look that over if you can. The thing that confuses me is not so much them, but us. Who the hell are we representing?" There was the kind of silence you have when there is no answer to the question. The quiet hung heavy; Holden never spoke.

"Is it John? Tom? Lino? You? Weinberg? Charest? Panju? Norshield? Who?"

"I think it's every one of them," Holden finally said.

"Wow, what a coalition. Talk about a horse from every county. Some of these people hate each other, and that's our client?"

"They are all best off if this thing goes away. They have a common need."

"Jesus Christ, how are we gonna herd those cats?" I said.

"Carefully," was Holden's response.

I worked the scenario over and over in my mind. The dynamics were astounding, but it might actually make sense. John needed this problem to go away, and he had access to money to help solve the problem. Tom didn't have many resources left, but he could be counted on to be onside. Lino would know the importance, but he would almost certainly try to put himself in the center of the negotiations, and he wouldn't contribute money to the solution. Weinberg had money and would like to get the mess over with; ditto Charest. Panju was in self-imposed exile; he had money, but no heat around his neck. Norshield had money and needed the problems gone. As I penciled out the schematic, I realized this just might have a chance.

I called John and let him in on our thinking. I asked the obvious question quickly and directly. "John, how much could you come up with for a solution? From all sources of funds, foundations and the business? What can you scrape up?"

"Twelve million," was the response.

"Can you get it soon?"

"Yes."

When the conversation was over, I knew the biggest piece was in place. Now the question would be how much could be pledged by Weinberg and Charest, then of course, Panju . . . and what Snyder would accept.

The conversation with Weinberg was like a fencing match. "How much has Panju committed? What has John agreed to? I don't think it's my responsibility to —"

I interrupted. "You're now the defendant in a $56 million suit, and we have a chance to settle everything in one fell swoop. What am I missing about your motivation level here? If this effort fails, there is going to be a $5 million fund to chase you guys for the next decade. What are you thinking?"

"Call me when you know what the others are doing, then I'll decide." The conversation was over; Weinberg hadn't committed. In some ways, though, he was important with or without the monetary commitment because he was the largest shareholder in the pending deal. Ironically, he was actively working with Snyder and Hirsch in the transaction, so he would have an information flow that could be valuable.

"I'll participate for $1 million," was Panju's response. Cold, distant and with an English accent, he would commit on a transatlantic call.

As the file began to grow, Lowell and I figured we'd better get Lino updated. No one keeps Lino in the dark, or out of the loop. Some called him "The Pope," others "The Don of Ville-Émard," but no one called him either to his face. The meeting started badly. We sat in front of him as he yelled at one of his operating guys over the phone. Then the background books and the outcomes of my conversations were revealed to him, and the tone of the meeting was about to turn sour, real sour. Both Holden and I had been through Lino's tantrums before, so we were prepared for the possibility.

His voice was low, slow and gravelly, but like a train as it gains speed, the power increases, the volume moves up and it becomes impossible to ignore as all other sound is drowned out. With John X unable to manage the crisis, Lino took control.

"What are you guys doing? Who put you in charge of all this? Who authorized you to talk to these people about money? What makes either of you think you can run these negotiations? These people will take your pants off and strangle you with the legs, and all of us will pay the price for your errors and naivete. The way this is going to work is . . . I will tell you what to offer, when and how, and you will follow my orders. Do you understand?" With that he started grabbing anything he had on his desk, tearing it and throwing it in every direction. We sat there dumbfounded. When he was finished, he returned to his emails and the double screen computer and said, "Get out."

Unfazed, Holden and I went to our first meeting with Snyder. After cautious pleasantries and introductions, it became clear that Snyder would prefer a deal as well.

"Who do you guys really represent?" Snyder asked.

"I think we represent everyone whose life would be better off if this thing were over," was my reply.

"Well, that doesn't include the lawyers and accountants, does it?"

"No, it doesn't. But I think it does include your board, your shareholders, former management and the business' future, because this is an unnecessary distraction to a real operating business. Do you have a number that can get this resolved?"

"I think I do; I've talked to enough people that I believe $14 million will make the problem go away. Assuming it's cash and concurrent to the closing of the sale."

The meeting would last another half hour, but for all practical purposes it was over with that statement. Now Holden and I knew what we had to do. We needed to

convince Lino that $14 million would solve this nightmare, once and for all.

He refused to see us. It was after 6:00 p.m., but he did take my call at his home. The conversation was brief.

"There is no way that we're offering $14 million, so don't even bother to consider it. I don't know what makes you think John can get all this money together, but I'll authorize $11 million total . . . $9 million from Norshield and $1 million each from Weinberg and Panju. Now, get Snyder to take *that* deal."

The line went dead. Holden and I looked at each other in amazement. Lino had accepted no comments, no supporting information; he had allowed no discussion or debate. How would we deliver this news to Snyder?

Snyder agreed to the meeting, but he only had 20 minutes and it was already 8:30 p.m. He was juggling three meetings at the same time, and taking phone calls. The place had the energy of a pending closing. The lawyers scattered around the various offices, rushing documents and drafts.

"We've talked to our clients and explained exactly where you are. They've gone through everything they've got, turned over the cushions on the sofa, emptied the cookie jars and broken the piggy banks. We've got a lot of money together, but not $14 million. We've got $11," I said.

"That's too far away, boys. You've got to do better," Snyder said and left the room.

We sat quietly and said nothing; not a word was spoken for over five minutes. I felt keenly what kind of disaster would follow if negotiations broke down. Finally, I said, "We need to hang in and make another offer."

"We're not actually authorized to. That's our limit."

"It doesn't really matter right now if we don't get a target to shoot for, it's finished anyway. If we can get a number from him other than fourteen, we've got something to sell with, and if we don't, we'll fire ourselves and I'll go huntin'. Can you get Snyder to see us again tonight?"

"I'll try," Holden said and quickly left the room.

Snyder agreed to meet us again at 10:30 p.m., so "the boys" never left the conference room. They just pretended to dial phones and call their "clients," talking animatedly to themselves in case the room was bugged. They pleaded, cajoled and downright begged over the phones. Every once in a while Snyder would walk by or one of his associates would nod. Bill Urseth and Lowell Holden couldn't have looked busier, or more frustrated.

When Snyder entered the room, it was late. Both of us were still on a "call." As they sat down, I said, "We've made progress. I think people know that this is the last best chance, and they've dug deep. I know you're not going to like our answer, but it doesn't do any good to make an offer no one can deliver on. I know you can't say yes all by yourself, so I'm going to ask you to please *not* say yes or no immediately, but just agree that you'll take this new offer to the board and then let us know. Is that fair?"

"Yeah, I guess so," Snyder nodded.

"Okay, we've got $12.5 million rounded up, and we can close at your closing date." Then I just shut up, didn't say another word. Slowly Snyder said, "We're closing now. I'll present it to the board. Let's get some sleep."

The meeting was over; it was 11:00 p.m. If there was an affirmative in the morning, then we'd need to get our clients on board and quickly document a deal. At this point the boys had stuck their neck out and spoken for no one, but at least the deal was still alive.

"I want to do this with Lino over the phone, not in

person," I told Holden. "The threats will be fewer. Can you make the Panju call? Who should call Weinberg?" Lowell responded that he'd call Panju, and I should call the other two. I picked up the phone and rang Weinberg first.

"Ron, if we're going to get a deal done, I'm going to need a million five from you. Are you in?"

"I don't think so, but I'll call you back," was his response.

The call came in from Lowell. "Panju will go $1 million but only if he gets a release from Snyder. Immunity from certain suits."

"Well, that's backward. He wants more and offers nothing additional? These guys don't get it."

I figured I'd better call Lino. "When are you coming to see me?" he asked quickly and directly.

"I can't. I need to talk to you now, on the phone," I said.

"I don't want to do this on the phone, come see me," and he hung up. Five minutes later the phone rang again and it was Lino. "Are you on the way?"

"No."

"What have you got to say?"

"The deal is dead unless you get more money; everything is over. I'm planning a hunting trip. There's no need to be here." This was a classic take-away, and Lino was softening over the phone.

"How much will it take?"

"This deal will get done if you have $12 million. Anything less is a substantial risk. Weinberg is a skinflint; Panju will probably double deal. Any amount less than $12 million, you're taking a big chance with everyone's lives, especially John's."

"Okay, we'll go $11 million. But I want two truckloads of Caillou dolls or no deal."

"What did you say?"

"Eleven million dollars, but I want the settlement and two truckloads of Caillou dolls. Have a nice day."

"How did it go?" Holden asked.

"He'll go $11 million and he wants two truckloads of Caillou dolls. Unbelievable! It's not even his money; he has the chance to settle everything and he's got us going for truckloads of dolls. How do you think the board will like that?"

"Well, at least we've got the $12.5 million covered. That's better than where we were last night."

Negotiations are a fine art. All parties look for strength, weakness and movement, but most importantly they're trying to figure who's really in charge and whether you can believe them. I knew full well that Lino's demand for the dolls was intended to show Snyder that I wasn't calling the shots. Panju's demand for the release was even more complicated.

The phone rang.

"Mr. Urseth, Micheline Charest here. Are you dealing directly with John? John must know that this settlement has to be made or he's finished. They'll track him down and skin him alive. He must settle!"

"Will you do the $1.5 million? I'm worried about Panju going south. Can you help keep him in order?"

"Nobody can keep that son of a bitch in line. You can count on us for at least one million." The conversation was over.

To the accountant, the numbers were $11 million from Lino, $1 million from Weinberg and Charest, and $1 million from Panju. The $12.5 million was covered. But what

would Snyder say? We waited for what felt like a year. Then Snyder was on the phone.

"Bill?"

"Yes."

"Thirteen is what they want, but they'll entertain an offer of $12.5 million, not one cent less. Can you deliver?"

"Let's write up the documents, Stuart, I think we're on."

Almost

On the morning of Wednesday the 24th of March, 2004, Stuart Snyder and I would agree to proceed to documentation on the settlement deal. Max Mendelsohn, a respected and seasoned Montreal attorney, would represent the composite group of Weinberg, Charest, Norshield, Panju, Muir, Daviault and whoever else there might be. Lino had remained grudgingly quiet, knowing intuitively that it would be best if this problem passed and everybody got back to real business. Crisis is an amazing dynamic; many people run from it as quickly as they would from a fire or a bomb, but there are others who are energized by crisis, find their focus best when pushed by adrenaline and deadlines, just as there are people who'll rush to the heat of a crisis or storm into a river of controversy. Lino was one of the latter. He loved the crisis and hated to see it end. The moment it was over, his power over the team of John, me, Tom, Lowell and Mario would diminish, but still he knew that it was best over. He would let Max and me finish it up.

The board meeting was scheduled for Sunday at 7:00 p.m. Snyder would, in that meeting, get the board to approve the transaction with Michael Hirsch, which would make Hirsch and his company the new owners of Cinar. With that approval, Snyder would resign, the board of Cinar would resign, and the shareholders would receive checks and be bought out. The untold portion of the closing was whether the board, with Snyder's recommendations, would approve the settlement agreement. Under those terms, Cinar would receive almost $12.5 million, drop its actions against Norshield, John Xanthoudakis, Weinberg, Charest and Panju; they would stop Clifford Johnson and the liquidators in the Bahamas, and life might return to normal for all those people caught up in the Cinar mess.

If there was no agreement on this settlement, then the Contingent Cash Entitlement (CCE) would be created. To be funded with $5 million from the proceeds of the purchase, the CCE would be run by three yet-to-be-named individuals who would hire lawyers, accountants, private eyes and PR types to pursue any and all pockets for money that might be owed or thought to be owed. The CCE would have three years to pursue its goals and would split the net proceeds — thirty percent to Hirsch and seventy percent to the old Cinar shareholders, who had financed one hundred percent up front of the $5 million. The "net" number would be of recovered funds *after* the expenses of the lawyers, accountants, private eyes and PR types.

Holden and I left Montreal and flew back to the Midwest, me to a hunting tournament, Holden to his home. Mendelsohn and Brock would work on the agreement on Friday and Saturday to ensure its presentation on Sunday night. At midday on Saturday, I would discover my cell phone only worked at the top of a 3,000-foot hill in the South Dakota prairie. Each call was going to be an annoyance, but off I went to climb to the top.

"Max, are things moving?" I asked.

"Yeah, the points are coming together. We'll have a draft in a couple of hours. Are you reachable?"

"Yeah, I have a fax back at the lodge, but here in the field it's quite a climb!" I hung up and looked around the vast prairie just west of the Missouri River where the land begins to roll and the ravines can be deep.

When I saw the draft four hours later, darkness had crept in, and while other hunters partied, I read. The deal seemed as agreed, except there was still no mention of Caillou dolls. "I'll buy them myself if I have to," I finally decided. The deal was simple: $13 million — $11 million from Norshield, John, Tom, or whoever, $1 million from Charest and Weinberg and $1 million from Panju. Within 24 hours the nightmare they had all been living would be over. Panju could continue his life in London, Weinberg and Charest could start over, John X could move forward with positive energy and build his now powerful financial business, and Tom Muir could restart his life. Lowell Holden could get onto another deal. The Cinar shareholders would have $18 million more to split up (13 plus the CCE's five), Lino could focus on Mount Real and I could spend more time hunting. Everyone slept better that night than they had in a long time.

Everyone except Panju. With a six-hour jump on everyone else, he decided to let Snyder know on Sunday morning he was backing out of the deal . . . no $1 million from Panju. I would learn of it after climbing the 3,000-foot hill after some early morning hunting. The voice mail would say, "Bill, it's Max. Please call soon. Panju has backed out. We're $1 million short for tonight." The news struck like a blow to the stomach; bad news flows to the gut — it's a subtle pain, but real. With a deep breath I called Lino's home. "Is he there? It's Bill, I need to talk to him." After a wait, the young boy came back and said, "Papa is taking his nap and can't be disturbed." I then dialed Weinberg and explained the situation, asking what Weinberg would do to help. "Just half a million more could make all the difference. I think I can get the other half million from the other parties."

No response for a moment, and then Weinberg said, "I'll call you back."

"Max, what do you think?" I burst forth the second Mendelsohn picked up.

"It's serious. Without $12.5 million Snyder won't present. I'm certain of it. Can you get the money?"

"I'll get it," I said. "Max, keep the documents moving. I'll call Snyder and tell him we're still on." I just didn't know how I'd find that money. A call waiting beep came into the cell on the high hill.

"Hello?"

"Bill, this is Micheline Charest. I need to talk to you."

"I'm on another line, but I'll be right back. Please hold on."

"Max, I've got to go. Keep things moving . . . Hello, Micheline, thanks for calling."

"Bill, you must convince John to come up with more

money. I know he'll do it. If he doesn't his life will be a living hell. These are not nice people we're dealing with. They will chase him down and cut his heart out. If this litigation committee is formed, it will crush us all. There has never been anything like this, a $5 million fund, run by lawyers whose only purpose is to get big fees and chase innocent people. This is bigger than the law and worse than government. You must reach John and get him to commit more money. You must!"

"I'm trying, but what are *you* willing to do? Will you come in for just five hundred thousand more?"

"Talk to John. Talk to John!" and she hung up.

I knew that John would say yes. But if I went to John and then told Lino that John had said yes, Lino would go ballistic and say no. So, I called Lino again; his wife answered. "It's Bill. I have to talk to him," I said imploringly. We liked each other, and I understood Lino's "no calls on Sunday" rule and his wife's role in enforcing it. Despite Lino's curious or even bizarre behavior, he was a family-values guy who guarded time with his family on Sundays, went to church, went to his mother's for Sunday dinner. He would get to all the kids' soccer games and even coach or referee to help out. For all the bluster and show, there was a soft side that could make you forget the abuse and the craziness. He came on the line.

"Hello."

"It's me. The deal's in trouble. Panju backed out so we're $1 million short. I've talked to Micheline and asked her for half a million. I need you to think this through carefully. If you say yes right now to $1 million more, the problem can be over and I will still work on Micheline and Ron for five hundred thousand while the documents move forward. If you say yes to half a million, we might end up half a million short and I don't think Snyder will present. If you say no to anything more, the deal is dead and there's a fight coming. What do you want to do?" He hesitated for only seconds.

"We'll go half a million more and I want those two trucks of Caillou dolls."

"This may not solve the problem."

"Weinberg isn't that stupid, he'll pay. I've got to get back to a game I'm playing with the kids," and he hung up.

I went down the hill with a bad feeling. I decided I would hunt some more and then climb back up.

"Ron, I've got five hundred thousand more. I need your commitment to make this certain. Do I have it?"

"Call John. He'll never let this fall apart over half a million."

"Ron, I don't think I will reach John, and we're out of time. His people won't go any higher. If you don't agree, Snyder may not present and starting tomorrow you've got $5 million aimed right at your nose. What do you want to do?"

"I'll go a million, just like I've always said." And that was that. He'd shut the door; there was nothing I could do but report the damage.

"Max, we have $12.5 million. Please revise the agreement to reflect the change. Hopefully, Snyder will present."

"Okay," was the response.

The day that had started with such a beautiful sunrise and hope was now turning dark and stormy. The prairie can produce thunderstorms that inspire awe and fear; the lightning can come with surprise and speed.

The Problem
Is Still There

The board of Cinar would never even vote on the settlement money. Their focus was on the closing of the sale to Michael Hirsch, and the professionals in attendance had no motive whatsoever to have the settlement take place. With the creation of the CCE, there was an unprecedented funding vehicle and a chance "to put the rascals in their place."

The first call was from Micheline Charest. "You've got to do something to get the settlement back on track. I don't think the board ever even saw the proposal. Can you call Snyder? We'll come in with up to $3 million if you can get things reopened."

I thought how helpful that $3 million would have been

48 hours ago. The reality was that the deal had closed at 8:00 p.m. on Sunday night and this was now Monday afternoon. Charest was afraid, and she had every reason to be. She seemed to understand better than anyone what the CCE really meant.

"Ron? Ron! I've got Bill on the phone. Talk to him." It was obvious they were at home.

"Hello, Bill. Yeah, I agree with Micheline that we should try to get this reopened. If John will keep his offer at $12 million we'll put in $3. That should get some attention, don't you think?"

"The problem, Ron, is I don't know if we have an audience. The people who had the power this time yesterday have all resigned and they're out. You know that."

"Call Stuart Snyder," Ron interrupted.

"I will."

I reached Snyder, who was already at his home in Connecticut.

"Bill, I think the horse is out of the barn. There's no one left to deal with. You could try Michael Hirsch, but the fact is there's a new legal entity and I don't think they'll have a voice or a decision process for months. We had our window and now it's gone. I'm sorry, and I know you tried, but there were five million reasons some people didn't want a deal. I thought a settlement was the best thing for the old shareholders and that's why I worked with you, but they aren't anyone's concern anymore. Good luck, Bill, but I think your clients are cooked." I thanked Stuart and hung up.

I now had to relay the news to Lino, John, Dale, Mario, Lowell, Ron, and the one who took it hardest, Micheline. "I can't believe that these smart people could have let this chance go by. I simply can't believe it. This will prove to be a worse day than the day we sent our first dollar to the Bahamas. Thanks for trying."

The structure was in place at the closing of Cookie Jar's purchase of Cinar. Five million dollars of the proceeds would not flow to the sellers, meaning the shareholders, Weinberg and Charest. Instead, it would be used to fund a litigation committee, which would be responsible for chasing whoever they could, for whatever money they could find linked to Cinar's investment in Globe-X. Of the $108 million invested, $86 million had been repaid to Cinar by Bob, Tom and John, despite Lino's protestations and warnings. Just as Lino had envisioned, Cinar used some of those funds to chase Bob, Tom and John and their businesses in a big game of "whodunit," enriching lawyers, accountants and PR people along the way. The rest of the funds had gone to stabilizing Cinar. At this point, four years later, they had sold the business, made their shareholders somewhat happy, resolved their governmental issues, put some money in Stuart Snyder's blue jeans, fattened Barry Usher's retirement plan and got back to producing cartoons again. Many rumors abounded that this had also made Bill Brock the country's top billing attorney. Most important to Brock, however, was that throughout it all, the blue ribbon board was never brought to task for sleeping on the watch and letting the fort get ransacked.

It was decided that the chairman of the CCE's three-member committee would be Wes Voorheis, a highly regarded Toronto attorney from the law firm of Voorheis & Company. Voorheis was 51 years old, articulate and qualified. Ultimately, his most important qualities would be tenacity and ruthlessness; if he couldn't get money, he would be certain to get something. David Drinkwater was

THE PROBLEM IS STILL THERE

also an attorney and very respected in the arena of securities law. When openings would come about in top spots in securities regulation or the top spot at the Toronto Stock Exchange, Drinkwater's name would be on every list. Eventually rounding out the committee was the former head of the RCMP, Norman Inkster. He would bring an experienced law enforcement eye to the committee, a huge Rolodex and a quasi-governmental tone that the committee would enjoy. The assumption was simple to make and easy to believe: if three guys of such substance, background and repute are on one team, they must be the team with the white hats. Therefore, the other team must have black hats, making anyone the CCE chased the bad guys, according to most press reports and onlookers.

Wes Voorheis had built a reputation for taking on tough jobs. In 1998 he had earned his stripes while working on the YBM deal. Embroiled in a visible fraudulent mess, YBM Magnex International was controlled by Russians who weren't afraid to play rough. Voorheis would later admit he was in over his head and would ask himself and partner Norman Inkster "if he'd ever do something like that again." "Yeah," was the response, "we'd do it again, but differently." When he was first approached about the CCE possibility four months before the CCE existed, he listened carefully to the bizarre story of Cinar, Norshield, Globe-X and the orbiting cast of characters, including Panju, Weinberg, Charest, Xanthoudakis, Muir, Daviault, Brock, Johnson, Matteo and Smith. He would later acknowledge that he thinks the list of people who do what he does is pretty short and that inquiries usually start with the question "Who's stupid enough to do this?" Then someone says, "Wes Voorheis, he'll do it."

Behind all the last-minute attempts at a settlement before the closing, which would have eliminated the need for and existence of the CCE, was a coalition consisting of Weinberg, Charest, Panju, Xanthoudakis, Matteo, Muir, Daviault and all their related entities. So, certainly, these allies in settlement must be cohorts in the crime, or so the assumption would be. In reality the interactions of these parties was very complex. By the spring of 2004 Weinberg and Charest's relationship had suffered, but they were still together. They both deeply resented and blamed Panju for their situation. Tom Muir and Bob Daviault were not even speaking to each other, and, of course, Matteo and Daviault had hated each other for years. Lino also had no respect for Weinberg or Panju, and his relationship with John X was both mercurial and bizarre. His need to control John kept him immersed in the situation, and his loyalty to a friend was causing him to take risks far beyond what was best for his business. John alone seemed to be able to maintain at least cordial relations or better with all the various people, and the spring of 2004 found him at his financial and domestic peak.

Norshield Financial had prospered greatly over the previous three years because of the "techno bust" of 2000 and the contrarian investment practices John used. The business had survived the Cinar rumors and had grown to manage over $1 billion. They were the largest and most innovative hedge fund in the country, one of the world's best. Norshield had greatly expanded its size and returns by striking a unique and creative structure with its hedge funds in concert with RBC, the nation's largest bank. In this structure, Norshield or its entities would take $15 million in cash, receive $85 million from RBC in debt and then, with this leverage factor, they would greatly expand their

ability to reap larger returns due to the leverage. The result was impressive returns and the ability to attract more and new money. With the way the funds were structured, the investors never knew about the leverage against the hedge fund basket because neither RBC nor Norshield ever divulged it. It was simply a proprietary trading model. John rationalized the non-disclosure as being necessary thanks to various confidentiality clauses and because the documents clearly allowed leverage against the investments. What no investor would ever know is that before any of the leverage they would expect took place, the entire underlying hedge fund basket was already leveraged with RBC, who held all the securities in total.

The CCE's eyes were immediately drawn to deep pockets that somehow had been involved in the Globe-X deal. This meant Weinberg, Charest and Norshield. Any of these parties had the ability to write a big check, which would be split up among the CCE itself, the old shareholders (oddly enough Weinberg and Charest were substantial) and the new owners, being Michael Hirsch or Cookie Jar. The in-place operatives of the CCE from the pre-purchase days included Bill Brock of Davies Ward Phillips & Vineberg, Clifford Johnson and Wayne Aranha of PricewaterhouseCoopers, and other law firms in various jurisdictions. Now that they were budgeted and operating, Voorheis would take his mighty checkbook to expand and develop existing relationships and establish new relationships, targeting the places he believed could produce money.

As amazing as it seems with all the documentation surrounding the entire Cinar investment, Voorheis and company would be able, as one of their first victories, to continue the obfuscation of how much money was really owed. Despite the fact that Cinar only sent $108 million to Globe-X, there had been, from the earliest headlines in March 2000, a claim that "$122 million was missing," so the press always clung to that number as the invested amount. Brock and company naturally preferred the larger number as well. Both Usher and Snyder seemed to understand that the lesser number was the correct figure. Usher had been understandably pleased with the recovery of $86 million for very little effort on his part, which left a balance of $22 million. Not bad considering the money had been sent offshore, the relationships between all the companies were weird and complex, and the federal government had all but signed off on the problem. When the eleventh-hour settlements between Holden, me and Snyder were taking place, the $12 to $13 million would have resolved the issue in full, *and* it would have put between $17 and $18 million more in the pockets of the Cinar shareholders (the settlement plus the $5 million earmarked for the CCE). This would have brought the total to $103 or $104 million of the originally invested $108 million or ninety-six percent at a time when most portfolios had shrunk by twenty to thirty-five percent due to the market collapses between March 2000 and June 2002. The newspapers and the CCE disinformation machine managed to keep the press, the public eye and even legal circles focused instead on the $122 million owed, the $86 million paid, with $36 million still due, which made their grievance appear more substantial. Some reporters were even willing to help spin the amounts further out of whack by converting the $36 million number, which is in U.S. dollars, into Canadian dollars, which at the time would cause the reader to believe that over $43 million was owed. Throughout the early life of the CCE, they would actively

seek publicity on the matter while Weinberg and Charest were publicity shy and Norshield, needless to say, wanted to keep everything out of the papers. John's business was going great and the only thing that could detract from it was negative publicity related to Cinar.

The AGM
Smackdown

By law, public companies must hold annual meetings and issue certain annual and quarterly reports to their shareholders. While it is certainly a requirement, it is also an opportunity that most CEOs and corporate executives look forward to . . . a chance to inform and educate shareholders, brokers, regulators, opinion leaders and the press about what the company has achieved and where it's going. The Mount Real annual meeting, for years, had been carefully scripted sessions of employees, friends and satisfied investors who were very pliable and shaped themselves to Lino's molds. After a well-seeded question-and-answer period, the group of 150 or so retired to the bar for free drinks and appetizers, small talk and gossip.

For many years, Lino had been the ringleader of the well-orchestrated circus. This year he would once again choose to play second banana to Joe Pettinicchio, the company's president.

Joe would do an excellent job of leading the presentation and helping the other executives explain their business, which was never easy because the company had never wanted to tell the shareholders what business they were really in. So, by way of obfuscation, the company would lead its shareholders to believe it was in the "financial management services" business, and then, reluctantly, that it was in the magazine business. The general impression was that the growth was due to the publishing side of the business, never that Mount Real was in the telemarketing business selling magazine subscriptions over the phone to American customers, which in fact was the business it *was* in.

Brokers, analysts, fund managers, employees, even board members were unable to describe the business succinctly. What they did know was the company was making money . . . lots of it . . . and that it had grown dramatically and consistently. It was in the financials that everyone found their strength and confidence.

As the annual meeting convened, an unusual anxiety had begun to affect the companies' key executives. Even Lino was concerned, so much so that he had asked me to sit with a fellow named Maurice Levesque. The rumors were that Levesque was going to introduce to the floor the concept of a stock buyback program. And like it or not, he did. The program as Levesque explained it would be funded by Mount Real and was a tool that could move share prices up. Since the financial statements reflected such significant earnings, Levesque assumed that the company would either have cash or access to cash to fund the effort. "After all," he would explain, "this company has done everything right, with excellent sales growth, outstanding earnings and good cost containment. The only problem is that the share price is undervalued."

As the concept was introduced to the crowded ballroom, many people began to nod their heads in agreement with Levesque's plan, but it was very obvious that Lino was becoming incensed. The question was why? Here was a thoughtful, well-meaning shareholder with a reasonable idea of how to move the company's stock price up. This man had used his own money to buy a significant amount of stock in the company, which he believed in. He wasn't challenging management's abilities, just introducing an idea. Was Lino angry because no one had ever broken the script before? Or was he angry because he hadn't thought of the idea? Perhaps it was because he had lost control of the meeting or that some of his loyal allies seemed to like the concept. As Levesque talked, the anger became palpable and finally Lino could contain himself no longer. He didn't thank Maurice for his thoughts, or for being a shareholder. He didn't acknowledge his program or the concept; he merely said, "We of the Mount Real management team are also concerned about the share price and are committed to improving it. We believe that there are a dozen ways or more to move the price up and we are focused on those twelve methods, not an ill-conceived thirteenth method that surfaces due to someone's need to give a speech in public."

The room became very uncomfortable and friendly questions and comments suddenly went silent. Grabbing the quiet moment, a very Francophone shareholder began directing technical, complicated, aggressive questions at

Lino, who had now lost the buffer that Joe previously had provided him. Lino's French is marginal at best, his understanding better than his spoken word. When the translations were complete, he would respond in clear English.

"It's obvious that you don't understand the financial statements. I'm not sure you'd understand them if they were much less complicated or downright simple, but your question makes me realize that you're not very perceptive and don't know anything about this business."

The room was silent. The meeting proceeded with another question tied to footnotes, which was equally complicated. Now Lino would lose it altogether and respond, "I'm not going to take everyone's time to answer silly questions like that, so here are some alternatives for you. You can sell your stock and I promise nobody will miss you, or you and I can meet after we adjourn and I'll answer your questions. Better yet, you and I can go outside, walk around the block and talk about it, or let's just go outside!"

The audience realized that the CEO had just called out a shareholder and suggested that they "go outside." The meeting adjourned, but Matteo didn't let it go. He went to the shareholder and asked him to step outside with him, with clear intentions of conversing with his fists.

Despite the disaster, Levesque's idea of the buyback had struck a chord. It seemed to make real sense, and since neither Lino nor the management team ever explained the other "twelve ways" of increasing share price, the buyback concept took hold.

One of the perplexing problems of business that even sophisticated investors and analysts seem to forget is that profitability and earnings don't necessarily mean good cash flow. Lino knew better than anyone that Mount Real could earn $12 million per year, but that it had chronic cash problems, and the idea of funding a buyback would only exacerbate his already sleepless nights. Growth requires cash; expansion of all kinds requires cash. Because his various operations were growing they were all consuming cash, not producing cash. The costs of the sales groups in telemarketing, the monthly interest payments for the MRACS (originally Mount Real Acceptance Corporation) and RealVest debts, the high processing costs, along with the fixed costs of the business, were chewing up huge amounts of cash monthly. While the books reflected profits, the cash ledger was going more and more negative and was reliant on a consistent flow of new money from debt, no matter what the source.

Over the next year, Lino would actually begin to support the buyback concept. While he alone knew he didn't have the resources, he couldn't refute the logic and he couldn't admit he didn't have the money.

CHAPTER   34

DATE   APRIL 2004

SCENE   Montreal

Micheline Charest

Micheline had finally realized that the only way to live life was to re-immerse herself in an active, full-time creative environment. While Cinar wasn't an option, she would find a viable substitute at Just for Laughs, the annual comedy festival that was now extending itself into television production and building its brand. While she and Ron had grown more distant and rumors abounded that they were separating, they remained together. Ron's life had become more withdrawn and insular with only litigation and family matters seeming to be the business of the day. His days were not full and there were times when depression would creep up.

The CCE was laying plans to tighten the noose around

Charest's and Weinberg's assets, including their home in prestigious Westmount, the unique Montreal neighborhood, and their summer home in Magog. Weinberg had developed some clever barriers to make their road difficult, but the CCE's grinding methods would seem to be unbeatable.

Charest's energy wouldn't let her be lured into the veils of depression and while she knew that life was now far from perfect, she could find happiness through her work. It was, after all, her talent, genius and energy that had made Cinar the most successful children's animation company in Canada and it would be these same attributes that could help another business grow. There are those private moments as people approach certain anniversaries when they stand in front of the mirror, naked and inquiring. They look at themselves with a detached eye and take stock. The individual looks at the overall impression, and then dissects the wrinkles, the bulges, the softness of the tummy, the bags under the eyes, the butt that has changed, the chin that now seems different. Some people are troubled by their nose, others their ankles; some are discouraged by their hair, still others their breasts. Charest's biting assessment of herself on this inspection as her 50th birthday approached was that she "needed some work."

Not one to delay a decision once it's made, Micheline would approach a plastic surgeon within days and talk with him about the prospects of "getting some work done." She, as have so many women her age, would say that she didn't like what's happened to her face with age and she was "just too big now and exercise doesn't seem to help get rid of fat in certain places." Then she would circle to the breast topic with "as long as I'm getting the work

MICHELINE CHAREST

done, I really should do these as well, for the good of everyone." She smiled as she said it. The doctor had listened carefully and made it clear that he could, in fact, do the surgeries, and he would be glad to. They would be expensive, but that didn't seem to be a concern for Charest. As he got out his calendar, the tone of the conversation would change.

"As I see the schedule, it seems that I could do the first surgery in about two months, on the 22nd. I think we'll start with the facelift. The procedure will be about three hours and I would say the recovery time will be roughly seven days. Then we could get the second operation completed; that would be the breast work about three months later, and that will be about two hours for the procedure and you'll need at least five days for the recovery, maybe ten. As for the liposuction, we could do that about three months after the breasts and . . ."

Charest interrupted. "Doctor, I haven't got all goddamn year to be cut and caressed. When I came here to talk to you about this process, I didn't come to plan my next twelve months. I'm busy and I want the changes now."

"I don't think you know what you're asking. Each procedure takes time and to do all three operations at once is impossible. Perhaps we could combine two of them, but certainly not three," he continued.

"Look, doc, if you can't do all three, I'm willing to bet I'll find someone who can. If not here in Montreal, I'll go to Miami, but somebody will do all three at once." Charest was emphatic.

"To do three surgeries would mean you'd be out for eight or nine hours; that's a lot of anesthesia and the recovery will be painful with three different operations to recover from." Charest could tell he was about to agree to do what she wanted. "Doctor, I think you have a small idea of what I've been through over the last four years, but I can assure you that it's been very painful. I can handle pain, lots of pain. I've lost the business I loved, the life I loved, even in many ways the man I loved. I've dealt with my son's disabilities and now I've lost the look that made Micheline Charest special. I need to be special again. If that means eight or nine hours on an operating table, fine. If that means two painful weeks of recovery, fine, but I need this done now . . . not in two months, or six months or nine months. My God, it took nine months to create me in the first place; I want to be recreated in weeks, not months."

"I've had a cancellation for next week. If I move some things around, I could do it then. I really don't recommend this, but I know you're busy and I don't question that you're tough."

Thank you, doctor, I'll see you soon." She left, feeling better than she'd felt in years.

Ron realized that no matter what his feelings were about the idea, she would do what she wanted anyway. He more than anyone knew how she had used her charms, her looks, her body, to change minds, motivate, excite and ignite. He was neither so old nor so defeated that he didn't know or remember her charms.

"Okay," he said, "sounds good. I'll plan on being around during the convalescence and try to help around the house."

"That would be great. Thanks, darling." She never told him about the conversation with the doctor or about his recommendation that the procedures be done as three separate surgeries over nine months. She never mentioned that it would involve eight or more hours under sedation. She wasn't concerned, so why should he be?

It was a normal day in Montreal as the city of three million woke up and went about its business. The Métro, which moved about a million people every day, was on schedule and taking people to their gainful employment. The buses, too, were full as were the Autoroutes that flow into and out of the city center. The bridges, as always, were congested and delayed as the commuters from the south and east made their way to work. Micheline Charest had gotten up early, followed her pre-surgery regime and was at the clinic ready to be recreated. She had said goodbye to her boys, whom she loved very much, and to Ron.

When the surgery was over, Micheline was moved into the recovery room. There was an alarm that should have warned of a lack of oxygen, but it wasn't operating. The nurse then left the room and left Charest unattended. The nurse re-entered the room and noticed that the patient wasn't breathing. Quickly, she notified the anesthesiologist. They immediately tried to replace the breathing tube, but couldn't get the mouth to open. While some doctors would have given the dying Charest a shot to relax the muscles of the mouth and throat, this wasn't done. After 35 minutes 911 was called and an ambulance was dispatched to the clinic.

On Wednesday, the 14th day of April, 2004, the mother who had built a billion dollar company, created television programming that other mothers could count on to safely guide their children, had died.

One woman who had worked with her for seven years said, "In all the time I worked with her she never even knew that I had children. Her focus was business."

The War Chest

Voorheis had requested the meeting with Lowell Holden, and after some back and forth, they agreed to meet in Minneapolis. Voorheis had flown from Toronto to Minneapolis. The Minnesota businessman now owned CIS and some other entities that he had purchased from Tom Muir. Through the entities he was taking actions in various jurisdictions to lay claim to certain Globe-X assets and also protect other assets from Cinar. The two would verbally spar for about half an hour and finally Voorheis would say, "You're pretty cavalier about all this. Aren't you concerned about what we're doing, what we intend to do and the fact we're committed to destroying you?"

Holden sat quietly and then said, "I've been watching you guys for almost two years now, not you, but the liquidators, Brock and the other Cinar parties. When I see the way you spend money and accomplish virtually nothing, I'm not very intimidated. I figure you guys are burning cash at the rate of six hundred thousand per month; at that rate you'll be short of money by November. When you're out of money, this will be over. There's no one here who is carrying on for passion or a cause or to make things right. This whole thing is purely about money. This isn't about justice, or right and wrong. It's only about money. You guys spend too much and you'll be out. So, no, I'm not intimidated." Holden got up and left.

Voorheis sat quietly and reflected on Holden's prediction. He penciled out the numbers and realized that the monthly costs were just about what Holden had projected. That meant that they could indeed be out of money by November.

Voorheis would then call Michael Hirsch and recount the story of his meeting with Holden. Then he would say, "I'm not interested in losing. I'd rather leave now than lose to these dicks in November because of budget. I want you to think real hard about how we get funding for this project way beyond $5 million. We may need ten or 15 or even more, and if I'm going to go ahead, I need to know that we can get it. I'll be back in Toronto on Thursday, so please think about it. They think this is all about money, but to me it's all about winning and I'm not going to lose."

The Report

Clifford Johnson and his cohort, Wayne Aranha of PricewaterhouseCoopers, had now been in control of Globe-X for one year, nine months. They had worked the file and researched where the money had gone, and by now they knew that the funds weren't sitting around in a big treasure box waiting for them. They would file their first report on July 5, 2004. In it they would make a stab at everyone they could: Norshield, John, Tom, Maria, Bob, Mount Real, Lino, Holden and the Mosaic deal. They were ready to punch Mother Teresa if they thought she had hidden money.

Their words were unflattering and while they never used the word "fraud," they danced around it using words and phrases like "camouflage," "cobbled together," "misfeasance," "breach of trust," "spurious at best" and "serious questions on accounting entries." The clever piece of the overall CCE was the use of depositions and their release to a well-prepped press corps. Because the Cinar story had captured so much attention and continued to pull front page or front page business section headlines, the story still had legs. The writers for the various papers were keenly competitive, within their own newspaper as well as with other papers. Brock, Voorheis and the talent block at the CCE knew that if they were to slug it out in court with the various and disparate groups they were pursuing, it would be a long, slow, expensive ground war that may not succeed. That's why the deposition strategy was chosen, in concert with the PricewaterhouseCoopers liquidators' reports that would surface periodically. Because Cinar was funding these reports in full, they could be certain that the liquidators' point of view would be in perfect support of the CCE position. As the reports and later the depositions of various parties would become available, the CCE would immediately make them news. The relevance of all of these reports or depositions in court was never a factor or ever reflected on in the press, only their existence and the information therein. So, suddenly a report about a bankruptcy trustee in a small Caribbean country that would not even be news in its homeland would be front page in the Canadian press. Or a deposition of a person as part of a case that would never even reach a courtroom in Canada would become front page stories in the business sections. The CCE had perfected and executed a "poison the earth" strategy, and the poison was falling all over the ground that John needed to walk on.

Excerpts from *First Report*
of the Joint Official Liquidators

6.27 The Liquidators are having some difficulty believing that there were managed accounts to the tune of US$85 million underlying these accounts, particularly since they have not seen any evidence external to the Norshield Group to support the existence or valuation of the managed accounts. It seems more likely that these accounts and the total return swap were "cobbled together" to inflate GXC's balance sheet and camouflage the payment of US$15 million to Norshield Composite.

6.28 The investment by GXC in MR Investments appears to have originated in 1995 when C$3,523,022 (principal of C$3,073,000 plus capitalised interest) was transferred from GX Growth in a merger – see Section II. By March 2000, the sum had grown to over C$5.5 million through the capitalisation of interest and after the further investment of C$100,000 in September 1997 and C$120,000 in December 1997. By December 2001, the balance had increased to almost C$6.6 million, there being no movement on the account other than the capitalisation of interest, as follows:

	CDN $
Balance 31 March 2000	5,559,497
Capitalised interest	549,950
Balance 31 March 2001	6,115,447
Capitalised interest	454,114
Balance 31 December 2001	6,569,561

[**Author's note:** The reader may notice that the first two numbers add up to 6,109,447, not 6,115,447 as written.]

6.35 The above accounting machinations indicate that the Company created an investment in Globe-X Emerald without having passed any funds to that company, and by the creation, in the main, of a liability that it termed US$ Commercial Paper that was issued to GXC, its parent. The effect of these entries was to present a false view of the financial position of GXC, and may have risen to the level of accounting fraud. Our investigations in this area will continue.

7.1 In section II of this report, the Liquidators list those records and documents relating to GXM that the directors and principals turned over. In addition to those sparse records, the Liquidators obtained from the GXM's bankers and brokers records of accounts maintained with them. The information in this section has been obtained and, to the extent possible, pieced together from these minimum records. Unfortunately, they have not been sufficient to enable the Liquidators to prepare a statement of affairs of GXM as of commencement of the liquidation. However, there is sufficient information indicating that funds of GXM were disbursed to persons and entities connected by way of common ownership or control or both, and to associates of those persons and entities.

8.2 Thus, of the US$108,000,000 received from CINAR for investing in an Enhanced Bond Strategy only US$21,420,173 was invested in bonds or similar securities.

[Author's note: The Liquidators refer here to the correct amount of $108 million, not the confused amount of $122 million they commonly quoted to the press. To this day, the press does not report the number correctly.]

8.6 It should be noted that three of the amounts received by GXM from CINAR purportedly for settlement of foreign currency trading losses, amounting to US$7,027,063, were credited with interest to 31 January 1999, amounting to US$22,247, by GXM and then transferred to GXC as an investment in GXC's US$ Debentures in the name of Killington Holdings Limited (Killington). Previously, Killington had invested US$3,000,000 in GXC's US$ Debentures on 12 August 1998. On 31 July 1999, those debentures matured and the proceeds, amounting to US$3,427,579, were reinvested. On 31 January 2000, Killington's investment in GXC's US$ Debentures was redeemed and the proceeds, amounting to US$12,001,996.81, were invested in GXC's US$ Second Management Shares. The Liquidators have not found from GXC's records in their possession evidence to support the redemption of these shares and will investigate this further.

11.4 The Liquidators have obtained the leave of the Supreme Court to apply to the Superior Court of the Province of Quebec seeking an Order that would:

11.4.1 Authorize the examination under oath by the Liquidators through their attorneys in Canada, of the following persons, reasonably thought to have knowledge of the affairs of the companies, their dealings and property:

Mr. John Xanthoudakis

Mr. Lino Matteo

Mr. Mario Ricci

Mr. Michael Maloney

Mr. Robert Daviault

Mr. Dale Smith

Mr. Steven Tsokanos

Mr. John Wickenden

Mr. Hasanain Panju

Mr. Eddie Koussaya

11.5 A summary of the reasons that the Liquidators are particularly interested in the various persons is as follows:

11.5.1 Mr. Xanthoudakis is or was a shareholder and Director of the Norshield Canada Companies most of which have their registered address at 630 René Lévesque West, Montreal, Quebec, and has received substantial sums of money either directly or through corporations interposed from the Companies, including without limitation the sum of US$800,000 as purported management fees. From searches which the Liquidators have conducted at the offices of the Registrar of Companies in The Bahamas they have found that the Directors of IAM are listed as being Mr. John Xanthoudakis (who also is shown as Vice President and Treasurer) and Mr. Lino Matteo (who also holds the offices of President and Secretary), both of whom reside and are domiciled in Montreal, Quebec, Canada.

[**Author's note:** IAM, or International Asset Management, was a shell company created by John and Lino in 1991 that was never more than a shell. The Liquidators have thrown in this dull bit of business to show a link between Lino and John.]

11.15.2 A Declaration that Mr. Muir is guilty of misfeasance and breach of trust in relation to the Company as a director in transferring, or permitting the transfer, of 1,700 shares of Univest Limited, owned by GXM (the Univest Shares) to ekal.

11.19 As noted above, Cardinal refused to turn over the Class B usd and Class C cad shares on the grounds that Silicon Isle had asserted a right to them. Cardinal has not cooperated with the Liquidators and seemed to have gone out of its way to bring about Silicon Isle's interference in the transfer of these shares to the control of the Liquidators; this is evident from Silicon Isle's letter of 29 August 2003, copy of which is produced and shown as **Exhibit 26**. There is nothing in the files to indicate how Silicon might have come to own these shares; its claim appears spurious, at best. It should be noted that Silicon's assertion of an interest is expressed by its then Anguilla solicitors, Caribbean Juris Chambers, as follows: ". . . following the acquisition of Globe-X Management our client Silicon Isle Limited became the beneficial owner of those shares and that they were placed as collateral following an agreement at the time of purchase." It is not clear whether the purported placement as collateral relates to the Security Agreement, dated 29 August 2002, which is discussed in paragraph 9.5.

11.20 The Liquidators will continue to seek turnover of GXM's shares in Univest, but consider it most likely that an application would have to be made to the Court in order to gain the cooperation of Cardinal. On 14 June 2004, the Liquidators, by their counsel, requested Ms. Castrechini to provide financial statements and certain other information to which the Companies as shareholders are entitled or which is required for the filing of the action in the Supreme Court that the Liquidators intend to commence in order to obtain relief for damages incurred by GXM in connection with the deprivation of its shares in Univest. Letters passing between the Liquidators and their counsel and Cardinal and its counsel are produced and shown as **Exhibit 27**.

12.3   The Liquidators will continue to press for the records and will seek the aid of the Courts in Anguilla, Canada, The Bahamas and, it seems more likely, also the USA to compel the turnover of the records. The Liquidators will also take advice on whether and the extent to which they might be obliged to file complaints with regulators, given the conduct of the former directors of the Companies. It appears to the Liquidators that a number of the parties do not take seriously the Orders of the Courts, and it is anticipated that action will be taken to gain effective compliance with Court orders.

12.4   The Companies, based on the records that have been turned over to the Liquidators, were being operated in a manner that appears to have been detrimental to its creditors, to say the least. There are serious questions on the manner in which accounting entries were booked for a number of the transactions. It is also unclear whether the Companies at commencement of the liquidation were solvent, and if not, the point in time in which insolvency occurred. The Liquidators do concede that their concerns and suspicions in this regard could be resolved by the disclosure of additional information by the directors and others but until then, this is a real concern.

12.5 The Liquidators also have grave concern over the manner in which the funds provided by CINAR were applied to activities clearly inconsistent with the terms of the original agreement. It is most disconcerting that the funds, by and large, were disbursed to parties that have been or appear to be connected to the principals (in fact or in substance, or both) of the Companies. This high concentration of connected or related party dealings precedes the Companies' involvement with CINAR; it is evident from their early years in business. The Liquidators propose to investigate these types of activities further.

John's offices had moved across the street from Place Ville-Marie where he had been for ten years. When the report came out that hot July day, the word went out to the people closest to the problem that everybody would meet up at Zesto's Pizza. This was the kind of place where the group would have met ten years ago, long before the high-flying days of $800 dinners and $300 lunches. Before it was remodeled, the pizza joint had about 60 seats, a marginal air conditioner and the kind of food no one really likes, but no one really dislikes. The tables aren't sized right for the chairs, so whenever you sit you're always uncomfortable, but no one knows why. The fluorescent lights flashed above the table, the way they do before the bulb burns out. At the table were John, Mario, Dale Smith, Lino and me. Some of us had seen the report, some of us had listened to secondhand feedback, but only I had read it.

"How bad is it?" John said.

"It's conjecture, innuendo and speculation," I said, "but it won't read that way in the papers. They've put everybody into the soup, everyone under the spotlight and everyone into doubt."

"Is there any question that the newspapers will run with it?" John asked.

"No question they'll run now, and it wouldn't surprise me if those guys were delivering copies to the press right now."

With his deep voice, Lino weighed in.

"Don't talk to the press, John, they'll misquote and cook you anyway. These guys have no interest in getting the story right; they only want a story that will make you look bad."

"I think you have to talk to them, John," I piped up. "This story is going to be completely negative if you don't. I think anything you say will get buried in the back of the story, but if you comment, they'll have to run it."

"But what in the world can he say, anyway?" Dale asked.

"He needs to tell people clearly and simply that the Liquidators' Report has been paid for by Cinar, who has paid over three quarters of a million. He needs to tell people that the Liquidators' Report in Section 8.2 clearly states the amount invested was $108 million, as we've said all along, and not $122 million as they've continuously tried to say. Finally, he needs to tell people that Norshield did provide services to Globe-X from 1996 to 2001 so there is no surprise that Norshield would be mentioned in the report. Cinar created this entire mess because their board let their management run roughshod over the company; this whole thing is a matter of Cinar's lack of corporate governance."

"The newspapers aren't going to run that!" Lino yelled.

"They'll run it *if* that's the only statement they get. They have no choice," I countered. "To say nothing will cause this to spin out of control. John has a good message, get it out there.

"John, I'm not saying he's wrong, but you can't trust these guys. In a few days this will blow over and nobody will remember it."

"Maybe I should send a letter," John said. Mario and I exchanged glances. Every time John decided to send a letter, there would be numerous drafts and the letter would never be sent. Finally, it was agreed that Dale would offer the messages according to what I had suggested, and John would remain silent.

Rooms
without Doors

Montreal summers can become surprisingly hot for a city
so far north. The humidity suddenly soars and the temperature climbs into the 30's. The effect is widely
variable, depending on social class and priorities. For the
affluent, they (like most wealthy people throughout the
world) have air conditioners in their homes, offices and
cars. For the not so fortunate, the high temperatures can
mean sleepless nights, hot commutes on the Métro,
crowded buses, or the freeway heat in their steaming cars.
The hot spell can last up to ten days and is usually dissi-
pated by a big, roaring thunderstorm that makes the skies
black and begins with an hour or two of downpour followed by a cool front.

John's home was air conditioned, so there was no obvious reason for the restlessness and sleeplessness. His days were full, his family time okay, but the bickering and fights were increasing and the making up wasn't as loving or as enjoyable as it used to be. For years John and his wife had gone by the old rule that they "wouldn't go to bed mad," but now they'd never get to bed if they stuck to the rule.

When he would hit the bed he'd fall asleep right away; unlike some who can't fall asleep in the first place, he'd drift right off. He'd hit a deep sleep cycle and begin his recharging process, but by about 2:00 a.m. bad dreams would set in and by 2:30 he'd be startled awake. The dreams may have had nothing to do with business, but once awake, it would be business that would occupy his thoughts and mind. The deep anxiety about what the newspapers would write next. Would the stories scare away the best employees? What if redemptions began to increase? How could he keep sales up and returns high? Always his mind would drift back to redemption concerns. Throughout the next couple of hours he'd toss and turn, unable to regain his sleep. Sometimes, he'd get up and try to eat or drink something, but it rarely worked. Mostly, he'd just toss.

There were times when just before he was about to fall back to sleep, his legs would cramp, reawakening him. At other times he would begin to feel fear, not in his mind, but in his stomach and solar plexus, pain so severe he'd curl into a fetal position and lie that way for half an hour at a time.

These nights would sometimes last until around 4:00 a.m., but then a welcome drowsiness and blessed sleep would arrive. But this was no certainty and at other times he'd finally surrender at 5:30 or 6:00, get up, shower and

ROOMS WITHOUT DOORS

start the new day, even if it had already begun at 2:30 in the morning. The difficulty for the entrepreneur is that the cause of their sleeplessness is usually known only to them and the thoughts are so frightening that they dare not share them with anyone lest they reveal the unknown problem or weakness to others. What John was feeling in the hot summer of 2004 was the typical summer heat, but also the first heat applied by Wes Voorheis and the new CCE.

Now that the CCE had fired their first shots with the Joint Liquidators' Report, Lino was predicting the next stage would be depositions with some of the key figures. Their report had made it clear that they had a list of people they hoped to talk to. With John first and Lino second, not far down the list was Bob Daviault, and while everyone might eventually have to be deposed, it was Daviault whom Lino feared would be the first to talk and the one who would spin the tale anyway he wanted to. He was now living in Calgary and while he didn't want to be re-immersed in the whole matter, neither would he evade it. John had hoped that Bob would just fade away, but Lino was vociferously insisting that wouldn't happen and that Bob couldn't be trusted. The confirmation arrived through me that Bob had been subpoenaed and he intended to cooperate.

If there were Daviault depositions, it would be the first time that the press might get a look at the inside workings or structure in which John X had operated. A unique structure of relationships, based on long histories of trust, combined with weaknesses of personality or character. John had carefully cast his associates, as well he should have, because in law and in fact they really owned the businesses they operated, and while John acted like a CEO with full authority in many of these businesses, he was without legal portfolio and operated by an unwritten code. John, for example, knew that Tom Muir would always defer to his ideas, direction and initiative, which he in fact did, even though Tom held all the legal authority. John knew Bob was lazy and would find the easy way around a problem so he was selected to be Tom's partner. As long as things went well that partnership worked, and again John maintained control easily because Bob wasn't looking for more to do; he wanted less to do.

The same would be true for other people he would surround himself with. Terri Engelman was great at detail; John was not. Peter Kafalas could do the tedious side of trading; John could focus on the flashy. He had carefully surrounded himself with people who complemented his strengths and weaknesses, but with whom he could maintain control. During the long sleepless sessions he would remind himself of these people and the casting sessions that had led to the peculiar structure . . . the structure that now, if Daviault was deposed, would run the risk of being exposed. Worst of all, the structure would be exposed to people who seemed more intent on hurting him than collecting money.

There had been several times since the creation of the CCE that John had asked Lino or me to send out feelers and see if they had a price in mind to get things settled. It would, after all, be nice to get the Cinar mess behind the businesses. Since the last-minute breakdown with Snyder before the sale was complete, there had been no settlement talks at all, just the liquidators' efforts, the funding of lawsuits, the public relations fees and the fees flowing now to Voorheis, Inkster and Drinkwater. The budget was full and the consultants had big appetites. Why would

ROOMS WITHOUT DOORS

anyone talk settlement . . . the pay was too good! There actually seemed to be no one willing to talk about a settlement at any price.

So, slowly, John began to realize that there may not be a way to compromise, negotiate or mediate this increasingly volatile situation. More and more his nightmares would end in rooms with no doors, with windows that couldn't be opened, or bridges that suddenly ended rather than reaching the other side. Most business problems have a solution; the solution may be unpleasant or undesirable, it may be expensive or time consuming, but there is a solution. John's middle-of-the-night sessions were causing his conscious and his subconscious to realize that he was now caught in a huge billing machine with lawyers, accountants and consultants putting in hours and creating invoices that were very good for their businesses, partners and families. They were working for a nameless, faceless client with $5 million and, in time, that amount would more than triple. There may have never been an opponent like this in business history because the concept of a fully funded litigation committee with multiple millions at their disposal is relatively new. There have always been deep-pocketed parties, but they would usually respond to economics, or there was the government, but they would usually respond to political agendas.

The way I saw it, John was the unwitting opponent of a hybrid: a privately funded, quasi-governmental, newly formed, multifunctional, litigious publicity machine working to the benefit of their own self-perpetuation and enriching themselves as they proceeded. Small pieces of this revelation would come to John at different times during the tossing and turning. While he would never cognitively recognize his exact dilemma, the pains in his stomach and chest would remind him that whatever he was fighting was serious and peculiar. The night that Daviault's depositions were announced, the thunderstorm that would break the heat wave roared for two hours. The temperature dropped by 15°C. The city was cool and glistening with the recent rain. People opened their windows and enjoyed the cool breezes. Most people hadn't had a good night's sleep in a week, but tonight they would sleep fast. John, too, turned off the air conditioning and opened the windows. He felt the cool air and could smell the refreshing rain. He went to sleep about a half hour after Kathy. They had fought again that night. The fight had been about money. They had a lot, but she spent as if they had even more. If they hadn't fought over money, they would have probably fought about something else. John fell fast asleep in the fresh air and cool breeze. At about two o'clock the nightmares started and at 2:30 in the morning, he was wide awake.

CHAPTER 38

DATE SEPTEMBER 2004

SCENE Montreal

Frayed Nerves and New Opportunities

When Tanya and I entered Gabriella's office to interview her as a profile for the Mount Real annual report, the meeting seemed as plain vanilla as meetings could get. What we wanted was a one-page interview about her and her life. Gabriella was born in Czechoslovakia when the East was still the East and behind the Iron Curtain. She had worked hard, learned four languages, developed excellent organizational skills and always had an eye for detail. Her children were attractive, smart and athletic; her son was playing tennis at a Junior National level. When she had started at Mount Real some eight years earlier, she was Lino's assistant, but she had been bullied and intimidated the entire early portion of her life by the

Communist system and wasn't going to put up with that same kind of behavior in her new world. So, after several warnings, she told Lino she was done with him. His response was to put her in a new position where she would be the administrator and intermediary for Mount Real and all its related entities with the governments, stock exchanges, regulatory bodies and securities commissions that the companies interacted with. She excelled at her job, and her eye for detail matched the task well. Lino tended to leave her alone, and her domain was quite firmly under her own control.

Tanya had been in the organization about a year; she was young, attractive and ambitious. She was hoping that hard work would move her from being one of Lino's four assistants into writing and editorial for the magazines. She was a good writer and she hoped to do most of the writing for the annual report. She was nominally under my tutelage for the project, and I helped her get the interview set up with Gabriella, who seemed to be avoiding it.

With Gabriella sitting behind her desk in her first floor office and with Tanya and me in front of her, the meeting began. Hundreds of times Gabriella and I had chatted, laughed and joked in the same room, but today there was a coolness, an iciness about the meeting.

"What do you want to know for this story?" Gabriella asked.

"A little bit about where you are from, how you got here and a little about your family. It's a profile story about people," Tanya responded.

"I will talk about work and only my work. I and my family will not be written about and I've told Lino this . . . no stories, no pictures. I would prefer my last name not be used and I will definitely not allow the last name of my

children to be used." She was emphatic.

Caught completely off guard, I said lightly and with a smile, "Gabriella, this is just a fun talk and a fun profile. The angle will be to make you look good. You can read it before it's printed."

She responded succinctly. "I will only talk about work, not my family, my history, children, no pictures, no last names. Do you understand?"

"I understand. Tanya, there's no reason to continue the meeting. Let's find someone else to profile." I rose as I was talking. Tanya left the room. But I felt very confused and I lingered at the door.

Then Gabriella said, "The things I do here, not even I always understand. I don't want to be brought any closer or more visibly to it than I already am. I'm sure this seems odd to you, but I know what I'm doing." Uncharacteristically, I closed the door when I left.

On the West Island Jimmy del Greco had already put in a six-hour shift with one telemarketing operation and now he was arriving at Lino's Honeybee operation to do six hours there. It was a Tuesday, so he knew that Lino wouldn't show up. His "surprise" visits were always on Wednesday afternoon. That meant that no one scammed on Wednesday afternoons, but on Tuesday afternoon Jimmy punched himself in, as well as his friend, Ricky Dellacolla, who was at the racetrack placing bets for himself and Jimmy. Yesterday Ricky had done the same thing for Jimmy while Jimmy was at the track.

"Hey, Jimmy, how did the morning go, you big hitter?" The questioner was Bronco Grabowski, a big smiler, big talker and a big hitter himself. "I landed three so the week is off to a good start, Bronco." They exchanged high fives.

"Were you doing sweepstakes or Derogs?" Bronco

asked. Derogs are basically telemarketing pitches for and to people with bad credit and "derogatory" notes on their credit reports.

"Derogs," was the reply. "I was working some real losers. These mooches were total fucking saps. They had lips like carp," he mimicked a fish as he said it. "Can you imagine Eric over there has me doing a pitch where I tell the guy he's going to get a credit card, but before I can send him the credit card he needs to send me five hundred bucks to clear his bad credit, plus five hundred to create a positive balance on his account, plus a hundred dollar application fee. It's all cash or money order by FedEx. We tell 'em it's because the person fixing the credit is leaving their job in only three days so this is a once-in-a-lifetime chance. Well, the mooches go nuts. They go borrow from their relatives, pawn their shit, steal from all the cookie jars. This is candy, Bronco, candy. The deal is so hot, I'll probably do a deal or two this afternoon while I'm pitching mags for the Pope. Whenever I get a mooch on the phone I switch the pitch 'cause the deal is so hot."

"Jimmy, why don't I tag-team my mooches to you?" Bronco asked. "Maybe I can get some of that action."

"Deal! Hand 'em over. We'll tell them they can use the credit card to buy mags when they get it." The bell rang. Jimmy and Bronco rushed to their cubes and began to dial.

"Hello, Mrs. Dangler, I'm James del Greco calling you from International Publishers Clearing House right here in New York City and I want you to know this is your lucky day because Mrs. Dangler if you decide you want to be smarter, bright and better informed than Mr. Dangler you can become that way for free! How does that sound? Pretty good, eh? Well, I'm sure you're familiar with magazines like *Good Housekeeping, Better Homes and Gardens.*

No, ma'am, I'm not selling magazines . . . hell, I'm giving 'em away! Now, wouldn't you like me to give some to you? Oh, yeah, that sounds good doesn't it?"

The pitch went on and before it was over she had ordered ten different subscriptions. She thought she was paying for five of them, but once Jimmy had her credit card number, he dinged it for ten subscriptions for four years, or a total of $1,440. Mrs. Dangler had good credit, so her card could hold the whole amount, and he put it through. If her card couldn't hold the entire amount, he'd put through what he could and put the rest on monthly payments. That afternoon Jimmy wrote three magazine deals for himself, one for Ricky and, sure enough, hit up one more mooch on the credit card scam for his other employer. At 7:30 p.m. he punched out and called Ricky.

"How did we do, pard?"

"Jimmy, we is in de bucks! Laredo came in as a long shot at eighteen to one and we were there. Meet you at Wanda's in an hour."

At Wanda's the boys could drink beer, do shots, get lap dances and burn through over $400 in four hours, without even trying. But tonight with money in their pockets and a little coke in their noses, they spent $1,000 and then stumbled home. Tomorrow was Wednesday and on Wednesdays everybody worked because Lino made "surprise visits."

CHAPTER 39

DATE SEPTEMBER 2004

Vulnerable

The young assistant investigator would meet with Eric Robichaud because through their research they knew he had worked with Lino, and after ten years in telemarketing he knew the business very well. Eric was now serving time for dealing drugs, something he resorted to when his sales offices collapsed. This was the same Eric Robichaud that Lino had thrown out of his office so many times and had humiliated with missed payrolls, bad checks and tantrums in their years together. Robichaud had been told that the guys he would meet with could do him some good to shorten his term. Eric was led to believe that the head of the RCMP would be along. They met in a small visitor's room.

"How long were you in telemarketing?" The first question came quickly.

"About ten years. I grew up in it. I was pitching by sixteen and shooting by seventeen. I've always been good at it."

"What kind of things did you sell?"

"I've sold 'em all . . . Derog, mags, Identity Theft, You Just Won, credit cards, travel . . . I've sold them all."

"Why does Lino sell magazines and not the other stuff?"

"'Cause he likes to be clean, and mags are the cleanest. The buyer really gets a product at a pretty good price."

"Is he really clean?"

"Oh yeah, he's too straight and not a good enough salesman to be dirty. If he let me sell and do things my way, he'd be a lot richer than he is now."

"Isn't he pretty rich now?"

"Oh yeah, but he'd be better off if he listened to me."

"Why?"

"'Cause in telemarketing you need a mix of products and margins. To get and keep good people, one product with tight margins won't do it. You need a mix."

"If you're so smart, how come you're in here?"

"You're a smart-ass, aren't you? Processing is the key to the business, not salespeople, product or back room. It's all about processing. Mine went bad and now I'm dead. It's just that simple. Like Lino; he's got good processing so he's alive even if his operation is half-assed. He's got guys that do nothing all day, nothing but apply and work with processors to have backups for his backups. Do you know what I'm talking about?"

"Keep talking."

"When he writes an order, he needs a processor to turn

it into cash. He gets a credit card number, no signature, just a number and an expiration date. The order is pre-approved within hours. Then the processor runs the card and gets the money. The holdback might be fifteen to twenty percent, the processing fee six to ten percent, and then every week the processor wires the net funds to Lino's bank. Some processors wire daily, some weekly, whatever, but they keep the holdback in case there's trouble."

"What kind of trouble?"

"If chargebacks are too high, like if customers are calling to cancel or claim they were misrepped, that leads to a chargeback. Too many chargebacks and they shut you down, bam, just like that. They keep your cash, they keep your holdback and you're out of business. Lino keeps so many accounts going and he's always getting new ones so he can spread out his risk and keep operating if there's trouble. A guy like me usually has all his eggs in the same basket. Do you follow?"

"Yeah, what you're saying is that without processing Lino is dead, just like you."

"Exactly!"

"What causes processors to shut you down?"

"Chargebacks, customer complaints, rumors about police raids, federal investigations, banking irregularities. Some of these pricks are just waiting for an excuse to grab your money. They're the worst whores!"

"Well, thanks a lot. That's all we need."

"Hold it, wait a minute. Where's your guy, the head of the RCMP? He's supposed to be helping me. That's why I'm talking. Where is he?"

"First of all, I don't know what you're talking about. My guy used to be the head of the RCMP, but that was years ago. Your hearing must be bad, 'cause he'd never

help a maggot like you. No, you're just where you should be." He walked out.

The assistant went back to the car and called in. "Good job on putting together this whole magazine connection to Matteo. He's in the business, all right, at least for now. It turns out, according to our convict friend, that the industry is very vulnerable to a certain type of disease. It's called 'processingitis' and now I know how to spread the disease."

A few inquiries would reveal the various processing accounts that Mount Real relied on. With some strategic phone calls and memos, the processors would feign alarm and act with decisiveness. Suddenly, the orders that cost so much to generate were becoming valueless, or at best, distressed. Lino's processing was shut down.

There may be no day more traumatic for a businessman than the day the processor cuts you off. Some may say, "Oh no, the worst is when you have the IRS or Revenue Canada seize your assets," but the tax agencies, even if they do seize your assets, virtually always talk to you and will usually settle for a payment plan that keeps you alive. Others may say the worst is when the mob shows up and extorts payments. While that may be horrible, they basically want money and you're no good to them dead. Others claim it's a product recall, but they're not usually fatal.

When a processor cuts you off, they do it without notice. They are the banks without whom you can't continue operations. You expect the cash wired to your account after a five- or ten-day hold. They've already held back fifteen or twenty percent of your money, plus their fees of six to ten percent, so you're only getting seventy-five percent or less of your gross sales anyway. When they cut you off, you also realize that not only are you not getting paid for the money, which represents your sales two weeks ago, but all the orders written in the last week are lost as well because they'll keep that money, plus the holdback. Soon, your competitors will hear you've been cut off, so they'll begin to recruit your best salespeople and managers within hours. If the operation runs close to the vest, it's likely that there are checks outstanding, so there are going to be overdrafts and that may mean a missed payroll. More than one telemarketing entrepreneur has locked himself in his office and called the police for protection as his furious employees used axes and bats to knock down his double-locked doors because of a missed payroll.

Sterling Leaf

"Joe, I'd like to meet with you today, if possible. Where are you?" Lino's voice was deep and calm, no hint of problems or panic.

"I'm right downstairs," was Joe Pettinicchio's response. He had offices on the West Island and at Mount Real because, as president of Mount Real and iForum Securities, he was wearing two hats. The Mount Real job was pretty easy because the company was well established and successful, and the iForum job was a very good fit for his skill set . . . sales management and deals. With over 100 brokers and agents selling insurance, investments and securities throughout Quebec, the company was one of the country's fastest growing; it was also trading publicly and was solidly profitable.

"Come in," Lino said in response to the knock on the door. "Joe, we need to accelerate the Sterling Leaf deal and get it sold and closed." Sterling Leaf was Lino's creation, an income trust trading on the TSX Venture Exchange and sold by iForum brokers.

"What's the rush? Anything wrong?" Joe inquired.

"No, no, not at all. It's just that these things have a way of dragging if we don't keep them moving. Most important, income trusts are hot now and we need to play off of that momentum."

Lino knew that the processing problems were draining all the organization's cash reserves, that MRACS and RealVest weren't really growing anymore and that the best chance of bringing in cash was the Sterling Leaf offering. Cash that the sales operations would need to stay in business, because when processing problems begin, they usually don't go away soon. The meeting ended quickly. Joe had gotten the message; Lino had offered no hint of a current or pending crisis, just a subtle reminder that they needed to keep this offering going. It was a year ago that Sterling Leaf had been first issued and $10 million raised. That $10 million had fueled the sales engine for the previous year, but now the hunger pangs were reverberating because the sales engine was consuming more and more, and its own cash was suddenly gone.

With complete calm and distinct clarity, Lino would call Daryl Dagenais, who ran his human resources department on contract.

"Daryl, there will be no raises at all this year, none," he said with deadpan earnestness.

"We'll lose people, we'll lose good ones," she responded.

"You won't lose anyone; you can do this. You've got titles you can give out, you can shift desks and cubicles and even offices for some people. Give promotions and make 'em feel good. Daryl, you aren't going to lose anybody. They'd rather work for me than anybody else. They know they're going somewhere when they're here. Say, did you see that article about Maria Vavrikas in the *Gazette*? I told Madeline about the article and how she started out here with *Ocean Drive*, learned the business with us. These first breaks are important for people. You won't lose anybody, Daryl. The old ones are afraid to leave; the young ones are too ambitious to leave. You know, I'm really disappointed that Maria didn't call and thank me when they wrote that story about her. She really should have thanked me."

"Lino, you didn't even pay her the commissions she was owed when she left," Daryl interrupted.

"That's the way you are, Daryl, always focusing on money. You just don't get it! Now get going on the meetings and don't lose a goddamn person. I can't be losing a bunch of people right now." He hung up.

When Daryl sat down with Madeleine Kojakian, the cute spark plug who was lighting up the sales front for *Overture* magazine, it was Daryl's twelfth meeting and just as Lino had predicted, no one had quit, not one résumé was circulating. She knew Madeleine wouldn't be easy. When she was hired, Madeleine had gone through all the tests and interviews but for some reason she wasn't getting the offer from Lino. Finally Daryl pushed him into making an offer, as lowball as it was. Maddie was the daughter of a Dubai businessman, well educated, ambitious and not without financial means. When she got the offer, she countered with her "final offer."

"I'll work for three months for free to prove to you I can do the job. As a matter of fact, I can do the job better than anybody else you've ever had. When the three months are up and you realize I'm right, the salary must then be double what you've ever paid anyone."

Never to be one-upped and needing to always remain in control, Lino countered with, "We'll hire you *only* if you take the salary now." Madeleine had her job.

Her first day at work had been a Saturday. She had arrived first as she was supposed to and went up the stairs to her desk. She had been warned by the other assistants that on Saturdays Lino yelled, screamed and abused even more than on weekdays. As she ascended the stairs, she left a trail of snow and water on the stairway. When Lino arrived, he immediately took off his boots and marched up the stairs, his socks absorbing the water and snow as he walked.

"There's water on the damn stairs, Maddie. Find whoever didn't wipe their feet and throw them out. Tell them to never come back again!" As he yelled, Madeleine was ripping off her boots. He would yell for five more minutes as she scrupulously wiped down the stairway from bottom to top.

Daryl looked Madeleine in the eye and said, "Madeleine, we're making you sales manager and associate editor. Congratulations! I wanted to be the one to tell you myself."

"Wow," Madeleine responded excitedly, "that's terrific. My father is going to be proud, but my mother is going to ask how much of a raise I got. So what am I going to tell my mother?"

"Madeleine, sometimes you just can't keep both of your parents happy. You should know that by now."

"So, I'm getting a Johnny promotion, is that it, Daryl?"

"What do you mean?"

"Every six months for four years now, Johnny has gotten a promotion but never a raise, and now I've just been 'Johnnied' and I don't like it!" Madeleine left the room and the meeting was over.

Shortly after, Madeleine met with Lino. He was in one of his moods. He'd heard about the meeting with Daryl and knew that Madeleine thought she was being "Johnnied." She walked into his office with a confident swagger. He scowled and said, "The magazine was late, distribution is all late. I won't put up with this."

"Distribution is late because the printer didn't get paid," Madeleine offered.

"That's bullshit. The printer was paid; things are late because you haven't worked enough over the holidays. That's why things are late. Now you listen to me, Madeleine, I don't care about your holidays. Your family is not my priority," he blustered.

"My family is my priority; your damn magazine isn't. When I came to work here I was told my job was to make Lino P. Matteo's job easier and make him happy and I've worked my ass off trying to do that. I don't know why people are so afraid of you, but I'm not. You've got my two weeks' notice right now. I'm done!" She turned and left. As she descended the stairs, she and everyone in the building could hear Lino yell: "I'm glad you quit because you're not a good employee, anyway . . . I'm glad you quit!"

CHAPTER 41

DATE   OCTOBER 2004

SCENE   Montreal

Processing Failure

Bronco knew he needed a second job. He saw how much more money Jimmy had because of his other gig. He was waiting in the reception room hoping his interview would start soon because he didn't want to be late for his shift at Honeybee.

"Mr. Grabowski?" the friendly voice intoned.

"Yes?"

"Please follow me."

He had never been asked to do something as pleasurable. Her outfit was spandex and it clung as tightly to her well-exercised butt as anything he'd ever seen. She walked like she knew this 23-year-old "shooter" was right behind her. As she walked the long hallway, his eyes never left her ass and when she turned to knock on Hughes's door, he almost piled into her. Hughes was sitting behind his huge desk. His office walls were tastefully covered with original paintings. Bronco sat down in front of Frank Hughes.

"Are you from out west, Bronco?" Hughes asked with a slight French accent.

"Yeah, Alberta. I've been in Montreal about two years and I like it," was Grabowski's response.

"What do you pitch?"

"Mags," Bronco responded.

"Are you any good?"

"I write good business and good numbers. I can keep a story straight and I can talk American real good. I can work New Yawk," he said with a good New York accent. "I've always been close to the people of the great state of Texas," he drawled, "because Texas and Alberta are like cousins with oil, cattle and hot cities, so the whole South loves me. The Midwest is mine because they think like the farmers in Alberta, except they say huh instead of eh. Yeah, I talk American and I can sell. What's your program?"

"We make dreams come true. Don't get me wrong, you have to sell, but our program is better than office supplies, better than Derog, smarter than Identify Theft and a hell of a lot easier than magazines. Have you seen the pitch?"

"No, not yet."

"Well, it's . . . You've Already Won! You just tell 'em that they've already won ten thousand dollars in the North American You Just Can't Lose Sweepstakes, that their check is here, you have it in your hands. You spell the name out loud so they can confirm it's really theirs, then confirm the address and explain that to send it, you need the shipping costs and taxes; the taxes are seven and a half percent and two percent and the shipping cost is

$50. We accept bank transfers, cash, traveler's checks and money orders. They have five days to respond or the money goes back in the pot. To make it simple that's $750, plus $200, plus $50 or a total of $1,000 USD. You get $200 per sale and I'd say a shooter like you who knows New Yawk, is loved in the South and knows how to say huh instead of eh should do three deals a shift. Can you live on three thousand dollars a week?"

"Oui, but I'll keep my other job, too, 'cause I can grab paper out of there and keep the girls happy with the chump change the Pope pays me. When do I start?"

"Tomorrow morning, big shooter, 9:30 sharp."

Now Bronco had a second income, too. He'd continue to work Lino's magazine program as a steady income, but his big bucks would come from You've Already Won! And most importantly, when he was talking with the Honeybee customers he could figure out who the mooches and marks were and slide those names into his backpack. Eventually, he'd figure out how to pull lead lists off the Honeybee computers that he could sell to Mr. Hughes. He'd make more money from that than if he were stealing a couple of shifts a week, like Jimmy and Ricky.

The key to making money legally in telemarketing is to maintain processing. That means the ability to take a written order and convert it to cash through Visa or MasterCard. Over the years, the credit card clearance operations have made it tougher and tougher to process the MOTO (Mail Order Telephone Order) orders. These are sales generated over the phone, Internet or from catalogues where there is no signature; the rate the merchant pays on these transactions is very high. Six to fourteen percent is not uncommon, versus two to two and a half percent for most retail transactions. Beyond the high pro-

cessing costs come holdbacks and chargeback fees. The holdback might be twenty to twenty-five percent of gross sales and chargeback fees may run $30 to $50 per chargeback. But, most important of all, if the chargeback percentage runs too high (two to three percent of total sales), the processor will cut off processing completely, seize the funds owed and retain the holdback money for a year or more, creating huge cash flow and liquidity problems for the sales agent.

Lino was at the head of the boardroom table at Honeybee. His audience was Jeff Klein, Honeybee president, Eric Clement, head of sales and administration, and Peter Sobotkiewicz, computers and data processing. His deep voice mesmerized his audience. "The economics of telemarketing are basically these: product cost, sales cost, processing cost and overhead. It's really pretty simple . . . the magazines are cheap because the publishers need to build paid circulation to attract advertisers so they subsidize the business. Sales costs need to be less than twenty percent, including salaries, commissions and managers; processing needs to be ten percent or less *and* consistent; overhead should be fifteen percent or less. When you add it up it's sixty percent. So, that's forty percent for profit, less five for bad debt. That's how we'll make money."

Lino loved explaining his formulas to others. But everyone at the table knew their sales costs were closer to thirty percent than twenty percent. The overhead was twenty-five percent, the phone bill alone was fifteen percent and processing was unreliable and running at eight percent with a twenty percent holdback. No one knew what they were really paying for the magazines because Lino did that himself and kept it all very close to the vest. Even if no one had dared to say it out loud, it was known that sales, overhead and processing were chewing up eighty-three percent of gross sales and that was before cancellations and bad debt. Because Lino wouldn't and couldn't be running a failing operation, everyone nodded and approvingly agreed with his formula. Somehow he had managed to keep it financed and, after all, the holdback monies were going to flow back to them "someday."

The financing, which no one seemed to really understand, was built around the sale of installment contracts. When a sale was generated it usually involved a cash payment and a series of six to ten installment payments. Because the sales operations required current cash to operate and generate sales, the orders would be sold at a discount to a third party with cash. The purchasers were largely MRACS, RealVest and now Sterling Leaf, three of Lino's big financing arms that sold commercial paper to the public at high interest rates, originally with a Mount Real guarantee. Eventually, the guarantee would go away as the years went by and many of the purchasers and their brokers became comfortable with the new owners of the debt — MRACS and RealVest — and the payment streams they enjoyed. By 2004 the two entities owed over $130 million to various, mostly small, investors.

The entities sold debt, received cash, advanced the cash to the sales offices that used it for operations, covered their costs and paid Mount Real a management fee. This gave them access to cash and they sold the ownership of the consumer installment contract to the lenders, being MRACS and RealVest.

Unlike most transactions of this kind, where receivables, mortgages or installment sales contracts are bundled then sold, title transfers and the new owner collects them out. These transactions were never "tied up"; the actual

contract was never legally assigned or transferred. Instead, they remained as a pool, were collected or not collected as a pool and true ownership was never specific. "After all, it didn't really matter as long as the whole organization is still together," was Lino's casual assessment.

The practical effect of all this was that none of the lending entities had either collateral for their loans or assets for their purchases. They had advanced the cash to operating entities and received nothing in return. The success of the operating entities was then the best and only means of recovery for the financing companies. The operating company that was most important of them all in that process was Honeybee, the sales room on the West Island where Ricky, Jimmy and Bronco worked as Big Hitters when they weren't selling Derog or You've Just Won!

When the processing failure of November 2004 hit Honeybee and the Mount Real network, Lino didn't lock himself in his office or drive off a bridge. He was calm, like few can be in a meltdown. He internalized the problem and told virtually no one. All information was on a "need to know" basis, so all the parties essentially knew nothing. Few people could operate that way, but he did it and did it well. He quietly cut costs, used his liquidity wisely, kept the entire mess a secret and even managed to have a profitable year, according to the annual statements. For the first time in his high-risk career, however, he felt vulnerable and knew how it felt to have weak knees and sleepless nights.

CHAPTER 42

DATE DECEMBER 2004

No Appetite

The Daviault depositions had been delayed again, much to CCE attorney Neil Stein's consternation. They were finally scheduled for December 8, 9 and 10, 2004, in Montreal.

I was meeting with Daviault regularly and he felt that Neil Stein, who would interview Daviault, had made it clear that all his client wanted was a settlement: "To get the money they were entitled to." When I heard the comment, without instructions from Lino or anyone else, I told Bob to relay to Stein that "the parties involved were ready to lay a settlement offer on the table and to ask to whom they should tender the offer."

The next day, Daviault did just that and Stein

responded that he actually didn't know who to make such a proposal to. Over the next two days Daviault would ask Stein for the answer about who the proposal should go to. Finally, Stein said, "I don't think there is any appetite for a settlement at this point."

The CCE attorneys, accountants and consultants were billing so many hours and doing so well on this file, there was no interest in discussing a settlement. As long as the file was paying, the professionals preferred to do their work rather than have it come to a screeching halt because of a settlement.

A Way Out

"Mrs. Lepin, this program is my recommendation for your RRSP money and your rollover from the Wood Gundy account. It will deliver a good rate of return on a monthly basis, and it can be liquidated easily because it's actually publicly traded on the TSX Venture Exchange. The units are ten dollars each and I'm recommending you put about fifty thousand in total into the income trust. What's the question? The return? Oh, the return is about eight and a half percent annually paid out monthly at seven cents per unit. So, you get about three hundred and fifty dollars per month paid to you, which will cover over half of your house payment. How do you feel about my recommendation, Mrs. Lepin? You like it? Great, I'll get the paperwork going and drop by to see you next week. Thank you. Bye-bye."

In the two minutes he'd spent on the phone with Mrs. Lepin, Grant Wood, an iForum broker, had made $3,000 in commission. The deal paid 60 cents per unit and she'd just bought 5,000 units. The story was good, the return strong, the liquidity seemed excellent and Grant had given Mrs. Lepin good advice in the past.

"Frankie, this Sterling Leaf is hot; people want it. I'm just dialing away and rolling people in. Have you tried to pitch it yet?" Grant was yelling over his cubicle wall to Frankie Manko on the other side.

"No, but I'm listening to you and it sounds smooth. I think I'll start pitching it this afternoon. How much have you placed?" Frankie shouted back.

"I'm over two hundred grand and I just started. That's twelve big ones in my pocket and I really needed a pile driver like this."

"No shit! Twelve big ones already? I might start pitching right now!" was Frankie's response.

Sterling Leaf Income Trust first hit the market in early November 2003. It was designed to raise $10 million and raise it fast. Now they were in a second phase and ready to raise another $10 million. Wood was on the front side of this effort. The InvestPro Securities guys were in it and so was the iForum sales force. People realized quickly that it was an easy sale and momentum grew fast. The underlying strength of the deal was the installment sales contracts or consumer magazine orders being generated on the West Island. At no time did the Sterling Leaf pitch explain that the telemarketing orders were being written by people like Jimmy del Greco, Bronco Grabowski or Ricky Dellacolla, some of the Island's hottest shooters.

Montreal and telemarketing had enjoyed a tempestuous love affair for decades. Since the Quiet Revolution when unilingual Anglophones were effectively squeezed out of mainstream employment like government, construction, large companies and retail, it meant that this portion of the labor force needed to leave town (over 400,000 did) or go to the gray market for their daily bread. As a result, telemarketing thrived. For a time, Montrealers dialed into the United States and throughout the rest of Canada, selling ad specialties, business products, flogging credit card applications, magazines and scams.

With cheap available labor, cheap office space (by 1990 the city was 40 percent vacant), reasonable phone rates and a sagging Canadian dollar at 67 cents to the U.S. dollar, the environment was perfect for the ambitious undercapitalized entrepreneur to open an office and begin to dial.

The Canadian government had grown weary of the practice by the mid-nineties and the RCMP fielded a special force called "phone busters" to close down, chase down and break any operations dialing into Canada. But the border created an entirely different problem for the phone busters in that the issue wasn't even on the radar screen for U.S. law enforcement. The practical effect was that the Montreal phone businesses moved all their focus to U.S. sales where there was no "heat," more people and a stronger dollar.

While many of the rooms sold decent products with decent delivery in a fair and ethical way, even the most honest were always tempted to set up a team of "shooters" who would dial for cash on a small scale to supplement the bottom line. They would be physically separated from the main sales group. They were paid differently, super-

vised differently and they held a mysterious status within the sales culture of the room. Often they would dial on unmarked cell phones rather than the main company phone system so caller I.D. systems couldn't track them down. The shooters would scam for cash, oftentimes changing pitches and their own names so they could circle back to the "real suckers" every six weeks and pitch them another ridiculous story.

The hardest part about being a businessperson in telemarketing is that one always knows how hard you have to work to make an honest buck and how easy it is to make a buck when you're dirty. Lino and the boys on the West Island never wanted to be dirty, they never wanted to scam, they didn't want "shooters" with mysterious packages of cash . . . they wanted a real business. The rest of the telemarketing world builds their business and sets their pay scales on a blend of business, some straight, some dirty. They want the straight business because it creates a front and a training ground for future shooters. The practical effect is that the shooters often subsidize the straight operation in whole or part. The reality for the room that's completely straight is that they are at a major competitive disadvantage because they must pay higher labor rates to attract good people; they don't have the cream to help offset it so their best people inevitably ride off into the sunset attracted by dirty money and opportunity.

There are two age-old questions in business. Will a good business make a bad businessman look good? Can a good businessman be beaten by a bad business? No matter how much the team at Honeybee struggled and attempted to make a bad business go good, the bad business just kept overwhelming them. Processing problems, soft orders, cancellations, sales force turnover, rising labor rates, the strengthening Canadian dollar, dishonest employees and the increasing "do not call" movement in the U.S. all added up to overwhelming problems.

The only thing that was working was Lino's calm demeanor during a crisis and his accounting magic, which somehow always kept the cash coming and the numbers looking good, despite the fact the problems never seemed to get solved.

Sterling Leaf's success would buy even more time for the sales operations to get their act in order. Between the brokers and sales agents, the clients like Mrs. Lepin and the ingenious structure, the cash would continue to roll in the back door, even if it couldn't roll in the front. Honeybee seemed to be doing "just fine" to anyone who looked.

CHAPTER 44

DATE MID-DECEMBER 2004

SCENE Montreal

Reloads

Frank Hughes walked into the building with a peculiar smile on his face. He passed by his knockout assistant carrying a mid-sized box and went directly to his office.

"Bronco, can you come in here right away?" he asked over his intercom.

"On my way," came the response.

"What's up, boss?"

"Well, my man, I've got us some rocket fuel and I thought you just might like to know about it," was Hughes's reply.

"Rocket fuel?"

"Here are six cell phones, completely untraceable. Here's a brand new lock box address and I've got two hundred reload leads that are solid gold. Forty of them are yours. You're sittin' on the edge of the big time, Bronco. You should be buying me lunch, taking me to Wanda's and generally kissin' my ass 'cause I'm about to make you big bucks. We're talkin' *reloads!*"

"*Reloads!* You're piling forty in my direction? Man, boss, that's great. You won't regret it. With paper like that I can make you proud. What are we pitching?"

"These are real mooches, like they've already been down most paths, so we're going brand new on this one . . . Identity Theft. Only with these phones we're doing it different." The way Bronco ran the scam was this: "Ma'am, you've got a problem. I'm calling from the police department of Los Angeles and we've learned that your identity has been stolen and that over twelve thousand dollars of charges have already been racked up. I know your statements don't reflect that yet, but that's only because it's just happened. Now, I've been in contact with Visa and MasterCard and they're willing to settle everything in total, reissue your card and zero your balance with no effect on your credit, if you remit now, directly to our Crimes Unit Settlement office, $2,500. It can be cash, money order or traveler's checks, it's up to you. Now, I'm Lieutenant Wilson and the only way you can reach me is this number. Do you have a pencil? Call me within one hour about what you want to do. What I would suggest is that you check your current balance and see what you already owe. There have been some people I've talked to that owe more than the $2,500 settlement amount, so they're actually pretty happy about their identity being stolen, if you know what I mean. Do you know what you owe right now? My phone number is 1-888-438-4338, that's 888-IDTHEFT. If you just want to

settle now, zero all your credit card balance, get new cards and new accounts, then all you do is overnight $2,500 and all of your current credit cards to Crimes Unit Settlement office, 1445 Hollywood Boulevard, Los Angeles, California 23152, Attention Lieutenant Wilson." The person on the other end would carefully write the address and thank the "lieutenant" for the call and the help. "I only wish my local police department was as buttoned-up as you guys in L.A."

The reload was as sharp a pitch as Bronco had ever worked. The leads were real suckers, just the way he liked them. Being a cop was real fun and after a day of getting the marbles out of his mouth, he even bought a policeman's cap and a badge so he'd have a number, in case anyone ever asked for one. No one ever did. One elderly lady told him on his third day, "I know exactly when it happened. I was at the casino and I left my purse at the slot machine when I ran to the bathroom. I've worried about it ever since, but that machine was so hot, I couldn't leave it and half an hour later, I won four thousand dollars." Her settlement cost with Visa and MasterCard was $3,500, according to Bronco.

The scam was perfect because it worked both front side and back side. The cash and money orders arrived in L.A. where Hughes's partner took care of all the banking and forwarded all the front side cash to Hughes. Then he took all the credit cards and identity information and proceeded to run the cards to the maximum and really steal the identity. He paid twenty percent to Bronco's boss on the back side, which amounted to over $200,000. Once he had the sample signature, the social security number, the mother's maiden name and all their credit cards, he would file new applications for additional accounts, take out loans, negotiate limit increases and even buy appliances and automobiles for the unsuspecting mooch who sent their cash, credit cards and information to Lieutenant Wilson.

Bronco got $1,250 per sale and within a month he had made over $40,000. At the end of his leads, he would take his phone and ceremoniously walk out on the Champlain Bridge where he would thank his phone and throw it in the St. Lawrence River. It was now even more untraceable. He had never had so much money; he bought a new car, some new clothes, some jewelry, some cocaine, 73 lap dances and he fully stocked his bar. Now that Bronco was a real shooter and a reloader, he would never again pitch magazines or anything else completely straight. It wasn't as much fun as being dirty. There was no high that came with a straight pitch . . . there was no edge, no mark, no mooch, no sucker.

Daviault

When it came time for Daviault's deposition, I would go to Daviault's hotel every night as they took place. We would smoke cigars and unwind with a drink. It seemed so unusual to see Bob without a cigarette, something I had never seen before. A lot of things in Daviault's life had changed. He hadn't worked since Norshield International in 2001, three years earlier, and he had gotten involved in his church and moved to Calgary to start over. He was involved in his children's lives and had quit smoking. When he left Norshield, he had struck a $900,000 severance deal with John X and had been paid two-thirds of it. His wife was working, but Bob hadn't found the "right opportunity."

I would debrief Bob each night about what direction the depositions with the CCE lawyers were going, what questions were being asked and how Bob was answering them. Bob had previously testified under oath that he was the CFO and voice of Globe-X and Norshield International, that John Xanthoudakis was not his boss, but a provider of services. He was clearly the captain of his ship and the decision maker in those depositions. Now, as I listened, I realized that Bob was heading in a different direction with these depositions.

"They know about Killington," Daviault would offer. "They know about FOREX; they seem to know about everything!" He was showing anxiety.

"Bob, they've had over four years to look at all the books and records. Why would you be so surprised that they know these things?"

"I didn't think they could get that information from the records they had," he responded.

"What's wrong with Killington anyway?" I asked.

"Killington were the accounts prepared for Weinberg, Charest and Panju that would have let them get pieces of the various other deals that flowed through Globe-X and CIS. It was kind of a 'juice catcher' if you know what I mean."

"Why did you set them up?"

"Because it's what they wanted. In fact they never really got going because of all the problems of March 2000, so Killington never really amounted to much, but it could have and these guys know about it."

When these debriefings were over, I would have to report the general outcomes to Lino and John separately. Lino would insist on his briefing being first and he didn't want to do it together because "John will ask too many

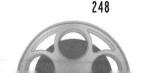

stupid questions." With more frequency, there were beginning to be breaks between Lino and John on both a strategic and tactical level. John's business continued to thrive, but only as long as the Cinar fire was contained. At the same time, Lino's operations were secretly dealing with liquidity problems due to credit card processing breakdowns.

"There is no doubt that Bob is afraid; he's very impressed with what these guys have found out and he's intimidated," was how I began the debriefing. Lino's low voice was on the other end of the line. He was now taking calls at his home with more and more frequency and talking later into the evening.

"Has he turned? Has he made a deal?"

"I don't know if he's made a deal, but he's definitely turned. Eventually he's going to tell them that John or John and you were responsible for everything . . . Globe-X, the cis loan, the back-to-backs, Killington, restructuring the assets, the books not being up to date . . . everything."

"I knew that son of a bitch would turn. Do you remember when he swore to the qsc that this was his business, that he and Tom made the decisions?"

"Yeah, I remember, but that was three years ago, and now he doesn't want or need any trouble in his life."

John's briefing would take three times as long every night because John always had a lot of questions. What was certain was that by December 10, 2004, Bob Daviault was telling the cce attorneys exactly what they wanted to hear and that was quite simply that John Xanthoudakis of Norshield Financial Group in Montreal and Lino Matteo of Mount Real Corporation were the brains, architects and engineers behind the Cinar–Globe-X deal and the other complexities, obfuscations and roadblocks that they were dealing with. This meant that John and Norshield were now fair game for the CCE pile driver and destruction crew.

The headlines would begin to break shortly after Christmas 2004. It was a rough way to bring in a new year. The Daviault transcript would be leaked to the press before it was even filed in court. The nation's press would have a field day as they now would begin to tie John and Norshield into the earliest days of the Cinar–Globe-X story. In the transcript Daviault would claim John X was the "architect" of the enhanced bond strategy and that Lino was involved in recasting the balance sheet of the Mosaic entities. The Cinar crisis had now landed squarely on the doorstep of Norshield and was lurching closer to Mount Real. In over 900 pages of deposition, most of what Daviault had said was technical background and essentially unimportant. Voorheis would deny it, but appearances are that the CCE public relations team would take the transcripts, break them down and deliver high-lights to the key reporters on the story who would willingly rise to the bait, like hungry fish on a hot summer day. Some of these reporters (like Bert Marotte of the *Globe and Mail*) had been around for a long time and had never seen such spoonfeeding, so their intuition told them to be careful, but other reporters lurched at the easy bait and wrote their stories with blind confidence.

It was in the aftermath of the Daviault leaks that John would make his biggest tactical error. With his home life now in a shambles from the pressure, he had moved away from his family. He was increasingly turning up late for meetings and seemed preoccupied; for the first time in his life things were not getting better, they were getting worse. John and his attorneys had concluded they should

proceed immediately with a court action to block the printing of or references to the Daviault deposition by the press. But that would be tough to accomplish. There are few things the press hold more dear than their freedom to print what they choose. Any attempt to block their right to disseminate information would be a declaration of war.

I was in Texas on a hunting trip when my cell phone rang unexpectedly. It was John, Dale Smith, his attorney and a PR adviser. They proceeded to explain what they were about to do in court, to block any further usage of the Daviault deposition. I was stunned. "Guys, don't do this. It's a big mistake. The only thing you can say that would make me feel worse right now is that they now have photos of you naked in a swimming pool with a bunch of fourteen-year-old girls. This is the stupidest action I've heard of; it will only make the story bigger, for a longer period of time. You're declaring war on the press and now they'll declare war on you. Don't do this!" The signal was weak and the call cut off.

I'd wasted my breath. The action would be filed in the court that afternoon, and after that, the press would turn on John and Norshield with a vengeance. They would not violate the court order by using the Daviault deposition. Instead they would do profiles on John and the company that would bring out any negative twist, turn or angle of the previous 25 years. Even Saint John of Xanthoudakis couldn't look good every moment for 25 years. The "Teflon Hedger" had now experienced the wrath of the press, and it would not stop.

One Photo
Too Many

At the 2005 annual meeting of Mount Real, everyone was hopeful that the proceedings would harken back to "the tranquil old days" of tightly scripted presentations and planted questions from the floor. No one was interested in repeating the volatile session of the previous year. There were already rumors of Norshield's weakening position and there had been several newspaper stories that were very unflattering to Mount Real. The CCE's efforts to feed negative information to a receptive press had begun to reap benefits and while Mount Real was still tangential and not square in the crosshairs of Voorheis' group, they were clearly on the radar screen.

Waiting for the meeting to begin was Francis Vailles, a

reporter from *La Presse*, Montreal's leading French newspaper, and along with him was a photographer. Vailles had covered the Cinar, Norshield and now Mount Real stories for years, and he had written several very negative stories over the previous six months. Since he didn't own shares himself, he would typically solicit the help of shareholders and feed them questions to ask during the Q&A session following the presentations. He had instructed his photographer to get pictures of all the officers and directors; "lots of them" he would counsel.

As the meeting was called to order by Joe Pettinicchio, the highly scripted portion of the meeting would begin. When it was completed, Joe would begin his less formal presentation. At this point, the photographer swung into action and began moving throughout the room, taking photo after photo of the attendees. A variety of shots were taken with flash, only a few feet in front of Joe's face as he was presenting. Suddenly, Lino could take no more.

"That's enough!" he said loudly. "That's enough!" The photographer continued to snap away. "Do you hear me? I said no more photos. That's enough!" The room was becoming very uncomfortable for many of the attendees. The photographer seemed to ignore or not understand what Lino was saying, but there was no question Lino was going to make his point.

As Joe continued his presentation, Lino rose and began to walk toward the photographer. As he strode, he seemed to puff up and become even larger than his 6'2", 250-pound body. Suddenly, the photographer realized he was being approached by the CEO of the company, who was rapidly and ominously getting closer and closer. He quickly began to retreat, and within seconds, he was forced out of the room. There were some in the room that thought the photojournalist got what he deserved, but most now realized that they had just seen the CEO of a public company chase a newspaperman out of an annual meeting with the unspoken threat of physical violence. Joe resumed his speech and Lino went back to his seat, feeling quite proud of himself.

When the questions began to flow, it became obvious quickly that the 2005 annual meeting was not going to be a return to the "old days," or even revisit the constructive comments of Levesque from the previous year. Now the tone had become hostile, and Francis Vailles' planted questions were cutting.

"Is it true that Mount Real is consuming more cash than it creates?" "Why is Mount Real's balance sheet so difficult to understand?" "Are all of the companies' contingent liabilities clearly spelled out in the annual report?" "Is it true the company has had seven consecutive years of negative cash?" "How collectible are interest and investment accounts on the balance sheet?" "Why are all the profits of the company from interest and investments, not operations?"

As the questions rolled, Joe did his best to field them and Lino continued to fume. Finally, he would order Joe to stop answering questions and he would begin to stare down Francis Vailles, who had fueled the brushfire.

The newspapers the next day would run a front page business section lead that proclaimed that "Mount Real's Management Won't Answer Questions" and ran photos that made Lino look menacing and bully-like. The word would travel quickly among the CCE gang that Lino, despite his tough demeanor, had thin skin and could be provoked into a fight quite easily. For the lawyers and accountants who composed the CCE, this was welcome

news because they were beginning to realize that Lino was as much their opponent as John Xanthoudakis was. There would never again be a "good old days," smoothly run, scripted Mount Real annual meeting. Those days were done.

An Objective Eye

I was very afraid that Norshield had spun out of control and that decisions were not being made. Over the years there were two brothers I had grown to respect who I felt might be helpful. I called David Brown because I sensed that if Norshield was to survive it would take a tough and experienced pair to deal with creditors, regulators and investors. David and his brother Michael were just that: two sixty-plus New York–born Ivy Leaguers, with degrees and résumés that would impress the unimpressable. They both had experience as athletes (both all-American), in academia (one attorney, one Harvard MBA and CPA), and in business (both CEOs of major businesses). What I found most appealing was that they both had experience in crisis management and weren't afraid of conflict.

We had served together, the three of us, in the pre-crisis period of General Development Corporation in Florida in the late eighties. GDC would become the largest case of bankruptcy in the country in 1989 and the multi-billion-dollar failure would be a bell cow that would attract national media attention, including that of *60 Minutes*. While both Browns would be out with the fall of the company, I would stay on for another two and a half years.

They came without a fee and while their expenses were covered by John, they were acting on more of a favor to me than anything. For four decades these two brothers with their powerful arms, thick necks and cauliflower ears would catch attention as they entered rooms, offices or elevators. Mike's Marine Corps years still showed on his face and David's charm was incredible, despite his some-what intimidating stature. For 24 hours they would study, meet, interview and assess whether, now in early May of 2005, the Norshield situation was too far gone to make a meaningful recovery. Matteo told them that if the Cinar pressure could lessen, the business could survive. He said that there were assets, but a new management team would have to firmly freeze redemptions and regain the confi-dence of investors and institutions. John X told them that things were busy and challenging, but "just fine," deliber-ately understating the scope and severity of the problems. I told them that "if new leadership doesn't take over soon, there will be nothing to take over; current management is overwhelmed and already in the bunker. They can't even establish the situation, much less develop objectives, strategies or a tactical plan to move them forward. Much of the talent has voted with their feet and walked out. The rest are basically mooching paychecks, while they're floating their cvs all over town."

After 24 hours, the Browns spoke to me. David explained that "It is too far gone and the assets too hard to monetize and stabilize. Current management isn't ready to realize where they are and they're more of a liability than an asset." Mike weighed in, too, in his military vernacular. "This is a cluster fuck! Without a gung ho, fight-loving sonofabitch to slap the pissants and get the rest out of their foxholes, it's dead. You should watch this shitcan; I think something of value will eventually float to the top. Maybe we can talk then."

While to some this summary might be ambiguous, as a former Marine, I understood exactly what Michael was saying. Watch the file; there will be opportunity. So, I would watch the file.

CHAPTER 48
DATE MAY 2005
SCENE Montreal

Ripple Effect

Of course, what the press didn't report from the Daviault depositions was what the effect of the stories would be on the Norshield and Mount Real investors. Only the most careful study of the deposition would, in significant detail, illuminate how Lino would never acknowledge bad news, record assets or admit to failed investments. The same information was directly linked to Norshield. The deposition coverage never revealed how the valuations of assets were done under Lino's instruction using a discounted cash flow model. The valuations were written by a well-meaning junior analyst who had never done this type of work before. The cash flow information almost never came directly from the company being valued, and if the information was wrong, the entire valuation would be valueless. At no time did this analyst ever visit any of the companies being valued or talk with any of their officers. Yet, these were the valuations that would be used on the balance sheets and would, surprisingly, pass muster with the audit firms, which included Grant Thornton, Deloitte Touche, RSM Richter and others, depending on the company and the year.

The newspapers ran with the highlighted morsels fed to them by the CCE, whose agenda apparently had become: If we can't collect, we'll destroy. Within days of the court ruling that the newspapers could print the December Daviault deposition, Norshield was weakened. The story line would shout that John Xanthoudakis and Norshield had helped Weinberg, Charest and Panju send over $8 million to the Bahamas through fictitious transactions, money taken from Cinar. The stories talked about how the Globe-X liquidators, who were paid in full by Cinar and the CCE, had serious concerns about the way Cinar funds were allocated, and how they felt they'd received very little cooperation from the administrators of Globe-X. Previously, the stories had dealt with how John X and Lino Matteo had worked to create false documents and to justify the Globe-X investments or clean up the Globe-X financial statements.

In the QSC deposition, Bob Daviault actually admitted that he had helped Panju with the foreign exchange transactions, that it was he himself who had signed postdated documents with Panju. One of the curiosities of Daviault's deposition for the CCE. was that he now would claim that he wasn't the one making the decisions or setting direction. In his deposition of July 2001, he had emphatically stated to the QSC under oath that he was in

charge and that John had nothing to do with his operation. At that time, even with immunity from the QSC, he had sworn that he hadn't helped Weinberg, Charest or Panju in any untoward transactions and that he hadn't made any secret pacts with Panju. Now in December of 2004 with no offer of immunity, he was testifying to the CCE and clearly showing himself to have been a liar with the QSC. What was Daviault's motivation for this extreme about-face?

The effects would be felt within days once the court order was lifted and the press could print what they wished.

The Wheels
Were Loose

John had grown distant from his wife, Kathy, and their separation became increasingly acrimonious. His oldest son was starting to have trouble in school and was hanging with guys who were making things worse. The younger boys were faring better, but the stress was hard on everyone. Kathy was still spending at the rate she had become accustomed to and didn't really perceive what John was starting to feel . . . that things were sliding out of control. Redemption requests from investors were rolling in and there were no new funds arriving. John's CFO laid it out for him.

"We're in full blast net redemption mode, John," Dale Smith explained. "We've paid out about $135 million and now the liquidity is getting tighter and tighter."

"How many more redemptions are there?" John asked.

"Five hundred dollars would be more than we can pay, but the answer is more like $100 million and growing. Worse yet, I don't see how we'll get an audit done."

"Dale, Dale, you've gone too far now. The structure will allow for the audit to get done. There are still good assets in Mosaic that underlie the funds. Remember the Univest assets are the Mosaic preferred shares. They're still in place. We can get through this, plus I've got over $60 million of good business in the pipeline that will flow in. We're just in a trough right now. We'll be fine."

"John, you'd better be a fuckin' miracle man because without some big hits, we're goners. These redemptions aren't going away and we're out of tricks."

Over the previous months Norshield had pulled some of the most sophisticated stunts ever concocted to create liquidity and try to stabilize themselves. They developed a structure for a deal with Merrill Lynch to create $30 million of liquidity by selling off an option on part of the Mosaic Hedge Fund portfolio. The deal, called Multi-Strat II, was as innovative as any financing ever contemplated, and true to form, John and his team pulled it off. To do it, they needed to tell some of their institutional clients about it and get the approval of RBC to proceed with the deal. The Teflon Hedger still had the confidence and charm to make it happen. Multi-Strat II would buy more time. Quick ideas and clever strategies were his strength and he kept coming up with them. From January to May the pressures had been unrelenting. Ever since the Daviault deposition and the war with the press had begun, the no-stick surface of John X was getting scratched and steel-wooled. The reporters were fueled by their own anger at his actions in court to block their access to information, and the information flowed into their notebooks from the CCE researchers.

The stories would vary, but in only months the

entrepreneurial philanthropist who had built from scratch the nation's largest hedge fund and helped thousands in the process had become the subject of ridicule and allegations. Various stories would expose a filing infraction from 20 years previous; another would posit him to be a control freak who was also fond of séances and tarot cards. Piece by piece the striptease would tear away his polish, his attire, his reputation, business acumen, integrity and hard-won lore. Another newspaper would caricature him as a joker, another as a clown. Old enemies would be found who would gladly offer quotes and sound bites that would further remove the veneer. Throughout the assault various investors and institutions began to shift their assets from Norshield-related products to other things and these redemptions were creating a literal run on the bank.

John was always good with a sales force and he needed them now more than ever to turn the tide of "hot redemptions." In the spring of 2005 with his home life in ruins, the guy who could charm a full room was fast becoming more and more reclusive. He would spend long hours with Lino, several days each week, rather than time in his own office or with the salespeople who might lead him back to liquidity.

"John, you've completely screwed the pooch on this scrap with the press," Lino said. "They're just kicking your ass, exactly like I told you they would. You are the guy who is trying to take away their most valued prize — freedom of the press — and they hate you for it."

"I'm just trying to protect my business. You know that Daviault is full of shit. The court has ruled on my side. I'm right in court, but do they print that? No, they tell the world about some ridiculous thing I did in 1986! I was barely out of school! They don't tell people about the millions I've donated to help kids, schools, hospitals, and my volunteerism. They

try to make me look like I was helping Weinberg steal money from his company! They are even trying to get the police — whose programs I've funded — and the schools that have gotten computers from us, to say bad things about me, but most of them are too smart. I'm so tired of the press blasting me and never offering my side of the story . . ."

Lino interrupted. "John, how could they? You never talk to them, never respond to their calls, never issue statements. All you do is fight them in court and, worse yet, you win! That really pisses them off. No, you deserve to get creamed, slammed, tarred and feathered! You don't follow good advice and you get suckered by these high-billing bullshit artists. You've got too many lawyers and consultants. I want you to fire these idiots now!"

The back-and-forth part of the conversation was over, and Lino's directives were now flying. "That PR flyboy is a joke. Get rid of him. This aura analyst is a charlatan. Can him. You can't afford Torralbo anymore. You need a new attorney and not one so damn expensive."

John sat dumbstruck. Lino was slashing away at the people and advisers he relied on and had no desire to dismiss or fire. John had become indecisive, and having all the various advisers allowed him to sort information and constantly get new perspectives on what were becoming unsolvable problems. All of the advisers were glad to sit with John for hours on end. They were paid by the hour and at this point he was still paying his bills. His lawyers, consultants and analysts were running over $60,000 per month, and most of John's time was spent with them rather than running the business. During these crucial months of crisis, he mistook activity for accomplishment. Lino, as he was inclined to do, had cut through the crap and told John how things needed to be. But John was slow to act, still indecisive, and he felt unable to fire or dismiss anyone.

Several days later Lino's temper was stoked and the confrontation was inevitable. "John, when are you gonna get here?" he asked over the phone.

"Soon, I'm on the way."

"Bullshit. You haven't left your office yet. Now, don't lie to me. When are you going to get here?"

"A half hour."

After that, Lino called me in. It was Lino's way. He would virtually never go to see John or anyone else. He would always make us come to him. "Bill, I want you in this meeting with John and me. Can you get in here right away?"

Like John, I was downtown, but Lino demanded that we both leave our downtown offices to go to him to meet on his turf. Amazingly, we both would comply.

"John, I've told Bill to be here for this meeting because that makes it less likely that I'll lose my temper and pound the shit out of you than if we're alone. More than that, I think he can do some of the nasty jobs you don't seem to want to do."

John sat silently.

"Now, about these advisers of yours. You just don't need them anymore, John. I'm not going to argue with you so don't argue with me. Bill, I need you to fire 'Chopper Boy' for John, because he can't do it himself. How much do you pay him, John?"

"Twelve grand a month," was the response. (Chopper Boy was a PR man in Montreal who had worked for twenty years as a helicopter traffic reporter for CJAD radio.)

"Then I need you to fire the soothsayer . . . who does *what*, John?"

"Reads the atmosphere, analyzes the aura," John responded.

"Okay, so the fortune teller is out the window. How much does he cost?"

"Ten thousand dollars," was the answer.

John was getting aggravated and relieved at the same time. "Now I'm cooling down the divorce lawyer myself, and I'll meet with Kathy. How much is that going to save?"

"Fifteen thousand a month."

"As for Torralbo, he's done a hell of a job and serving as your attorney during these screwed-up times might get him sainthood, but as you continue to get bashed, you're more of a liability than an asset to him and soon you won't be paying your bills. So, I'm doing him a favor when I fire him. How much will that save?"

"Twenty to thirty," John responded.

"So, we're gonna save you fifty to seventy thousand per month and make your life less fucked up. How does that sound?"

"When are you going to do it?" John asked.

Lino turned to me. "Bill, when are you going to do it?"

"Today, tomorrow," was the answer.

"Today, tomorrow," Lino repeated. "Now you go find one new lawyer who's affordable, no more of this five hundred dollars an hour bullshit. Find one that is reasonable. From now on pay attention to your staff and don't take advice from anyone but me." The meeting was over.

By the second week in May, it seemed as if there would never be any good news again. For over six months John had been spinning instead of leading and the crisis hadn't gone away. But finally John's focus came back and he developed some new ideas.

"Here's what I'm thinking," said John X. "If we formally freeze redemptions and keep the structures in place, if the hedge fund basket holds together, then the funds will survive. They're gated; they'll be reduced in overhead dramatically. There will be over three hundred and sixty million dollars at work for the investors; with even fifteen percent returns over the next five years, that's over two hundred and fifty million, plus the current equity of fifty-five million. The funds will be okay. Not great maybe, but okay. The International funds are okay as is, and the hedged assets are producing good returns. It might take five years to work our way out, but if our performance is good we can make it and pay off the redemptions over time."

The audience included Lino, Dale Smith and me. The plan was simple, draconian and had a chance. The key component was that RBC, the lender on the hedge fund basket, stay in place. Without that there would be trouble.

The conference call was set for a morning in May. John, Dale, myself and a compliance officer working for Norshield Financial Group would be in the conference room. The call would be short, but questions ran another half hour. The message was simple: the Olympus Univest fund was freezing redemptions, as were other Norshield funds, in an attempt to save themselves and the investors from a total meltdown and liquidation. At the time of the meeting John truly believed in his plan and thought he could execute an organized structured liquidation that would lead investors, bankers and the business to eventual health.

The business press would welcome the news of a freeze of redemptions, and the stories would break everywhere. But there was no mention of a structured liquidation or an orderly future. The structure John had envisioned was lost in the chaos of each day. Ever since January the press had viewed John X as their nemesis and the "evil hedger" who dared to trample on the freedom of the press. Now they were very glad to see that they had played a part in his destruction and were glad to portray his demise as a fait accompli.

In Toronto, Voorheis would get the news by phone.

"Norshield has frozen redemption on their funds," the voice said.

In slightly more than a year, the CCE had determined that they weren't going to get any money from Norshield so they might as well knock it down. There was no consideration of the people affected. Within weeks, over $350 million of investments would cease to exist. Retirement funds would be wiped out, savings plans kaput; institutions pressed their noses against the window as they lost fortunes. Industrial Alliance alone would lose $82 million, Bank of Montreal $30 million, Banco Atlantico $25 million, Chagnon Foundation $20 million. As well, the cities of Laval, Sherbrooke and Jolicoeur would lose $18, $12 and $15 million respectively, to name just a few. There would be vacations cancelled, retirements delayed, purchases stopped in mid-stream, down payments lost, people forced back to work. Some would even need to sell their homes. The investors in the International funds would fare better, but the $1 billion of assets under management were now reduced to rubble.

Within a few weeks, RSM Richter would be named receiver for the Norshield entities and would control whatever remained. The furniture in John's office had been purchased for over $100,000; the paintings that had adorned the boardroom had cost the same. In the liquidation, Richter would get less than $100,000 for every asset including computers, flat screens, chairs, desks, Persian rugs, file cabinets, sofas or pieces of artwork in over 46 offices throughout the corporate headquarters. At public auction people would walk away full of smug satisfaction with their purchases.

As the weeks went by the whispers coming out of Richter were that they were finding very little in terms of assets from the portfolio. They struggled to understand the extremely complex structure that was Norshield. Eventually, they realized that there was very little left. On June 1, 2005, in an innocent-looking four-paragraph letter, RBC Dominion Securities of New York, the entity that had financed Norshield to a great extent since 1998, decided they were pulling out of the "swaption" agreement that had buoyed the Norshield funds. When that happened, the preferred shares of Olympus Univest in Mosaic Composite would become valueless, and the hopes of investors for meaningful recovery or a sensible work-out were over. With the action, RBC would take over $300 million to its benefit and cause the permanent closure of the business.

There were numerous lawyers and executives working for RBC who waited, ready for pleas, proposals, threats, suits and actions as soon as they made their audacious raid, but none came. John and his staff were still in shock. Richter's staff were too new on the scene and the regulatory bodies were seemingly unaware of what RBC's actions would really do to the average investor.

It's doubtful that even the cadre of high-billing geniuses the CCE had assembled actually knew or understood the financial structures set up by John X and his colleagues. As they pounded away in the courts and newspapers, they probably didn't know how susceptible Norshield and its investors were to their attacks. When people see the strength of mountains, few search behind the image to make sure strength is really there. Norshield's strength lay in its unique ability to make complexity acceptable, not because you understand it, but because you believe that someone else does.

Mechaka

He had worked for a variety of banks over a span of 15 years and, after watching carefully the growth and improvements of Norshield, he had decided to join the business. He had entered the company as an assistant vice president in Norshield Asset Management. In 1994, they primarily sold mutual funds and his job was to develop a sales network of brokers who could sell mutual funds and other products. Smart, likable and persuasive, Yves Mechaka would build, over the next two years, a sales group that could sell funds, securities and insurance, and sell them well. He would attract established brokers with a "book of business" and as the Norshield alternative investment line of products grew, he would encourage the growth of value-added proprietary products that clients could purchase only through his organization. Among these products would be offshore funds, Univest (eventually called Olympus UniVest), the Canadian fund and commercial paper from Mount Real.

He worked with legal teams to find exemptions and methods to offer these special products legally to his clients without prospectus. Within a few years he had built a sizable organization and in 2001 Norshield Fund Management was sold into iForum and taken public as an independent entity.

By this time he had invested a sizable amount of his own money into Norshield and Mount Real products and many of his clients were now heavily invested. The following three years were heady and exciting for Yves and his colleagues. The returns of the Norshield funds were strong and impressive. Mount Real was reliably paying interest quarterly to its MRACS and RealVest clients. The iForum structure was working and attracting new brokers and clients. As time went by, virtually all clients were pleased with their reinvestments, so redemptions were rare and rollovers extremely common. What was also taking place, invisible to Yves and other brokers because once an account was established brokers were excluded from the paperwork flow, was that Mount Real had changed its debt product. Originally, the commercial paper was issued by Mount Real Acceptance Corporation, a wholly owned subsidiary of Mount Real at the same address, and the paper was guaranteed by Mount Real. Now, quietly, the obligation shifted to a new corporation called MRACS, not owned by Mount Real, and the corporate guarantee had shifted down to an "intent to support." The paperwork of established accounts on rollover moved

directly from MRACS to the client and to a trustee, B to B Trust (a major independent trustee). The brokers like Yves were out of the paperwork loop. Renewals were done between Mount Real, B to B Trust and clients. So, Yves would never know about or see the changes to the Mount Real product.

Simultaneously, the Univest structure from Norshield had gotten even more complicated and the fact was that the returns Univest now held for their cash investments were in the form of preferred shares in a fund called Mosaic Composite. Mosaic, in turn, had assets of its own and a huge hedge fund basket that included a loan, which would eventually reach $350 million with RBC Securities U.S. The other assets of Mosaic would include the Olympus Bank, Norshield Asset Management, the managed accounts and about 13 different private equities. The other assets served as collateral to the RBC loan. RBC was also secured by the fact it held all the securities in its own accounts of Mosaic Composite. Actually, RBC was in custody of all Mosaic Composite investments and held the securities themselves. This included the securities that offset their own loans, as well as the equity of Mosaic. They were fully secured. For all the cash put into it, Univest had not much more to show for it than some preferred shares in Mosaic Composite, and Yves, his brokers and even the president of Olympus Univest didn't know these were secured loans against Mosaic. The complicated structural changes John and Lino had made were unseen and unnoticed. Yves and the brokers were selling in good faith a product they had known, but that no longer existed.

The collapse had now taken place. It was mid-May 2005 and Yves realized that things were about as bad as they could get. Norshield was folded and reports were grim.

"For me it was hell when Norshield collapsed. What will happen to clients' money? It was a big panic. We began to take things into our own hands. The communication and comforting was full-time, nothing but crisis management. People got divorced and separated because of it. Family fights were common. There was no sleep, so tired people would fight day after day. Now I realized that my clients needed Mount Real to thrive. They couldn't afford a double whammy. Thank goodness in May of 2005 Mount Real was thriving. That's why keeping Mount Real alive was so important. We never expected the Norshield collapse. Imagine dealing with two betrayals and two collapses in the same year."

For Mount Real, in the summer of 2005, there was smoke. Lino said it was a liquidity problem that should be solved by October 2005. Yves asked that a letter be sent to clients, and he received a draft, but an official letter was never sent out. In October, brokers were told there must be an interest freeze until February. Finally there was an agreement, but that too was never done.

Moving on to
the Radar Screen

"Why are you even thinking about this? You've done some wacky things, but this is ridiculous." I sat in front of Lino's big leather-covered desk while Lino sat in his usual place. He was peculiarly silent. "So tell me, what do you hope to gain by meeting with Wes Voorheis? Why put yourself on the radar screen like that? What do you have to gain? What can you possibly accomplish? Do you realize that you have responsibilities to others . . . your family, your shareholders, your board, your investors? This guy is out to destroy whoever is in his way, and that will soon be you. You're an asshole, don't you realize that? When he meets you, when he talks with you, when he sees your derisive sneers and your arrogant air, he'll know you're an asshole and that's all it will take to be on his radar screen. This is stupid! I think you even know it's stupid, so why are you even considering this?" This was as directly as anyone had talked to Matteo in years. I was holding nothing back.

"Are you finished?" Lino asked quietly.

"No, I'm not finished," I shot back. "Are your billings to Norshield up to date? Because if they're not and you're not getting paid a lot of money to do what you're doing, then you have no excuse for taking the risks you're taking. The only explanations are that you're making a lot of money in fees, or you're covering up a lot of money you've stolen or you're just plain stupid. Even if you just love a fight, which I think you do, you're not so selfish as to drag all those other innocent people into your pastime; it's just unfair."

"Are you finished?" Lino asked for the second time.

"Yes," I barked.

"I will get my billings up to date. I'm not stupid and I will get the better of this guy, if I just meet with him. You don't know or you forget how good I am. He'll come here, I'll be quiet, he'll start talking and before he knows it, I'll know more about what he's up to than he does. These lawyers are all the same. They talk more than they listen, especially when they're on the visitor's court. This meeting will be on my home court, right here in this office. I'll make him wait ten, maybe twenty minutes. He'll show up with another person who I haven't agreed to meet with and I'll refuse to let them in the meeting. Finally, it will be the two of us and he'll start talking and I'll start listening and then the meeting will be over. You're wrong again, and I'm right again. I'm not going to make you apologize for calling me an asshole because I know you're trying to

help me, but don't worry about everybody else. They're my worry and I'll take care of them."

"When is the meeting?"

"Tomorrow at 10:30. He's in town to see me and some other people."

"If he wants to talk to you, let him depose you and do it right."

Matteo shot back, "You're so stupid sometimes. I'll never get him talking in a deposition. That gives him the licence to question me, pepper me with questions. No, I'm right about this one." I shook my head because I knew Matteo; he'd never back down on this.

It was a Wednesday morning in mid-May. Among the scent of blooming flowers and apple blossoms, Voorheis could also smell the sweet smell of victory over Norshield. In a little more than a year he hadn't collected any money from Norshield, but through his agents in the Bahamas, the lawsuits and the public relations efforts in Canada, he had destabilized the once thriving, largest hedge fund firm in Canada. They had just announced that they were freezing redemptions, the precursor to closing their doors. He had pummeled them into extinction because they wouldn't submit to his demands for money, even though it was never clear how exactly one might submit to his demands, even if they wanted to.

Voorheis was running a well-financed, quasi-governmental collection-and-destruction squad that was full of bright, high-billing professionals who were accountable to him. He stayed at the best hotels, ate at the best restaurants, expected the best service and got it. As Voorheis and Inkster arrived at the Mount Real headquarters in Ville-Émard, he noted his surroundings. The office was across the street from a Couche-Tard convenience store with graffiti on its walls. Further down the street was a bowling alley; in the other direction was Aldo's Italian delicatessen. The building was a converted fourplex.

"This doesn't look like a hundred-million-dollar business to me," was his first comment to Inkster as they climbed the entrance stairs.

"May I help you?" was Paulina's friendly greeting from behind the reception desk.

"Mr. Voorheis and Mr. Inkster to see Mr. Matteo," was the stiff reply. Scattered on the tables in the reception area were copies of the various magazines from Lino's publishing empire, *Menz* and *Overture.*

Paulina said, "It'll be a few minutes. Please make yourselves comfortable." Voorheis began to thumb through the magazines. Five minutes soon became ten, then 15. The phone on Paulina's desk rang; it was Lino.

"Mr. Matteo will see you now, Mr. Voorheis, but he says he has a meeting with you and you alone, not a meeting with two people. You must go upstairs alone, sorry." Voorheis shot a look at the former head of the RCMP and Interpol. He reeled back, frowned, and then shook his head. Finally, he said, "This guy is something." He proceeded up the stairs.

At the top of the stairs Jill, Lino's senior assistant, met Voorheis, knocked on Lino's door and opened it. Voorheis entered the office and Lino directed him to the chair in front of him and to his left. They shook hands and said "Nice to meet you" at the same time. There was no sincerity in either voice. Lino sat quietly. Voorheis opened his notebook and asked, "How did you get involved in this whole Cinar-Norshield affair?"

Lino responded, "John is a friend and client of mine and he asked me for help back in March 2000. How did

you get involved?"

Voorheis acted as if he hadn't heard the question. "Would you describe yourself as the chief strategist for Norshield over the last five years?"

"Well, since Norshield is apparently up on the rocks and out of business, I don't think anyone except John can lay claim to that flag. Have you met with John?"

Again Voorheis acted as if he hadn't heard the question, which was beginning to annoy Lino.

"When did you first learn of Cinar's investments in Globe-X?"

"I read about them in the newspaper in March of 2000. When did you first learn about them?" Lino asked.

"When did John originally call you about being involved?" Voorheis responded.

"Hey, what's with you? I thought we had agreed to have a meeting. At meetings people have conversations. You're acting like this is a deposition and that's not what I agreed to." Lino was heating up.

"I was asking you when John originally called you about being involved," Voorheis said coolly.

"This meeting is over. I'm not answering your penny-ante questions. You come to my office to have a conversation; you show up with someone else unannounced and uninvited, walk in here and start an unscheduled deposition. You won't answer any of my questions, so screw you. Get out of here."

Voorheis was stunned. His mind raced. "People don't talk to me like this," he thought.

"Get out of here!" Lino's volume increased. Voorheis got up and left. No one said goodbye, good day, good luck, *au revoir, ciao* . . . no one said anything. The meeting had ended in patented Lino style.

As Voorheis and Inkster got into the car, Inkster spoke first. "That didn't last five minutes. What happened?"

"That guy is the biggest asshole I've ever met," was Wes Voorheis' only response.

As they drove away, Voorheis would note that while sitting in the seat Lino had assigned him to, he noticed on Lino's bookcase a black three-ring binder entitled "RBC Option Agreement." If Lino knew of the swap agreement and understood it, this meant he could in fact be "Mr. Big," the guy who knew more than anyone about this complex mess.

"I've become convinced," he'd say, "that the Option Agreement is key; if it comes undone it will unhinge everything else for these guys. I'll push on that. We have no axe to grind; we just put together information and everything takes its course."

Six hours later you could find Voorheis at the St. James Hotel, the posh boutique hotel in Old Montreal that Voorheis used as his Quebec headquarters. He was having a drink in the first floor private meeting room he liked to use. He was due to meet Mario Ricci that evening for another session of threats and coercion in an attempt to get Mario to tell whatever he could about Cinar's investments and Norshield's business. The cat-and-mouse game had been going on for over a year now and Ricci was always being threatened with suits or discoveries of wrongdoing, no matter how untrue or unprovable. Ricci entered the room and they shook hands and said hello. Voorheis offered Mario a drink and then began to talk. Mario sat down in this well-appointed private salon. Voorheis stood and paced.

"How long have you known this Matteo character?" he asked.

MOVING ON TO THE RADAR SCREEN

"Since 1994," was the response.

"Tell me more."

"I used to work for him as controller at Mount Real."

"What?" Voorheis interrupted. "You worked for him? That means you worked for all three of them . . . Matteo, Weinberg and Xanthoudakis! That's unreal! You can sure pick 'em, Mario," he said with unusual familiarity.

"Well, yes, I did work for him until I went to Cinar."

"What do you think of him?"

"He's a character all right. He's controlling, smart, very confident, a good planner, and he's very good with the debits and credits. He drove me nuts at times, but then you'd see him do something really brilliant and you'd forget about all the other junk."

Voorheis was suddenly quiet. He held his drink in his hand and sat down in front of the fireplace in the salon. He didn't look at Mario; he looked into the fireplace and said, "Well, I met him today for the first time and he's an asshole. Now that asshole is mine. I'm going to bring him down. I'm going to bring him to his knees and he will know within the year that no one treats Wesley Voorheis the way he treated me today. He's finished."

Rubblification

Lino was behind his big desk and very animated. It was a beautiful spring morning; lilacs were blooming and their smell permeated the air of the residential neighborhoods of the city. Ville-Émard was full of lilacs, as are most of the older neighborhoods. Many people planted them in the thirties, forties and fifties as hedges and boundary plants, and every spring people are reminded why they keep the rather unexceptional bush around.

"I have a new term," Lino said with a proud smile. "Rubblification."

"What?" I asked.

"Rub – li – fi – cation," Lino said slowly and phonetically.

"What the hell is rubblification?" I countered.

"It is the process of rubblifying, of pounding something into rubble; it's like Berlin in 1945, Warsaw in '44. It is the reduction of something of substance into dirt and powder. You follow me?" I just shrugged. "At this point, Norshield is toast, they're finished. This redemption freeze and the mistakes John is about to make will make them extinct. Now that they can't be saved, it's better if they are rubblified."

It was dawning on me that this was Lino's way of hoping that if the heat and regulators maintained focus on Norshield, he and Mount Real might just stay off the radar screen and sneak into a cave of temporary obscurity until everything quieted down.

"So, you want to see the rubblification of Norshield?" I inquired.

"You're darn right I do. I might even help if I have a chance. With the way the rumors are flying and the gossip mills work, a good leak or a titillating piece of info can keep the circuit going for a week. The brokers catch a story, they leak it to management. Management twists it a couple of ways, it's back to the brokers, then the sub-agents, then the close clients, then the far clients and by then you start another one. Think about it. It can't be saved, so pound it into the ground. Like a story out there that John was having an affair with Maria would fly all over the place. Say that Daviault has a big stash of cash; people don't like him, so that will get legs. Hancock has destroyed all the records. A good leak here and there, along with the press that will be there anyway, and they'll be rubblified."

Over the next few weeks the rubblification Lino predicted would take place. The press would file story after story that would pound and pound like 500-pound bombs and leaks would take place to brokers, salespeople and employees because despite the fact the company was dead, John was unwilling to shut down the Toronto or Chicago offices until they had drained all the cash available to them. Incredibly, people would go to work every day, preparing résumés and job applications while being paid by Norshield. Lino was more and more confident his theory was working as the news of Norshield got worse and Mount Real faded off the radar screen.

There is an Italian restaurant in LaSalle called Bocci where Lino liked to eat. They knew him by name and would prepare his pasta exactly the way he liked it. They would even make whole wheat pasta for the days when that is what he craved. He had known Billy, the maitre d', for years and Billy would even wait Lino's table, if that's what Lino wanted. Mario, Lino and I went to lunch. John was lonely and calling everyone on their cell phone to figure out where lunch was that day.

"Don't answer it," Lino demanded when I reached for my phone. "No don't you answer it." I answered the phone anyway. Lino's eyes rolled back and his body language signaled disgust.

"Bill? It's John. Where are you guys?"

"Bocci," was my one-word answer.

"I'll be right there," John responded.

"I told you not to answer. Why don't you listen to me? He'll come now and mope and ask for advice that he won't follow anyway and ruin lunch. You shouldn't have answered the phone."

I said nothing. Ricci changed the subject to hockey — even in June, Montrealers can talk hockey — and suddenly the gloom left the table and Lino was reanimated, disagree-

ing with everything Mario or I said. When John arrived, he was welcomed by Mario and me; Lino said nothing, he just kept talking hockey. When my phone rang at the end of lunch, Lino said, "Don't answer it." Seeing it was Lino's office, I answered anyway and Lino scowled. John was never able to talk about much of anything except business, so he had been very quiet through lunch because all Lino wanted to do was have fun and chat lightly.

"Bill?" the voice on the phone asked.

"Yes," I responded.

"Mount Real has been cease traded; the AMF has announced an investigation and has cease traded the stock." The Autorité des Marchés Financiers (AMF) is the Quebec Security Commission. It has all the power to rule and regulate publicly traded companies.

"This call is for you," I said to Lino and handed him the phone.

Lino would now hear the same words. Suddenly everyone at the table had a ringing cell phone. The reality was sinking in as the four of us worked our phones, gathering information and seeking advice. The lunch would last two more hours. Plates that had once been filled with pasta and salmon salad were cleared away and the place became a crisis center, a communication crossroad. None of us were rookies at crisis management; we had all lived in that arena since March 2000. Now, over five years later, the last ship afloat had been hit, but how hard? The damage reports from the various attorneys rolled in and ranged from "This is serious" to "You'll be trading again in a day, just issue a press release."

At 4:00 p.m. the calls stopped and each of us reported what we had learned. Lino would listen at least for a while.

I spoke up first: "My securities guy says this will be a long, slow investigation. This is clearly political. As a matter of fact, he was on the train with these guys when they went to Quebec City to get approval. This was approved at the highest level."

John said, "My securities guy says issue a press release and you'll be trading in forty-eight hours or less. You just have to notify the public that there is an investigation . . . that's it."

Mario said, "My guy says the same thing, except in this case, the press will be all over this story and the press release won't be the only thing going out; the headlines will scream Mount Real Under Investigation!"

Lino was listening very carefully. He was realizing that "rubblification" hadn't worked, that now the bombs were falling on his city and he felt very alone and angry.

"This is that bastard Voorheis, isn't it?" The others nodded and I said, "Yeah, it probably is."

"That son of a bitch has hit me." Lino went quiet and for a minute no one spoke. "Can you write the press release?"

"Yes," Mario responded.

He looked at me. "Can you look it over and polish it?"

"Yes."

"I'll call the securities attorney you were talking to and ask him for a conflict check. I think he's probably our best bet." Then Lino looked right at John and said, "You know, my life was a hell of a lot better when you were the one getting all the bombs."

CHAPTER 53

DATE JULY 2005

SCENE Montreal

Gone in Moments

Since Mount Real had been "under investigation" by the AMF, there had been a few meetings on the subject and a lot of negative publicity. The stock trading was sluggish, but in large part things were okay. The legal advisers were basically counseling that the investigation might drag out a year or so. It was very political and at some point in 2006 it would be time to sit down with the Finance Minister, have a healthy chat and get the matter behind the company. Lino felt strongly that the investigation was brought on by Voorheis, but he was very aware that there were liquidity problems inside MRACS and RealVest, the funding entities that were causing brokers, investors and himself headaches. He had very carefully distanced himself and Mount Real from the funding entities several years earlier by changing officers, directors, even the names of the entities. In the process he had cleaned up Mount Real's balance sheet, eliminated or softened the Mount Real Guarantee from some of the debt and put the debt at arm's length from Mount Real.

All these machinations seemed important, but the perception of the sales force, the investors, even the employees was that MRACS was still Mount Real Acceptance Corporation, RealVest was still a subsidiary, Mount Real still backed up the financing entities and the money was still used to buy installment sales contracts. After all, you still dialed the same phone number to check on your account and you were still invited to the Mount Real summer picnic, so while everything had changed, it felt like nothing had. By July 2005, it was obvious to Lino that the liquidity crisis was getting increasingly worse. The newest Sterling Leaf offering had been shelved, so there was no help on the way. Holding his cards very close to his chest he began to meet with Lowell Holden and Laurence Henry, the presidents of RealVest and MRACS, about the pending crisis.

"I think we need to meet with brokers and tell them what the situation is," Lino said. "At this point if they don't keep selling and we don't defer some interest payments, we're going to slide into the sea."

Laurence countered, "These guys can't handle bad news like that. If we tell them that there will be an interest holiday for six months, that will send them running, and then a full panic will result; forget about them selling more." Laurence Henry was afraid, and he could see the problem worsening. A small man in his fifties, he had come to Canada from Egypt. A Coptic Christian, he

worked in his church and now was deeply regretting having gotten involved in this whole mess. Holden, being an American, was more distant than Laurence. The problems weren't going to happen in his home town; it wouldn't be his friends, family and neighbors reading about problems in the newspaper. Holden's objectivity was more in place. "If we don't declare the interest holiday and suspend payments, how much longer can we last?" he asked.

"Two months," was the answer from Lino.

Both Holden and Henry were surprised by the answer. "How much is the interest each month?" Holden asked. Surprisingly, neither of the presidents seemed to know the answer.

"Combined, about six hundred thousand dollars," Lino responded.

"That's a big nut. I didn't realize it had gotten that large," Lowell said. Uncharacteristically, Lino then said, "I'm not making the decision on this, you guys. These are your businesses, so you decide. Do we notify people or not?"

"What about the redemption requests that are due now? What do we do about those? I've got people calling me night and day about redemptions. What do we do about those?" Henry asked.

The room was completely quiet. Lino had decided he wasn't making decisions on this matter; the problem was Henry's and Holden's, so he quit talking. Finally, just to break the silence Holden said, "Well, obviously redemptions have to be suspended for now. We can't even pay the interest. Let me think this over for a few days. In the meantime, let's have Bill Urseth draft up some letters so we can see what they might look like."

"That's a good thought," Laurence shot back and the meeting was over.

I would draft a dozen letters over the next six weeks, all of them minor variations of the other, only to get a small change or some feedback. None of the letters were ever sent — no one dared to send them — and Lino was no longer making decisions. Even though the AMF investigation seemed to be slow, benign or nonexistent, the liquidity crisis was fast, malignant and very existent. Some clients were now contacting the customer service people daily, demanding meetings with Lino or Laurence, and the brokers were being barraged. I could now see that if they did nothing, things would spin out of control. The question would ultimately be, "Could Mount Real survive if the funding entities were put into liquidation?" Lino believed most certainly that Mount Real could survive because they were separate entities and MRACS and RealVest were *not* part of Mount Real. I doubted it, and I began to encourage Joe Pettinicchio to make a deal and sell iForum as quickly as possible. In fact, I'd begun to think as early as July that Joe needed to make a deal.

iForum had over the previous five years become one of Quebec's largest independent investment advisers, selling insurance, mutual funds and other investment opportunities to their client base. The company had been a consolidator of individuals and independent firms — finding merger opportunities was a key part of its business. With about 200 agents working with thousands of clients, the company had grown enough to be noticed in the financial community. As a public company trading on the TSX, the firm offered annual reports, quarterly

financials and annual meetings, and its stock could be used as currency for acquisitions. For the last couple of years, the local and national financial press had been paying positive attention to iForum.

Most important for John and Lino was that the brokers had served as a key distribution network for the financial products they had developed, including Commax, Balance Return Fund, Olympus Univest, MRACS, RealVest and Sterling Leaf. The agents knew and sold these products and had done so for years.

In a meeting with Joe, I laid it out. "You must separate yourself and iForum as quickly as possible. You must move fast. Just sell, you don't have much time."

When Daviault went back to give a second deposition in September 2005, he would once again testify to the CCE for three days. This time, on the first day, he focused his comments on his longtime nemesis, Lino Matteo, and when the newspapers covered this testimony, they would focus on Lino. Bob would testify how he and Ricci and Maria were "the worker bees" in Florida recasting the Globe-X balance sheet, following instructions from Lino Matteo. He would recount how Lino was in charge of managing the Cinar crisis for Globe-X and that included creating the false documents with Panju. He even implied that the clients who had invested in offshore funds to avoid taxes were somehow tied to Lino, a completely unsupportable accusation. Within eight weeks of his testimony to the CCE they had enough information to circulate to newspapers and government regulators.

By October the brokers were demanding meetings and wanted explanations about why redemptions weren't being paid. On the edge of a nervous breakdown, the customer relations person checked herself into the hospital.

Now Laurence was really in the line of fire, but still important decisions were left unmade. Surprisingly enough, some money was still flowing in so he had a little more time, but within a month there would be no money for interest, and all hell could break loose.

Joe was working frantically on a deal, hoping to separate the thriving iForum from the quagmire. He had four deals on the table. "Don't worry about the best deal, just get a deal done!" I would howl. "Time is running out. Work with people who understand that things go wrong sometimes, so when things blow they don't try to back out."

None of the brokers wanted to meet with Laurence or Lowell alone . . . they wanted Lino. They knew it was Lino alone who ran things, no matter what the minute book said. They were already dealing with the side effects of the Norshield collapse. Most of them had clients in those funds, clients who had been shocked and harmed by the rapid and surprising demise of John's business. Oddly enough, even though Mount Real was known to be smaller, it was thought to be more stable by the brokers who brought the money.

Finally, Lino agreed to a meeting. The conference room was full. Laurence Henry was there, but mostly the room was full of brokers, all of whom to varying degrees had brought their clients' money to a Mount Real entity, whatever the name. Simply put, they had sold Lino and Mount Real as a good, safe, high-return investment . . . a place to put one's savings. All in all, that simple pitch had raised over $100 million in seven or eight years and fueled Mount Real's growth. Lino explained that things were tight, that they'd get better soon, and that things would get better faster if people would get back to work and sell more debt. He explained that Laurence and Lowell were

working on some things as well, but most importantly he told them that the agents who were working and selling would see their clients' problems dealt with first. By implication, if you were bellyaching or bitching, but not solving the problem, your clients could wait. Most important was what wasn't said. No one said, "The funds are essentially out of money; there will be no interest paid for six months while we restructure and there will be no redemptions for at least a year. Even with these draconian steps, the funds may not survive because the installment sales contracts aren't really receivables in the traditional sense. They're more of an opportunity to collect and up-sell."

Lino then would pull out a sheet of paper, which served as a pro forma business proposal and spreadsheet where he tried to explain how all of the sales agents could open a telemarketing room of their own and sell their way to financial strength and stability, while helping MRACS, RealVest, Mount Real and their clients in the process. By the time the meeting was over, the attendees were more tired than worried, more confused than concerned. They had heard enough to know Lino was working on a solution, so things should be just fine.

The Mount Real board would meet on November 10, 2005. Joe would resign as planned and agreed upon, in anticipation of an as yet unaccomplished deal for iForum. The board still had faith in Lino and didn't really have all the information about the liquidity crisis, the pending failure of the funds and the deteriorating situation with the brokers. The ongoing investigation was a concern, but not one that seemed imminent. The more pressing issues surrounded year-end projections and the stock price.

For me November 11th was a travel day. I would work until about 1:30 p.m. at the office and then headed to the airport. The ritual was very routine: check in at the Northwest Airlines counter, proceed to duty free for cigars and whiskey, shuffle through customs, check bags and then go through security. The process takes between 30 and 60 minutes, depending on the day. As I was going through the check-in process, the events began to unfold at 2500 Allard (Mount Real's head office) and 2638 Allard (Michael Maloney's office). In one rapid stroke, the AMF was cease trading not only the stock of Mount Real, but *all* of them: iForum, Honeybee Technology, Gopher Technologies, Lakefield Marketing Corporation and Upland Global Corporation. In June, when we'd all been at the restaurant Bocci, it had been cease traded for a few days; then it had resumed trading. Now, in November, it was permanent, and the outcome would be delisting and halt on all trading. The shares would become valueless. AMF agents would arrive at the Mount Real offices and proceed to seize all the documents and properties of the company, send all the employees home and lock the doors. In short order, the same would happen to the attorney, Michael Maloney, down the block, as well as at iForum's and Honeybee's offices. The AMF would name the firm of Raymond Chabot Grant Thornton as receivers and begin to treat the empire of Lino Matteo as if it were in the past tense.

Wes Voorheis would say later about Mount Real's demise, "I began to wonder about Mount Real when I gave a friend of mine, who is a very successful investor, the Mount Real financial statement. He studied it carefully and said, 'I just don't know. I just don't know. I just don't know.'"

The phone call would come to Wes Voorheis in Toronto. "It's happening right now, the cease trade, the

seizures, the receiver, the closure. They're all happening right now. As of another hour, Lino Matteo will be crushed," the voice on the phone offered.

"Thanks for calling. This is a good day," Voorheis said quietly into the phone.

As I went through customs and security, I could hear my phone ringing, but I wasn't allowed to answer. As I emerged from the process, I drained my messages.

"Bill, it's Joe. The AMF is here at my office. They're closing us down. I know the press will be all over the story. Please call, we've got to talk."

"Bill, it's Paul. They're shutting us down." Paul was the CFO of Mount Real.

"Bill, I think Lino is in big trouble. This is John. Call me."

"Bill, I think something is happening to Mount Real. This is Mario. Call me in Ottawa. The AMF website says they're being shut down."

"Bill, it's Lino. I'm being thrown out of my own office. The press will be calling me soon." I'd become accustomed to the eerie calm Lino exuded in a real crisis.

As I reached my gate, the world I had left behind just an hour ago had now completely changed. The government had moved with a finality that roared. This was not a matter of a clever line or some spin control. In a matter of minutes, without a trial or court order, they had destroyed what had taken ten years to build, wiped out $100 million in market value and made over $130 million in investor notes valueless. There have never been criminal charges brought against any officer, director, employee or even Lino P. Matteo himself . . . just swift, dramatic, destructive, administrative blows to the head and vital organs of Matteo's business.

I returned as many calls as I could while I waited for my flight. I gathered the information as it came and passed it on to others as I learned it. I would write some carefully scripted lines for Lino and Joe, phrases they could stick to when confronted by the press — knowing all the while that whatever they said would be buried in the bottom of the juicy story that the reporters were concocting. When it came time to call Lino, I suppressed my anger at him for putting his companies and himself unnecessarily in the firing line. Only Lino and I really knew how much time, focus and attention Cinar and Norshield had taken and what a distraction it had become for Matteo.

"Are you okay?" I said.

"I'm a little shaken up," the deep voice responded. It was strangely without emotion.

"Anyone would be. Do you have any kind of a damage report?"

"It seems like the Monk office is still open and the West Island hasn't been badly hit. Otherwise, they've taken everything."

"Can you deal with them?"

"I haven't met them. I don't even know who they are, but I'll try. They'll need someone to teach them the business; at least maybe I'll be the teacher."

Lino had a shocked detachment about him. He couldn't comprehend that they intended to shut it down and kill it rather than try to find value or have some scaled-back, ongoing business. He clung to the idea that he would "teach them" about the business, and that could be his role. One of his strengths was the ability to cover his fear and find a clear calm in the midst of a crisis. He had, after all, been in a crisis mode almost constantly for the

previous five years. He had been in a severe liquidity crisis for the previous year and been under press attacks the previous nine months. None of that had rattled him, so it wasn't surprising that this knockout blow would find him still rational, calm and pragmatic.

"I'm sorry, this is very hard. I'll call you tomorrow." I hung up. I really did feel bad. I wasn't focused on the quarter of a million dollars of stock I held that was now worthless, or on the fights, arguments or mistreatment I'd been through with this one-of-a-kind bully. I began to realize that it was finally over; the Cinar thing was finally over. There would never be the victory dinner at Muscadet, the restaurant that Lino and John preferred when they were flying high. The dinner I had thought about, imagined over the last five years that would celebrate Cinar standing down and the whole chapter ending, so that lives and businesses could return to normal and focus on profitability, not survival. I was on the losing team. The conflagration started by Panju and Weinberg had just consumed everything — including Lino and virtually all his assets, along with the savings and retirement funds of thousands of others who had believed in the enigmatic Italian who spoke straight.

The boarding announcement jolted me out of my daydream. I rose, gathered my stuff and walked onto the plane, leaving behind the familiar Montreal I had known for so long — in what seemed like moments, it had ceased to exist.

CHAPTER 54

DATE NOVEMBER 2005

SCENE Montreal

The Little Guy

On the 11th of November 2005, Mount Real and six other entities it administered were extinguished without trial, testimony, debate, rebuttal or presentation. In the process, over $200 million in equity and investor debt became valueless. On the sworn deposition of an admitted liar, Lino and Mount Real were destroyed. Daviault's deposition had done it.

What so many investors in the various entities would ask is: "Where were the warnings?" The CCE expected the newspapers to tell the stories in Daviault's over 1,800 pages of deposition the way they wanted the story told; the newspapers accommodated that wish. If they had actually read the depositions in full, they might have realized that the security of thousands of investors — who had in good faith put their life savings and retirement monies into the investments — was now being destroyed by innuendo. These people had needed warnings and alarms to protect their capital from collapse. Some Norshield and Mount Real investors were actually Cinar shareholders. In other words, it was their money that had funded the CCE, which had now destroyed the savings and retirement funds in Norshield and Mount Real. On November 12, 2005, the CCE would turn its attention back to Weinberg and Panju, the only people left to either collect from or destroy.

As a young man, Robert Thompson had always wanted to teach. He loved the sciences and when he left university in 1961 he immediately went to work in the school system. He would never marry. He taught, lived alone and consciously chose to be frugal, always trying to save twenty percent of his paycheck. At first it didn't seem to amount to much, but after his tenth year of teaching he checked on this tidy little account and he was surprised he had over $30,000. Even more surprising was that after 20 years the amount had swelled to over $200,000. Never having had children, Robert would treat his savings as if it was his child, nurturing and watching it grow. While for some people keeping track of retirement income is a necessary chore, for Robert it was a pleasant diversion and a proactive pastime watching his "kid" get strong and big.

In 1999 he met Yves Mechaka, his investment adviser, and through Yves' counsel and some personal relationships he began to invest his savings with Norshield. The Commax fund was a Norshield managed fund that he came to trust and within months he had placed over $500,000 in Commax. Months later when Yves talked to him about Balance Return Fund, another Norshield managed fund, he was also impressed and invested yet another $500,000. When he compared how his "kid" was growing, he could clearly see that the funds he'd invested in Commax and Balance Return Fund were the stars of his portfolio. In 2000 and 2001 with returns over 20 percent, the funds were glowing stars in the investment galaxy. In 2002, he would shift more money into the Norshield orbit, almost $300,000 more, the rest of the money he had saved from teaching. Even with such substantial savings, Robert never took money out. He just rolled his interest into his principal and watched his "kid" compound to the point where his net worth exceeded $2 million. When he was shown MRACS, a Mount Real high-yield, fixed-return commercial paper product, he bought $100,000 worth of that as well, liking the story and the conservative ten and a half percent fixed return that MRACS offered. While neither John nor Lino knew Robert by sight or name, they were now in possession of over $1.5 million of his savings, scrimped from his teaching salary over 40 years. To them he was an account number.

The stories that Norshield was in trouble had begun to circulate in May of 2005, and were widely fueled by the newspapers. The stories had been constant since late December when the CCE had leaked Daviault's deposition to the press in well-marked, highlighted briefing packages. At the time, the reporters didn't understand the effect of their stories on either Norshield or people like Robert. They were, after all, in the news business and this was news. Just because it was served up neatly by the CCE's public relations people didn't mean that the public didn't

deserve to know, and it was the reporter's job to inform. Annoyed by John's action to block the reporting of Daviault's testimony in court, the reporters had become incensed about "freedom of the press" issues and the stories about John and Norshield would become increasingly ugly. When Olympus Univest, the "Fund of Funds" managed by Norshield, froze their redemptions, Robert began to have anxiety attacks. He was unable to sleep and in May 2005 he would walk the streets of downtown Montreal at night, sometimes all night, as if he were a parent looking for a lost child. Sometimes he would call out "Kid, kid," as if there might be a response, but there never was. Realizing he was sliding rapidly into depression, Robert sought medical advice, and on the 21st of May, 2005, he was hospitalized for clinical depression. He would make progress over the following months with psychiatric therapy and drugs. His condition stabilized.

"It was like my kid was clobbered by a car or truck," he recounted. He would hear voices that would haunt him for months, putting him back in the hospital a second time. He would at times call out to the voices. Robert knew that he had lost a good portion of his $1.5 million with the collapse of Norshield. He would find solace in the fact that the money he had placed with Mount Real was still there. In reality his life hadn't changed much; he was still living in the same home, still living the same life. His routine hadn't changed with the loss of the money. He had been quietly wealthy, not flashy, and very secure with his life, his accomplishments, his "kid." What had changed was that his health had deteriorated.

When Mount Real collapsed in November 2005, Robert would learn of it through the newspapers. He realized that over $100,000 may now also be lost. He again lapsed into hearing voices and walking the streets all night, calling out to his "kid" and answering the voices. He would be hospitalized for the third time, and now even more of his carefully saved fortune was gone. He would simply offer, "I miss that money. I never used it, but I miss it. I lead a simple life; that was my pleasure." Robert only knows that he lost the money "because of forces beyond my control that caused Norshield and Mount Real to go under. I'm trying to recuperate."

When Terry was building his business as a young man, he had chosen "to work hard now and play harder later." His small retail jewelry store had done well, but his routine involved 100-hour workweeks, including every Saturday of his life. By 1997 he had accumulated several million dollars and wasn't pleased with the return he was getting from traditional banks. His investment adviser recommended some commercial paper from Mount Real Corporation that paid a fixed return of ten and a half percent. "This was a very appealing product," Terry would explain. "I was tired of the banks screwing us little guys."

Over the next years he would move $500,000 into the MRACS and RealVest products of Mount Real, never taking money out, just letting the interest accumulate and compound. At the same time, he would learn about Norshield and their various funds, and by 2002 he would have over $2 million in various Norshield funds. Times were good. He left his business and retired. He and his wife of 45 years were now doing what they intended; they were "playing hard." Terry knew he needed an income of over $300,000 pre-tax to live the life he wanted and he

had that now by starting to take only the interest component of his investments. "In 2003 and 2004 I was even suggesting to my friends that they get into Mount Real and Norshield. I was very happy with my investments."

He would first learn of the Cinar problems in March 2000 through the newspapers and he knew that Norshield was somehow involved, but "I was reassured that it was nothing, not a serious problem." It was in late 2004 and 2005 that the alarms began to go off — Norshield might have real troubles. But again Terry was reassured. "If I had smelled anything I would have taken my money out. I wasn't close enough to do the smelling."

In reality, the CCE had started little fires that were hard to smell, but they definitely were burning. If in February to May 2005 Terry had tried to get his money out, it would have been too late because redemptions had already run out of proportion at Norshield, and Mount Real was about to be in the same situation.

"When I had money, I'd buy my son six shirts and three pairs of trousers, just for fun. Now I can't. When I go to the gym I'm asked to buy raffle tickets for charity. Now I have to say no and I don't feel right about it. Things I've done for ten or fifteen years have evaporated. Nice restaurants are out of the question, Le Coq Cheval and Gibby's are gone. Now we eat at home and are selective. I used to hear 'Terry, you have so much money, you'll never spend it all in your lifetime.' No one says that anymore.

"It's hard for me, but it's worse for my wife. She's distraught. It's hard to live with her now, she feels so restricted. My own health is affected by anxiety, sleep deprivation, depression. My wife now gets very bad heartburn and her depression is really serious. I'm very bitter. I feel that John betrayed me and Lino betrayed me. It was bad enough to lose the Norshield money, but then when Mount Real collapsed, I lost them both together. My God! Then the worst part came. I had to pay income taxes on the unpaid interest from the investments, even though the interest was never paid and the principal was lost. Can you believe that? Where is the government to help us? Nowhere! I'm not so sure they didn't actually cause some of this. Norshield collapsed because of the big banks. Mount Real was brought down by the government. Why would they do that to all of us innocent people?"

Terry would find it too hard to attend the meetings put on by the liquidators for Norshield and Mount Real. "It would just be too painful. Maybe I should just face it. If I had settled for six percent returns and let the bank keep screwing me, none of this would have ever happened."

The Shakedown

In Montreal the days become short in the fall. Being as far north as the city is, once daylight savings time ends at the end of October, the darkness arrives by 5:30 p.m. and by Christmas it's dark at 4:30. In mid-November, the evenings have a chill and the nights are below freezing. There are still colors in the trees, but most of the leaves are gone and the vivid colors have faded, leaving mostly browns and mottled yellows. John had been asked for a meeting by one of the now very worried investors of Olympus Univest. These requests were becoming more and more frequent as the reality of the collapse set in on people at different speeds and the visibility of the Mount Real collapse led to new headlines.

Most of the meetings were very similar. The process entailed John explaining in as contrite a way possible that things had definitely gone wrong and that at least for now the investor had lost access to all their money. Then he would explain that he hoped that there would be significant recovery of assets and that he was committed to helping in the process. The meetings were usually with the investor, sometimes with their family, and generally the broker or sales agent was there. Many of these investors had been involved in John's deals for years and had watched their net worth rise because of his work and success. Many changed their lifestyles due to the prosperity he had brought them. Some had paid for their daughter's wedding with money that John had helped develop; others bought new homes or condos in Florida. Until this debacle, they had been proud to say they knew "Johnny," as they called him. He held a cult-like status to these people who knew few celebrities or stars and fewer still who had actually improved their own lives dramatically.

Amazingly, at the end of these meetings when John would sincerely apologize and promise to "work for recovery of their assets," they would sincerely ask him how he was doing and express their sorrow about his life and what had happened. As long as they believed that he was a victim, too, these sessions remained civil, albeit sad.

"After dozens and dozens of these meetings, I'm amazed at how understanding people are," John said. "People may be angry, in denial, financially ruined, but the people who actually made the money are genuinely gracious. It's the children or the heirs that are hard to deal with. They've been counting on dad's or grandpa's cash all these years and now they realize it's gone. Those are the tough ones to deal with." On balance, the meetings were

THE SHAKEDOWN

taking four to six hours every day, but they seemed to be helping in some way.

A meeting was to be held at John's attorney's office in the largest office building, in the center of the city. The time was set for 4:30 and, as usual, John was running late. Dominic was an ex-broker who had sold some Norshield-related investments. It was Dominic who had set up the meeting because he had some clients who had invested money and as had become typical, they needed explanations. The waiting room of the law firm was large and well decorated, with the feel of importance that any law firm's interior designers try to create. As John entered the waiting room, he was told that his guests were already in the conference room and that he could join them right away.

The double doors swung open and John entered wearing a dark pinstripe suit, blue shirt and red silk tie. He looked strong and undefeated as he walked into the room. Dominic was there and rose to say hello with a handshake. The other three men in the room remained seated. They wore sport shirts with open collars and had piled their leather jackets onto one of the 12 conference room chairs. They looked like three unimportant gentlemen in a very important room. John sat next to Dominic, across the table from the three men. He said, "It's nice to meet you. I don't think we've ever met before." The largest of the three had a big head with combed-back, thick, dark hair and a goatee about three inches long that terminated in a point. His eyes were black; from the crow's feet, he looked about 40. His right fingers and his teeth had tobacco stains. It was clear from the way he swung in the conference room chair that he wasn't used to sitting in one.

"We're glad you came to see us today. We represent a group of people who aren't very happy. As a matter of fact, they are very unhappy and their unhappiness makes me very, very unhappy." He spoke slowly and with a tone of condescension and intimidation. "Now, you've got about $350 million and we want $5 million of it because we don't want these people unhappy anymore."

John could feel the shakedown through his body. This was no ordinary meeting with another investor or group of investors. This was an old-fashioned shakedown, the kind he hadn't been through since he was 13, when the 16-year-olds would shake down the younger kids for their lunch money.

"Guys, I don't have three hundred and fifty million. As a matter of fact, I don't have three hundred and fifty thousand. I've lost my business, my family, my investors' money, everything. Now, let me explain how this all happened."

"Don't bother. Let me explain some things to you. You're not stupid; you've helped people sneak money out of this country for decades. You've shown people how to avoid paying taxes and how to hide money. We know that . . . you know that . . . the newspapers know that. So, watch what you're saying when you talk to me. I know you've got a stash 'cause that's your business. So, if you don't have three hundred and fifty million I don't care 'cause all I want is five million anyway. So just get that and everything will be fine. As a matter of fact, your friend, Matteo, who has over two hundred million, can use some of that to solve your problem. We don't care."

John turned to Dominic. "Did you know this when the meeting was set up?"

"No, uh, I knew they wanted money, but everybody does."

The bigger guy cut him off. "It doesn't matter what he

knew, knows or didn't know. The only thing that matters is that you tell us when we're getting the five mil." Again, John turned toward Dominic, about to speak, but as he did, the smallest of the three men came around the big table unnoticed and struck John in the head with brass knuckles.

The cut above his eye was deep and bleeding profusely. The law office conference room was splattered with blood, the blue shirt now matching the red silk tie. Dominic was in over his head, offering John a handkerchief as a bandage. The big guy began to speak again.

"I'll be calling in the next few days. You had better know then when we're getting the five million. That eye of yours will take a while to heal and we want every cent before it does. Do you understand?"

"I understand."

The trio got up and left. No one in the waiting room or offices had any idea that in the conference room there was someone badly bleeding . . . the injured former CEO of what was once the largest hedge fund in the country.

Dominic discreetly went to the washroom and got towels and bandage materials. John would lock the conference room doors when Dominic left and reopen them only when he returned. Using ice water and soda, they would try to stop the bleeding, but to no avail. On Friday afternoons, offices have a way of emptying out early. It was now 6:30 p.m. and they hadn't been discovered, so Dom took a stroll and found almost everyone gone. At 6:45 p.m. on Friday night, November 13, 2005, John was escorted out of the office building he once called his home, with a towel over his head and his dark pinstripe suit, red silk tie and blue shirt covered in blood. At 7:00 p.m. he was admitted to the Montreal General Hospital.

In the waiting room was a drug addict who had badly overdosed. A gunshot victim from the east side was undergoing surgery, fighting for his life. There was an Aboriginal woman weeping because she had run over her boyfriend three times with his pickup truck . . . once while he was walking behind the vehicle, a second time when she panicked and realized he was under the left rear tire and the third time when she panicked again and pulled forward. She smelled strongly of beer and whiskey; it was unlikely he would survive.

Dominic had left John at the hospital, needing to get home as he was already three hours late and covered in blood himself. He had some explaining to do. John sat alone surveying the reality of the situation in the emergency room and how much things had changed. It was only 24 months ago that he had hosted the "We See Things Differently" party and showed the financial world how different Norshield really was.

Wipe That Smile
Off Your Face

The room was supposed to hold 300, but from the long lines, it might have to accommodate 500 people. The lines to register were supposed to be ten minutes long; they would be an hour long and the start of the meeting would be delayed an hour and a half. Lino was in a hotel room on the second floor with his attorney, waiting anxiously for the proceedings to begin. This was the largest assembly of business associates he would ever have. The annual meetings, the summer picnics, the parties and briefings would all pale in comparison to the turnout for this . . . the first creditors' meeting of the now bankrupt Mount Real.

The lines would reflect the ethnicity of the company's

following. There was a Chinese contingent, a Greek group, many Italians and Sicilians, French Quebeckers, English Ontarians, Lebanese and Filipino. The group would include soliciting attorneys, reporters and regulators; the tone was angry. These were the people who had lost over $100 million in loans to the company, and the stockholders whose shares were now worthless; over $100 million in market cap had shriveled to nothing.

Some people were both shareholders and bondholders, and others had hit the trifecta: they were also Norshield investors. At the appointed time, Lino was brought down from his waiting room. It was reminiscent of the way a prizefighter is led to the ring, surrounded by managers and seconds. He would wear a business suit and tie, not a typical outfit for Lino, even in his most prosperous days. He was accompanied as they climbed the dais by his lawyer, Claudine Murphy, and Lowell Holden. On the raised platform were four staffers from Raymond Chabot and a huge screen on which the report would appear. While proceedings were in French, there would be simultaneous English translations. After the written presentation, questions from the floor would begin. But the questions didn't flow to the presenters from the accounting firm; they flowed immediately to the deposed president whom they had believed in and trusted, and to whom they had sent their money. The packed room of 500 in a standing-room-only setting would now hear the voice of the man they had once admired but now had grown to detest. Most of them had never been in a room alone with him or seen his antics, puppetry, insults, abusive behavior or tricks of domination. They didn't know how bright he could be, how powerful his presence or how demeaning and cruel. Those who did know him from his days of power knew the vast

talents he possessed. There was an almost perverse feeling that accompanies a coup d'état or a war crimes tribunal, where the vanquished are paraded forward to be judged by their conquerors.

The first question was from a woman in her mid-thirties. She simply asked, "How can you sleep at night after what you have done?" There was applause from the 500 and catcalls filled the room; there was shouting and insults, and the chairman made little effort to create order. Matteo sat silently, waited to speak and did not say a word. Only when the room was quiet did he begin. "I'm not sleeping very well; this has been very hard on my family and me." He spoke with confidence, his powerful bass voice filled with the resonance of former days. "I never thought that the investigation that began in June 2005 could end as abruptly and disastrously as it did in November. I didn't believe that the company we had worked so hard to build for so long could be destroyed in such a short number of days by people who didn't understand it. They never learned what it did or how it did it and seemed motivated only to destroy it. I'm sorry for your losses. I'm sorry for the employees' lost jobs, and I'm sorry that the dream of Mount Real was lost." The audience listened politely, but there was much too much anger for an eloquent, well-spoken apology, too much anger for empathy or sympathy. They wanted a pound of flesh. The questions continued: "Is this really just a Ponzi scheme?" "Where is the money?" "They're saying they've found only a few million out of one hundred million. Where is the money?" "Did you start out to cheat us?" "Are you going to pay us back personally?" "How could things look so good and be so rotten?"

Lino was verbally attacked and pilloried as if in a medieval town square. Throughout, he remained in control, his voice calm and purposeful, his responses well thought out and clearly stated. Never did his infamous temper flare or his contemptuous arrogance gain control. He would talk at great length about how the value in the company was in the database and the installment sales contracts, which the receiver had declared virtually worthless. He would never vary far from this theme, despite the fact there seemed to be no tangible proof of value. The meeting ran until 4:00 p.m., over five and a half hours without a break for lunch, or the bathroom. Lowell Holden, president of the companies that issued the bonds, was asked only one question; Lino was asked over 80. It was Lino that they wanted to talk to, only him. When the meeting was over forty percent of the audience was still in the room; the rest had walked away, knowing in their hearts and in their minds they had lost everything. They would walk out to their cars in the hotel parking lot. It was March, and in March in Montreal, the cars are cold when you enter them. Snow was on the ground, and the roads were icy. Their hearts were cold now, too; the process they had just witnessed felt slippery, and there was an undertone that said they had also been snowed.

The Mount Real Creditors Committee would never recover much money. When the meeting was finally over, Jean Robillard went out to the same parking lot as the other attendees. He had been the senior partner from Raymond Chabot, the receivers. It was he who had stuck the stake in the heart of Mount Real; it was he who now had supervised its burial. He walked alone to the far corner of the parking lot where he had carefully left his car away from others. He slid behind the wheel of a brand new, warm, pre-started Mercedes Benz with heated seats. Virtually all of the money ever recovered in the Mount

WIPE THAT SMILE OFF YOUR FACE

Real liquidation went to Raymond Chabot and Grant Thorton, the receivers.

Lino would be one of the last to leave the room. As he was gathering his things, a woman in her mid-fifties approached him. He automatically held out his hand and introduced himself with a smile. "Hello, I'm Lino Matteo," he said softly. The woman looked at him and didn't offer her hand. She simply said, "I'm Francine Chagnon and I just wanted you to see one of the people you've fucked," she said directly. Startled, Lino's smile froze. Then she said, "Wipe that smile off your face," and walked away.

It was a lonely drive home, on the loneliest day of his life. When he got to his home, his little nephew was there. Almost three, Lino greeted him as the little boy toddled up to his big uncle. As part of the greeting he bent over to address the young boy face to face. As he did, the youngster mirrored his bow and was now even lower than the powerful Matteo. So, Lino dropped to his knees to be face to face, and the little boy immediately dropped to his knees. Lino then began to laugh out loud and said, "Angelo, thank you for being here. This is truly the best part of my day!"

Where Is
the Money?

It had been over a year since the collapse of Norshield. Every employee, except John's brother, now had a job and had started their lives over. John himself still wasn't working and had renewed fears of the death threats. He was always dealing with increasingly serious problems with his oldest son, who couldn't make it through two days of school without an expulsion. More and more his concentration had slipped and the interruptions from his kids made it difficult for him to be productive. After three phone calls from his son, the school and then the police, he excused himself from the meeting he was intending to have with Dale Smith and me.

Dale Smith had served as CFO of Norshield for eight

years starting in 1998 when Daviault had gone to Nassau. He had worked hard and believed in what the company was doing, what it stood for and how it operated. He was pissed off, and couldn't believe how things had ended up.

"Bill, what I still don't understand is how far away Richter is, how little progress they've made and how much they've been charging."

I just nodded. With extra time on our hands due to the unexpected cancellation of the meeting, no one was in a rush so I just let Dale keep talking.

"I offered to do a reconciliation," he said. "A wrap-up type of sheet for them six months ago. One that would simply show how much money came in, how much money went out and how the money was spent. It would seem to me that that is something a receiver would want to know, but it seems that they prefer ambiguity, procedural inquiry and a continued cloud surrounding 'hundreds of millions missing'! It's amazing that a year later they've found so little, but they keep looking in the wrong places. Do you realize that most of the money that flowed into the funds came in during 2002 and 2003? Those years were audited by Deloitte Touche and no one has even talked to Deloitte, much less investigated them. There was a little audit firm that audited the Channel entities. All they did was audit, but now they've been through eleven days of investigation and depositions . . . eleven days! Do you know what it costs to do an investigation per day? Twenty-five thousand dollars a day! Yeah, four people, full time, one at five hundred bucks per hour, one at three hundred and two at two-fifty. The depositions run seven hours per day, just for the accountants. On top of that are three lawyers, a court reporter, two researchers and, with preparation time, it all comes to twenty-five thousand a day. Now this little firm doesn't know anything and definitely doesn't know where there is any money, but they've tied them up for eleven days. They chose them because they need to run the billing clock, and investigate someone who won't send them any future business. Deloitte will send business, so they leave them alone. Do you think they'll do a partial distribution of the money they've found? The money they've got? Hell no, they'll keep every cent, in case they can figure out how to spend it all on their own investigation.

"It's the damnedest racket," Dale continued. "The court appoints you, you become the agent of the court, take over all the assets and pay yourself for as long as there's any money left to pay. They've made millions, admitted that they've recovered very little and distributed nothing, and they continue to pay themselves liberally. It's so obvious where there is money and where there isn't. Deloitte Touche has insurance, the law firms have insurance and the banks have insurance. I'll tell you who doesn't have any money . . . me and John! We have nothing and they'll get nothing from us, but they continue to spend their time investigating us. I wonder how many investors actually understand that it's their money that's funding not so much a recovery effort for funds, but a billing machine for the AMF, the OSC and other regulatory bodies.

"What I do know is we took no money, we have no money and that all the money we worked so hard for has now been paid to the people who redeemed early. That's two hundred million! The bank took three hundred million and now the liquidators will take anywhere from ten to twenty million, depending on how they end up. It looks like we and the investors have nothing." Dale then slumped in his chair, exhausted from his thoughts.

WHERE IS THE MONEY?

CHAPTER 58
DATE AUGUST 2006
SCENE Quebec Provincial Court –
Montreal

Brock

While litigation had run rampant for over six years and legal bills had risen to astronomical levels for virtually all parties, Weinberg, who insisted that Bill Brock be removed from the case against him, would now get his day in court. The press had trumpeted the accusations of Ron's attorneys. The witnesses were diverse, 19 in all, and many of the faces went back to the very beginning of the Cinar story: Robert Vineberg, the senior partner of the firm Davies Ward Phillips & Vineberg (now being enjoined to stop its unparalleled billing cycle); Pierre Lessard, chairman of Métro grocery; and Raymond McManus, chairman of the Laurentian Bank. In addition to Lessard and McManus, others subpoenaed included Henry Rosenhek, associate at Ernst & Young, and Laurence Yelin, associate at Fasken Martineau DuMoulin. The list was auspicious in the number of people on it, their power and their net worth. Also on the list were Lino and Mario, one vanquished, the other trying to get restarted anonymously in life.

For six days, Weinberg's attorney, Pierre Fournier (after subpoenaing this star-studded cast of witnesses), would bumble his way through his case. Fournier and his daughter had carefully crafted the firestorm for Brock, but no one knew if he could deliver the death blow to the man who had plunged the sword into so many others.

Brock had brilliantly guided the demise of Weinberg, Charest, Panju, Matteo, Xanthoudakis, Muir, Daviault, Henry, Pettinicchio and Klein, and was behind the destruction of Globe-X, Norshield, Mount Real, Honeybee and over 12 other entities that operated in their orbit. From the time he had entered the scene, between Cinar, Norshield and Mount Real alone, over $1.8 billion in market value or investment dollars had been destroyed. The CCE had become an unprecedented litigation and business-destruction machine. Run by three lawyers, Wes Voorheis, Norm Inkster (former head of the RCMP) and David Drinkwater (former securities regulator and now chief legal officer for Nortel), they had taken their original funding budget of $5 million and spent $14 million by the time the trial would begin. On the swelling of the budget, Voorheis would explain, "I haven't had trouble getting additional funding; every request has been met with the unanimous approval of the governing committee. We've now been authorized in excess of $15 million." Amazingly, they had recovered almost nothing and spent the money on attorney fees, accounting fees, private eyes and lavish expenses.

The courtroom was now Fournier's; it was his time to bring the case. The judge was Justice Brian Riordan, who was extremely smart and very capable of following the complicated and convoluted truths and half-truths that would be paraded before him. With Jacques Rossignol, one of the most reputable criminal attorneys in Quebec on hand to defend Panju, with Maitre Langlois as Brock's senior defender, and with all the other "seniors" and "juniors" on hand, there would never be fewer than seven attorneys in the court at any one time.

"Your Lordship," Fournier would offer, "while I apologize for the alleged aggressiveness of my charges, I firmly believe that Davies Ward Phillips & Vineberg as a law firm and Mr. Brock should not be allowed to continue their service in pursuit of my client." He would enumerate the reasons, including conflict of interest, improperly passing confidential information, and serving in too many roles on the file. He would explain at length the rationale and concern. Judge Riordan's attention seemed to peak at several points — points that Fournier himself didn't seem to view as his most compelling arguments.

This clever judge had figured out that one very important question at hand was, "Who was really Brock's client?" Over the previous six years, he had worked for many masters, but most strangely because of the odd structure of the CCE, he had actually been working on his own file, for his own billing interests and racking up record fees in the process. Fournier suggested that the clients had been the audit committee, the board of Cinar, and then the CCE. Interestingly enough, not one defence attorney or plaintiff ever suggested that he was working in the interests of the shareholders, who directly or indirectly had been paying his bills along the way. What the judge realized is that there was a significant difference between working for an audit committee and working for a board, management or the shareholders. The audit committee members were the ones who had thrown out management and stopped the pillaging of Cinar, but they also had allowed the pillaging to go on for so long without taking any action at all. This subtle nuance would elude Fournier, Weinberg's lawyer, and Langlois, Brock's defender, but it didn't seem to elude the judge. The boys who had built the fire were the first to yell "fire, fire, fire," hoping everyone would look elsewhere for the arsonist. These most distinguished, rich, powerful gentlemen had avoided review, criticism, blame, derision or prosecution because they had chosen the right guy to keep the heat off of them. Bill Brock was their man.

Weinberg would choose to never enter the courtroom, despite the fact this should have been his day in court. All would wonder why, but speculation is just that . . . speculation. On the third day, a surprise hit the court as Fournier announced he would be releasing seven of his witnesses, including the very visible, powerful and neglectful Messrs. Lessard, McManus and Yelin from the audit committee. Amazingly, Fournier was not going to get testimony from the people who could help him the most, if only he knew what to ask them: "Were you afraid of your own liability for having driven the ship up on the rocks? Why did you allow Ron, Micheline and Panju to run roughshod over the companies? Why did you stand by as they drained millions from the company? Why did you not catch them in the Israeli deal, when they siphoned $52 million out of the business?"

These questions could never be asked because it was Fournier's position that his client hadn't done any of these things and so, of course, the board wasn't guilty of malfeasance. He would posit that his client hadn't authorized transfers to the Bahamas, knew nothing of special accounts at a brokerage firm and wouldn't have authorized improper activities. In fact, Fournier would suggest that the audit committee members were "mutineers and usurpers" who improperly grabbed authority and acted outside of the proper role of conduct, people who were out of line when they'd dismissed management and who had created anarchy at a time of crisis for the company. While Fournier himself couldn't degrade the "usurpers" with adequacy because of the preposterous position of his client, he baffled the court when he suddenly announced he would not be needing the testimony of these gentlemen.

On the fourth day of the trial, Bill Brock would appear in his own defence. He would emotionally contend how devastating it was to see his name in the newspapers with such dastardly accusations.

"My mother would call me and ask if it's true that I'm a discredit to my profession," he would offer on the witness stand. Aggressively, he would contend, "I am not in conflict, nor have I violated the confidences of my clients." When Brock was finished with his attorney's questions, Fournier was allowed to cross-examine. "No questions, Your Lordship," was his response. Amazingly, the clash of these two nemeses — in which lawyers hope to convene the most powerful and rich in order to bring forth the truth about one of business' greatest failures and attempt to defrock one of Canada's highest paid attorneys — was melting down like an early stage rocket on a failed launching pad.

Despite Weinberg's absence in court, Brock not being cross-examined and six key witnesses not being put on the stand, Justice Riordan was still astute enough to know that there were some key points to be adjudicated:

"Had Brock acted improperly in allowing the CCE to breach its financial limit of $5 million?" (They had spent $14 million, and he knew it.)

"Who was Brock's client?"

"Had Brock just worn too many hats for too long, and being the plaintiff's attorney against Weinberg was one too many?"

While Fournier would never summarize the case so simply, these issues remained. Even though the judge saw through the smoke, Brock would be exonerated and allowed to continue his pursuit of Weinberg.

CHAPTER 59

DATE OCTOBER 2006

SCENE PricewaterhouseCoopers –
Nassau, Bahamas

Darkness

For John, a lot of time had passed since there had been any good news, or even news he could pretend was good. It had become increasingly clear that the Ontario Securities Commission was ready to take enforcement action against John Xanthoudakis and Dale Smith, the Norshield CFO. The amount of correspondence and the tone of it had increased and heated up. RSM Richter had made it clear that a new report was imminent and that it would be very negative. They were intimating that their work indicated that Norshield had been in financial difficulties earlier than previously thought.

Most people around the crisis felt that Norshield was indeed in trouble somewhere between January and March

2005, with redemptions rising and liquidity suffering. The first visible sign of problems was May 2005 when redemptions were frozen. A few people would speculate that the company was in trouble as early as November 2004, but Richter was now acting as if they thought the troubles could go back to 2003. They were indicating that the "in kind" transfer of indebtedness into Olympus Univest in 2002 and 2003 had caused Richter to conclude the funds' values may have been misstated and the net asset-values (NAVs) improperly calculated. The assets involved in these transfers were not being regarded three years later as being very valuable by the receivers and so a fundamental problem had developed between the deposed executives and the people at Richter.

Then a report surfaced the first of October that the liquidators of Globe-X, Clifford Johnson, Wayne Aranha and PricewaterhouseCoopers Bahamas, had resigned from the Globe-X accounts. This report was quickly followed by a report that the Bahamian Board of Accountancy, who had ruled a year earlier that the liquidators had violated their professional rules, was ready to hear from the Disciplinary Committee. The rumors were that the committee was ready to take strong action against the pair and the firm. The actions could include revocation of licences, suspension of licences, an order to return fees (amounting to millions of dollars), a recommendation that their work not be admissible in court and other actions.

When Bill Brock picked up his phone, Clifford Johnson was on the other end and he was yelling.

"Stay calm," Brock responded. "Maybe we can get our friend the Judge to realize how bad he'll look if this

disciplinary board has their way."

"Bill, this could ruin me. This is a small island and I'll never get through this if they sanction me. What could Judge Lyons do?"

"We'll ask for a restraining order against the Board of Accountancy. We'll actually ask them to not allow the committee to meet and not allow them to discuss your case amongst themselves."

"Is that even possible, Bill? Do you think the Judge would actually issue an order keeping a disciplinary board from even meeting?" Clifford's voice was calming because maybe it would work.

"Clifford, I'll get back to you. Stay calm." Brock hung up.

To any rational third party, the idea that Judge Lyons would grant a restraining order against the Bahamian Board of Accountancy seemed impossible, but this was the Bahamas and this judge had a reputation to protect. It didn't take two days before the order was written. The disciplinary sanctions would remain in abeyance.

To the watchful eyes, like mine, that were looking for recovery possibilities, the PWC opportunity was too good to be true. If a disciplinary board said Pricewaterhouse-Coopers had acted improperly in their concerted effort to destroy Norshield, there could be some big, deep liability pockets ready to open up. John had hired attorney Alain Gutkin, after Robert Torralbo. I immediately told John that his attorney should move now with the Richter people to let them know that if they report that Norshield was in a financial crisis pre–November 2004 or January 2005, the ability to recover funds from Cinar would be greatly diminished. With deliberate speed, Alain Gutkin called the RSM Richter attorney. Without a second of hesitation the Richter attorney picked up on the theme and said he'd call his client.

I called David Brown. He and his brother Michael had been there in the early days when we were trying to save Norshield. In only a couple of days David Brown and I would meet in New York with attorneys on a $350 million recovery claim against the nation's largest bank. Now, suddenly, there might be a new suit against one of the world's largest accounting firms. Out of the deepest dark can come the dawn, and 2005 had been a long, dark night for John Xanthoudakis.

CHAPTER 60

DATE OCTOBER 2006

SCENE Urseth's Office –
Montreal

Am I Somehow
Off Track?

Even if you're expecting bad news and you think you're prepared for it, the cold, black letters on the stark white sheet with the letterhead of a regulatory body can frighten the most hardened. I'd waited for four days, knowing that the shoe was going to drop, but who would kick it off first . . . the OSC or the Receivers? The Receivers had a filing deadline for their report and the OSC seemed to have a newfound desire to make headlines.

The notice would come from the Office of the Secretary of the Ontario Securities Commission. The 15 pages would allege that John and his management team kept inadequate books and records, filed a misleading/untruthful offering memorandum, improperly calculated the net asset-value (NAV) of the funds, misled and misinformed staff and had failed to deal fairly, honestly and in good faith with investors. The words were cold and indicting. I cringed at the thought that I had worked so long with people who were now alleged to be so bad.

When you take a step back from the fray and look carefully at the people around you, one must always determine or redetermine if these people are who you thought them to be. "Have I myself somehow wandered off track and surrounded myself with the wrong team? Have I grabbed the wrong colored jersey and put on the wrong hat?" How many people have been forced to this moment of doubt or reassessment, when suddenly reality demands a recount and the status quo is not the acceptable measure? I had worked with the amoral before and I was convinced I could see that quality. I had dealt with greed and knew that over the long haul it's always discernible, it always appears. I had seen naivete, short tempers, laziness and obsession, but none of these qualities seemed to be at play here. How could what seemed like such good people end up in such a bad situation?

When I took John through the OSC breakdown and the document, listing the history, the allegations, the potential penalties and the public relations reality, there was palpable silence on the phone line and only occasional acknowledgement. At the end of the half-hour conversation, a somewhat recovered John Xanthoudakis said, "It's simply not true. I've spent only one hour and twenty minutes with their investigators in the last year and a half. They haven't done an investigation!"

"They're also using Richter's information, John," I said.

"What they're saying simply isn't true. I have to fight it," John countered.

"Tomorrow I'm going to New York with David Brown to meet with the lawyers on the recovery suit. I'll keep you posted on the meetings, but there is one more thing you need to understand at this point."

"What's that?" John asked.

"Given the developments of today, there is no reason left to not have you be a defendant in the recovery suit. It will strengthen the suit for the investors. Do you understand?" I asked.

"Yes, I understand. Hopefully, it will help the investors," said the quiet voice on the other end of the line.

Sitting at the table high in the New York skyline was me, David Brown and three senior partners in the law firm of Zwerling, Schachter & Zwerling. The three of them were some of the United States' most successful plaintiff attorneys, sharp legal minds who had taken on some of the nation's biggest and strongest corporations and banks and beat them into billions of dollars of court actions and settlements.

Clearly and simply, Brown would lay out the case to his colleagues of the New York Bar. With a low confident voice and Eastside accent, he sat in a black suit with wide silver pinstripes. His 66-year-old body could still bench press 300 pounds and his powerful biceps could still curl 220. His audience knew that this Rutgers grad and fast climber was recruited into the Kravath Swaine & Moore firm in his early twenties; by 40 he would be General Counsel for City Investing, the multi-billion-dollar conglomerate. Then he would become the Chairman of General Development Corporation, Florida's largest developer.

"This case is pretty straightforward," Brown began.

"It was actually Bill Urseth here who developed it. I wish I could say it was me. Norshield was one of Canada's largest hedge funds, about a billion dollars in assets, when they went down in June of 2005. Everyone involved was severely damaged. The employees were all out, the investors lost everything, the brokers who sold the product lost their clients . . . everyone lost except for the Royal Bank of Canada. Somehow they came out whole. Now, Bill has been on this file in various ways for seven years and he still has the faith and confidence of those closest to it. He listens and begins to realize that the relationship between Norshield and RBC wasn't just a traditional lender/borrower relationship. It was very different and, in fact, RBC was in nominal control of Norshield. First of all, the contracts between the money managers and the managed funds weren't between Norshield and money managers as you would expect. They were between RBC and the money managers. Next, the decisions on investments weren't in the control of Norshield, but rather in the control of RBC. The fee flow also went primarily to RBC, which over the period of five years made fees of over $60 million, while Norshield's fees were only $20 million. To complicate things even more, RBC approved the product for sale by its sales force and sold the product. The prospectus never revealed, in any way, RBC's role in the structure.

"Starting in 1999 a lending relationship began where RBC loaned Norshield $12 million. Over the next six years, the amount would grow to $350 million on the basis of a second 'option agreement.' In fact, when someone did business with Norshield they were actually doing business with RBC without knowing it. Investors also didn't know that RBC had a $350 million secured loan against virtually

AM I SOMEHOW OFF TRACK?

all the liquid assets of Norshield and its funds, and that, in fact, they could seize the liquid assets, which they did in June 2005; thus, all the other structures would collapse, leaving everyone else penniless. RBC lent the money, had control of the operations and actually even had their retail division selling the offerings, without revealing it to anyone." Brown was interrupted by Jeffrey Zwerling.

"So, they acted in preference by taking all their money and leaving the others with nothing."

Zwerling was then interrupted by Robin Zwerling, "And because of the fact they were, in fact, running the business themselves there was equitable subordination required."

"Exactly," Brown smiled.

"Why would they fall into such a trap?" Zwerling asked.

At that point, I spoke up. "The Canadian laws on hedge funds and alternative investments are what caused such a convoluted scheme. With this structure they could be in the business and not be in the business. Most importantly they were by legal definition in 'control' of Mosaic and Olympus Univest."

The meeting went on for two hours as we exchanged ideas, legal points and strategies. I also backgrounded them on the complicated Cinar/Norshield history. As the meeting was coming to a close, the Ontario Securities Commission document came on the table and everyone reviewed it.

"So, as you can see," Brown began, "the OSC is saying that John hasn't done anything wrong." Everyone nodded. But I was dumbfounded. The document clearly said that he had kept inadequate books and records; filed a misleading, untruthful offering memorandum;

improperly calculated the net asset-values of the funds; misled and misinformed OSC staff; and failed to deal fairly, honestly and in good faith with investors. I wanted to say out loud, "What are you talking about?!" but I held back for the moment and let them talk.

Zwerling said, "Yeah, I see that. So they must not have much. He hasn't stolen money." Brown shook his head, indicating no. "He hasn't shipped money off to relatives or partners, he hasn't run away." Again Brown indicated no.

"These are charges that could be made against anyone who has ever done an offering and then been investigated by the regulators." Suddenly, I realized how these cold professionals viewed everything so differently from myself, much less the newspaper reading public. They had read all these charges and concluded that even though they meant John's financial life was over and he would face reprimands, restrictions and fines, "he had not done anything wrong."

CHAPTER   61

DATE   OCTOBER 2006

SCENE   JFK Airport –
          New York

Hopes

The call would come in as I was waiting for my flight back to Montreal at JFK airport. Gate 31 is a crowded departure gate for short flights out of Kennedy. The call was from John Xanthoudakis.

"How did things go?" he asked.

"Very well. They really believe we have a strong case for recovery and want to work on it."

"The story broke today in the French press."

"Yeah, I expected it would. The press breakdowns are waiting for me," I said.

"Gutkin told me this morning he has an Ontario attorney who will work with me."

The words struck me as déjà vu. "John, stop, just stop.

You need to realize where you really are. You can't beat these allegations; you can't even afford to defend yourself against them."

"What do you mean?" he asked.

"John, when you get a fee proposal from this attorney, you'll realize what I mean. They'll ask for $50,000 up front and then it won't be a retainer as you think of it, it will be a deposit. They'll expect you to keep the payments up as fees are incurred. He's also from Ontario. You're a visible case in another province and that makes you a potential collection problem. What's worse yet is that you will spend the money and lose anyway."

I glanced around Gate 31. This was not the place to have this conversation as a half dozen people were within earshot and quite fascinated by such a dire prognosis.

"You need perspective, John. Yesterday I sat in a room full of legal talent and when they reviewed the osc document, they unanimously concluded that the osc thinks you've done nothing wrong."

"What are you talking about? They've charged me with things that are horrendous!" John shouted.

"That's my point. To you they're horrendous, but to the cold, cynical eyes of those attorneys, you've done nothing wrong. Think about what the fifteen pages don't say. They don't say you took money for your own benefit, they don't say you sent money to a friend, partner or girl-friend. They don't say you left the country or can't be found. There is no prosecutor, John, no criminal charges. What this means is that you won't be able to serve as an officer or board member of a public company. You will be reprimanded and have to pay a fine. These people want headlines, not blood. They want the world to know that they'll get the bad guys. That's what they want . . .

headlines and champagne. Do you remember when Ron and Micheline agreed to their settlement? A million dollar fine, no boards for five years, no admission to any wrongdoing. Do you know how much of the million they've paid? Almost none of it."

"How do you know that?"

"I keep track of it," I said. "These regulatory bodies are better at handing out fines than they are at collecting them."

"But I can't let my reputation be destroyed like this," John insisted.

"John, your reputation *is* destroyed, and soon you'll be bankrupt as well. What you need to understand is that you can't defend yourself; you can't afford it. If you really have the ten million that your wife thinks you have hidden away somewhere, then go at it. If you don't, you need to figure out how you make a deal for yourself that admits no wrongdoing, accepts sanctions and agrees to a fine. I'm sorry to be the one to tell you this."

"You should be," said the large black lady who had been eavesdropping.

The reality of the situation was very hard for John or anyone to accept. The writing on the wall said, "Accept the destruction of your reputation, and realize there is no return to the business you know; allow the world and the life you've known to be gone forever."

"Bill?"

"Yeah?"

"How do I live? What allows me to come back?"

"Epiphany," was the response.

"What?"

"Epiphany, like Saul on the road becomes Paul. Like Chuck Colson, John Dean, Michael Milken. Some blame liquor; others blame bad marriages; some find God. They virtually all have to move and start new lives in new places. There is nothing new here. I've been saying this for a year and a half, but it's just that you're finally closer to the bottom and now you're more ready to hear it. Epiphany, John, epiphany." The conversation was over.

There was comfort for me in the fact that I really believed John didn't have a stash, that he still had the emotional strength to take the harsh reality offered and not crumble. As the plane left New York and headed north, I realized that I had chosen the right team; the jersey fit and while those who read the newspapers may not realize it, the best chance investors had of recovery was coming from my team and not from the sincere blue suits of the banker, the slick Italian suits of the CCE, the frumpy, ill-fitting outfits of the receivers or the off-the-rack three-piece suits of the regulators. After ten minutes in the air, I fell asleep.

CHAPTER 62

DATE NOVEMBER 2006

SCENE Toronto

Do I Regret It?

When the story first broke, many people found the actions of the Voorheis cabal to be heavy-handed. They had arranged to use subterfuge in order to serve a subpoena on Nassau banker Michael Morris. Morris was in Toronto visiting relatives and he was approached by a woman who said she wanted to talk about financing for a client in the packaging business. In fact, it was a sting. A process server showed up at the Starbucks where the meeting was to take place. The bailiff served Morris with a subpoena intended to pull him into the litigation against Ron Weinberg, in the CCE's continued effort to grind Weinberg into the ground and grab whatever money possible for their recovery effort.

Morris, who as a Bahamian banker is used to confidentiality protection as it concerns bank business, was angry and chagrined. While he was vaguely aware of Weinberg and the Cinar affair, being pulled into it had been something he strove to avoid. So off Morris went to Quebec Superior Court with his story.

"I was approached by a woman who identified herself as Ginette Brown of the firm F.G. Brown Hide and Associates. She wanted to meet regarding financing for their packaging business because they were involved in an acquisition. I agreed to meet her on November 28, 2006, when I would be in Toronto. We agreed to meet at Starbucks because Ms. Brown said it would be convenient for her. As I was waiting for Ms. Brown, and at the time we agreed to meet, I was approached by a bailiff server and issued a subpoena. The bailiff literally apologized to me for the subterfuge." Ms. Brown would never reveal herself and the firm of F.G. Brown Hide and Associates would prove to be fictional.

That Bill Brock and Wes Voorheis would get caught in this little prank wouldn't be amusing for either of the boys. Brock's position, despite the judge's reprimand and stinging criticism of the tactic, was simply, "We regret the judge's conclusion." He went on to explain that it was important to get Mr. Morris to testify about Weinberg's offshore transactions. "The judge's decision deals only with the manner in which the subpoena was served. It does not affect our right to examine Mr. Morris," he answered.

When challenged by reporter Bertrand Marrotte of the *Globe and Mail* about his antics, CCE chairman Wes Voorheis said, "Do I regret it? I do. Would I do it again? I wouldn't."

The CCE was in its third year of operation; from the time it was created, its task and charter had been to use the $5 million budget taken from the shareholder proceeds and recover money for Cinar. Recover it from wherever they could get it — Weinberg, Charest, Panju, Globe-X, Daviault, Muir, Norshield, John Xanthoudakis, Mount Real, Lino Matteo, RBC, Merrill Lynch or Barrington Bank — any pocket that had walked too close to Cinar. At this stage, the CCE had spent the $5 million they were budgeted and had blasted through $9 million more, totaling over $14 million in fees. Voorheis would summarize his functions simply: "The mandate was to investigate the culpable. In the process we've run across various issues. I've stuck to the mandate. We've been expensive and thorough. I've talked with all the key players along the line." The unguided fee missile had a momentum all its own.

Of the CCE's targets, Weinberg was financially crippled and was severely diminished in his court battles, Charest was dead, Panju had spent six years living reclusively in London, Globe-X was bankrupt, Daviault hadn't worked in seven years and Muir had been forced to leave the Bahamas and live a quiet life in rural Ontario. Further, Norshield was in receivership, John Xanthoudakis had been physically beaten, mentally abused and hadn't worked in a year and a half. Mount Real was bankrupt and put out of business. Lino had been crushed and humiliated by the collapse, and he was unemployable in his beloved city. In the process, Cinar shareholders had lost over $1 *billion* in market capitalization, Norshield investors had lost $700 million in savings and investments, Mount Real shareholders had lost over $100 million in market value and investors in commercial paper issued by Mount Real affiliates had lost over $130 million in savings and investments. None of the parties involved — Weinberg, Charest, Panju, Xanthoudakis, Matteo, Daviault or Muir — were either charged or convicted of any crime or wrongful action. No member of any of the boards of directors of Cinar, Norshield, Mount Real or its affiliates was charged or convicted of any crime or wrongdoing.

The CCE had paid money to law firms in over seven cities and accounting firms in multiple nations in its attempt to collect what it could collect and destroy what it could destroy.

Wes Voorheis said, "We have law firms working for us in New York, the Bahamas, Montreal, Philadelphia, Toronto, London and Anguilla. That's seven locales in all. In some cities there are multiple firms."

The collections would prove negligible after the initial $86 million repaid willingly by Globe-X prior to being forced into receivership; virtually nothing else of substance would be recovered.

The CCE would get stories into the newspapers that led to character assassination, public shame and investor panic, and ultimately to several businesses being so badly beaten they could not recover. Voorheis would explain: "I believe that the press figured out who the good guys are, so they supported our point of view." These "good guys" created suits in courts throughout the world that lined the pockets of possibly hundreds of attorneys, but never recovered money for the real victims of Cinar's scandals: the shareholders. Most important of all, the CCE would continue to deflect blame for Cinar's woes, begun in the year 2000, from the blue-ribbon board of directors of Cinar. These were the people who allowed their company to be

ransacked and run amok while they accepted congratulations and stipends for their "fine work." Where were these captains of industry, the professionals and the government when the robbery took place?

Wes Voorheis commented on the CCE's "success": "All our results are positive to date. We've won every battle, every conflict, virtually all of them. We haven't collected much money and we all wish we could have returned significant funds to the shareholders, but justice is slow. Justice is expensive and slow.

"The problem I've got now is after all the victories, when I get my victory against Weinberg, can I collect on the judgment? The victory will cost millions, but it doesn't mean we'll collect the money." Finally in February 2008 the CCE would settle out of court with Weinberg on the eve of the trial. All the witnesses had been prepped and the law firm had huge billings earned from the pretrial work. The amount of the settlement was not revealed and remains a well-guarded secret. The photo of Ron Weinberg at the announcement of the settlement is reminiscent of photos of lottery winners used in publicity campaigns. It's not likely the CCE recovered much from Weinberg.

After a series of bizarre moves by Weinberg's team, Ernst & Young would see the lawsuits against them dismissed and their name allegedly cleared, despite years of watching over a corporate mugging.

- The Globe-X receivers, PricewaterhouseCoopers of Nassau, would be found by the Bahamas Institute of Chartered Accountants (BICA) to have violated confidentiality and having improperly taken the Globe-X file in the first place. PWC would manage to suppress the determination and outcome for years after the decision.

- **Bill Brock** would become one of the highest billing attorneys in Canada and though he was emotionally hurt by the Weinberg court accusations, he would prevail and continue his battle with cancer.

- **Wes Voorheis** would attempt to get even more funding for the CCE litigation machine. Riding such a powerful quasi-governmental steed roughshod was far too intoxicating a gig to give up under any circumstances. In January 2007 he would become the CEO of the besieged Hollinger Inc., the company Conrad Black ransacked.

- **Michael Hirsch**, the new owner of the Cinar assets, knew that at some point his new entity, Cookie Jar, would need to distance itself from the old scandal-ridden Cinar, but hoped to enjoy some of the fruits of this long, destructive campaign he had largely financed. Since he intended to take the company public, his attention was now turning to positive news rather than the dark veil of Cinar.

- **Nick Assimakopoulos** had worked hard all his life. Born in Greece he immigrated to Canada where he worked long hours and built a small fortune. He had assembled enough money to move back to Greece and live the life he dreamed of. Nick would choose to put about $400,000 into various Mount Real and Norshield investment products, high-yield notes paying nine and a quarter to nine and a half percent interest annually, the kind of return that would allow him to live comfortably in Greece, off the interest. When the collapses took place, Nick was forced to move back to Canada and work in his brother's clothing business. Now separated from his wife by distance, and without his life savings, Nick could no longer travel, entertain or dine out. At 60, his world was not getting better and he recognized the life he was missing. It was only because of a generous gift from his children that he could get back to Greece for the holidays to be reunited with his wife.

- **Nick Mylonakis** had worked hard all his life to be a good provider and family man. He would become an investment broker, pass his insurance licence exam and become a successful agent. Nick would move closer and closer to the Mount Real orbit and do some joint ventures with Matteo and Mount Real. The year 2005 had been a turnaround year for Nick's operations, and his business became profitable. When the collapse took place, he struggled to survive in the post-seizure era, then broke his foot in an accident and lost everything. Nick would work the next year in a convenience store.

- **Rick Bruni** had worked with Norshield, Norshield financial advisers and iForum, a financial services company that was publicly traded and prospering in 2005, when it was named for the first time to the *Profit 100* list as one of the country's fastest growing companies. Over the years Rick had sold some Norshield investments and some Mount Real investments, always believing in the products and the businesses. When the collapse took place, Rick would first see the value of his clients' Norshield investments evaporate and then six months later the Mount Real investments would also be lost. He would subsequently lose clients, income, switch firms and then almost lose his wife and family.

- **Joe Pettinicchio** was the president of both Mount Real and iForum. An affable, well-spoken guy, he was very comfortable on the golf course and smooth in sales settings. As did all of Lino's associates, he yielded to Lino in virtually all circumstances and was as genuinely surprised as anyone about the condition of the businesses as depicted by Raymond Chabot Grant Thornton, the receivers. He worked vigorously to the day of the seizure to get iForum sold and separated. Despite suggestions that he had "cut and run" from Mount Real in the fall of 2005, Pettinicchio remained loyal and didn't resign until literally the last minute. Joe would be unemployable for the next several years.

- **Bill Marston** put more investors into the Mount Real affiliate paper than any other single person ($19 million). For years he was a noted and successful investment adviser, building a strong client base, largely on the West Island of Montreal. When the collapse came he would be reprimanded by the IDA and Quebec's AMF; his licence was suspended and numerous newspaper articles would implicate Marston as a major sales agent. Numerous client lawsuits pursued Marston. He and his wife would eventually separate as a side effect of the pressure. At 60, Marston doubts he will ever recover from the debacle, but he's trying.

- **Frank Iacono** was a visible and successful investment adviser who by 1996 had become a devotee of Mount Real and actively sold Mount Real and Norshield investment products, selling strongly on a friend-and-relative referral basis. The

proud Sicilian would work hard for and did well by his clients until the collapse. Stung by the circumstances, he would suffer a minor depression, but struggle through the mess, trying to find a new perch to fly from. While his family has survived the dark years, he doubts he'll ever be the same.

- **Bob LaFlamme** was the chairman of the Mount Real board for six years and president of InvestPro Securities, a regional investment firm in Eastern Canada. LaFlamme, a French Canadian with a quick smile and flashing eyes, genuinely liked people, and people genuinely liked him. Never a detail man, Bob took Mount Real and its structures, financing and business at face value and believed in Lino and the company up to the time of the seizures. After the seizures, Bob was derided in his own firm for not having perceived the "scam," as the newspapers had depicted it, and his role in InvestPro was diminished. Bob would be forced to testify in several hearings regarding the businesses' demise. He would die in his sleep on Saturday, December 16, 2006, of a massive heart attack at age 66.

- **Peter Kafalas** was a successful trader in commodities and derivatives his entire career. He was a cornerstone of Norshield's trading operations and as a successful senior player he would become very wealthy and respected. Kafalas would leave Norshield about six months before the May 2005 collapse to work for RBC. In 2003, Peter was Chief Compliance Officer for Norshield, and post-collapse he would be queried by the Ontario Securities Commission. In his deposition he would ill-advisedly state that he served as chief compliance officer in title only and never performed in that role or function. He would be charged in civil proceedings in Ontario along with Dale Smith. Kafalas was relieved of his duties at RBC and would try to start over as a trader.

- **Dale Smith** served as Norshield's chief financial officer for seven years from 1998 forward. As a member of the team, he would help to develop deal structures, financings, investments and acquisitions that would help fuel the companies' growth and reputation. As the underpinnings of the Norshield Financial Group began to crumble, Smith would eventually be forced to take the lead in the process of freezing redemptions in May 2005. Subsequently, he would serve as a director of several public companies and try to rebuild his own life. When the Ontario Securities Commission's actions against him surfaced as civil proceedings, among their assertions were that "Smith would never again be allowed to serve as an officer or director of a public company," which set back his hoped-for recovery.

- **Jaime Lao** had been a model immigrant citizen. Coming from the Philippines to Canada, he sold insurance and investments, largely to the Asian community, and truly cared about his clients. He sold more and more of the Mount Real debentures and always put others in front of himself. After the collapse, he was able to sleep only when heavily medicated; he then returned to the Philippines to try to get well. Unable to abandon his clients in the post-collapse tragedy, he returned to Montreal to be included in the AMF actions against him and other brokers. He would then take a job at a Chinese

grocery store, stocking shelves for $5 an hour, plus lunch and dinner, explaining that "now my mother doesn't have to worry about feeding me."

CHAPTER   63
DATE   JANUARY 2007
SCENE   Montreal

No, You're
Wrong Again

The AMF's files were full of pending cases ranging from the multimillion dollar Norbourg mess to small infractions of a technical nature. Mount Real was probably the second most prominent of its cases, with Norbourg being number one. The Norshield matter was being handled by the Ontario Securities Commission, so the AMF in Quebec didn't need to put resources into it.

Rumors would circulate for several weeks before the AMF made anything official. At first, the scuttlebutt was that Revenue Canada was going to be taking action against the sales force of MRACS and RealVest, on the basis that their sales agents helped people hide and smuggle money out of the country. Eventually, the rumors would subside when the AMF actually took the steps to proceed with their action.

The actions would be broad and sweeping against 24 former brokers of MRACS and RealVest. These former iForum employees had been charged with over 600 counts of selling products without a prospectus and misleading their clients. The fines would range from $1,000 to $15,000 per count, and the newspapers were calculating that up to $4.2 million in penalties and fines would be the outcome. These would be the largest securities-related fines in the history of the country. (When Weinberg and Charest made their settlements in 2003, it was a $1 million fine, the largest securities-related fine ever dealt, and the largest fine ever in Quebec.)

Now the 24 agents were dealing with the side effects, which for many included not just the deep anger of their clients, but also the fact that most of their new employers would, by corporate policy, be forced to suspend them. Thus, many were looking at a huge fine by the government, legal costs, loss of employment and the probability of not going back into the career field of their choice. The newspapers would print the names of the agents being charged and broadcast journalists would relay the story as "24 brokers charged with criminal involvement in $130 million Mount Real debacle. Over 600 charges filed in Quebec Court with fines of $4.2 million." Their children, wives, husbands, parents, neighbors and clients would see the charges, read and hear the stories.

Oddly enough Lino wasn't charged with anything, nor was Joe Pettinicchio, or Laurence Henry, the MRACS president.

I was in Reno when the story about the AMF's charges

broke. After having the stories read to me via phone, I called Lino.

"Hello," the familiar deep voice came over the line.

"It's me. Have you got any thoughts?"

"I've always got thoughts," was Lino's enigmatic answer, "but not on the telephone."

We would meet several days later. "Are you okay?" I asked.

"Yeah, I'm fine. It was a tough week, but I'm fine." Lino looked softer now than he had in the high-flying days. His clothes were clean, but not well chosen; his hair somewhat longer, his beard not as well trimmed. He drove his own car now, which he rarely did in the prosperous times, or he took the Métro where he could sit anonymously among other working people, with whom he now identified. His life had come to the point where he was refereeing kids' soccer games and referring to himself as "retired." Looking directly at him, I asked, "Are you ready to leave town yet? To get out, to be less visible and try to start over?"

"I'm fine here. This whole thing with the brokers just goes to show they don't know what to do with me or what to charge me with. I haven't done anything wrong, so why would I leave?"

"To get a new start. You'll never be anything but damaged goods around here. Most of all, you continue to cling to the old days, not the future."

"I think the brokers are going to need my help."

"What are you talking about? The brokers are the ones who are going to cut deals, to reduce their own fines and liabilities in exchange for stories that will make you look like Sinbad. Those poor guys are going to be the way the AMF gets you. By the time it's done, there will be 24 people

NO, YOU'RE WRONG AGAIN

swearing to the fact that you deceived, misled and told half-truths to yourself and them."

"I still want to help the brokers. It's like today I was talking to one; they're all very afraid, eh? And I told him that I can approach this two different ways. I can either say that 'Those were good, properly filed offerings according to our lawyers, auditors and advisers,' or I can say 'Those were good, properly filed offerings according to our auditors and advisers, but I always told the brokers to never put more than ten percent of a client's portfolio into them.' They're both true statements, but one will help the brokers and one won't. Right now I want to help the brokers. If they turn on me, I won't."

In his calculating way Lino Matteo was trying to stay in control of a world that had spun out of his control. I shook my head. "Frankly, it seems to me that framing statements like that means you're more concerned with helping yourself than helping the brokers."

"Maybe, but I think I can help them and I'll try. They don't have a leader. Maybe I can be that leader."

"You should move to Fort McMurray where you can start over, no one knows you, there's lots of money, and many people have pasts. If we had all 24 of those sales guys here right now and you told them at the end of the meeting it's cold outside, button up your jacket before you leave, half the group would put on swimsuits! Most of those guys wouldn't piss on you if you were on fire!"

"No, you're wrong again. They wouldn't put on swimsuits, but they *would* blame me for the cold weather."

"Did you know that Voorheis was named the new CEO of Hollinger?" I asked.

"Yeah, I heard that. He really kicked my ass."

"You shouldn't have thrown him out that day."

"I didn't throw him out, he just left. But what still kills me is how he screwed up my processing. You know with processing I never would have fallen; it was the processing that killed me. Yeah, he really kicked our asses," Lino finished.

On the eve of the trial, with the CCE lawyers in high gear and busily preparing witnesses, another CCE legal team was deeply immersed in settlement negotiations with Weinberg's attorneys. Without a deal in place, but with the certainty of settlement looming, they would appear in court and let the judge know that a settlement was imminent and that they'd like to delay the proceedings. The trial team was disappointed after years of preparation on this $116 million suit.

When the settlement was made, there was a strict confidentiality surrounding the terms and the amounts. It appeared at the time that the numbers would never be revealed. Many would speculate on why, if the settlement was favorable to the CCE, they would want it to remain secret. At this point they had spent in excess of $2 million largely in legal fees to chase Weinberg, Panju, Xanthoudakis, Norshield, Mount Real, Matteo and group. Weinberg was the last best chance for meaningful recovery. When Weinberg's photo appeared in the newspaper at settlement time, he looked like a man who had won the Irish Sweepstakes; genuine joy surrounded his countenance. So, despite the confidentiality, intuitive observers like myself began to speculate that this was no victory for the CCE. Usually, rumors and leaks surface after a few weeks, but not in this case. My own guess was around $4 million because this would be an amount that Weinberg could pay with assets he no longer needed, like his Westmount and Magog homes that Cinar already attached. But no leaks bubbled to the surface.

Then, in an odd set of circumstances, everything would flood into public view because of some bad commercial paper of all things, the very thing that started this bizarre tale in the first place. Sure enough, Ron had sold his Westmount and Magog homes and paid the CCE's bailiff $3,388,000 as proceeds to fund the settlement in full. The funds were now "in trust" with the bailiff and would pass to the CCE on the settlement date. The bailiff had invested the funds in commercial papaer, which he claimed he had the right to do. The commercial paper had not gone sour and the CCE couldn't get their money on the closing date. They actually tried to get the court to make Ron pay it again, but that didn't fly, so they would now have to wait to receive their $3,388,000 and the secret of the settlement was out. The CCE had settled their $116 million lawsuit against Weinberg for $3,388,000 and could no longer chase and harass him . . . something they had done for eight long years and made a fortune doing. They will probably get their money someday, when the commercial paper mess is straightened out, but it's safe to say that the former Cinar shareholders will never receive a cent for the $5 million they invested in the creation of the CCE. Ironically, some of them were shareholders, note holders and debenture holders in Mount Real, Norshield and Olympus UniVest, which were some of the entities that went spiraling to their deaths.

Timeline

1997

- Cinar is a high-flying public company — "Disney of Canada"; Charest is one of Hollywood's most powerful women
- Cinar begins to transact business in the Bahamas with foreign exchange transactions

1998

- Cinar is flush with cash; begins to invest in Globe-X
- Charest and Weinberg continue to work out schemes to avoid taxes, use tax credits illegally, use corporate funds to finance private deals, a practice they'd used since the founding of the business

1999

- The amounts to Globe-X increase; large transfers take place
- The Killington Strategy is developed to get corporate funds into their own pockets
- The social scene sees the Weinberg/Charest duo as the toasts of the town
- Panju continues to develop schemes to enrich himself
- The Cinar board seems oblivious to all the shenanigans; then in October, the investigations begin regarding padding the officers' nests and falsified tax credit issues
- The Cinar Audit Committee begins to realize that they are in a mess
- As 1999 comes to a close, the scrutiny increases and the Cinar board begins to realize that their founders and CFO might be crooked

February 2000

- Globe-X hunkers down; affected parties include Bob Daviault, Tom Muir and fund manager John Xanthoudakis
- Weinberg and Panju pretend that $122 million is deposited offshore in a traditional account; they never reveal the fund is leveraged and *not* liquid
- Panju requests that the funds be liquidated and returned to Canada
- Globe-X management reminds him they're invested until at least November and they're leveraged
- The Audit Committee sends a group of lawyers, accountants and advisers to Nassau to meet with Globe-X managers, Panju and Weinberg. Once again, the Globe-X managers state the situation

March 2000

- Panju, Weinberg and Charest are fired
- Newspapers scream $122 million "missing"
- Simultaneously Bob Daviault (CFO) reveals to John Xanthoudakis (fund manager) and Tom Muir (president), that the Globe-X books are not up to date, audits are incomplete and that Cinar's redemption demands will break the fund
- John Xanthoudakis brings in Lino Matteo as adviser and consultant on these matters
- Cinar names new president, Barry Usher
- Collection efforts heat up in Bahamas Supreme Court
- Bill Brock of Goodman, Phillips & Vineberg heads the collection, intimidation and litigation efforts
- News stories are run daily on a national basis, the general theme "Where's the missing money?"
- Late March the court action stops due to a settlement
- The world is told "where" the money is: Globe-X
- Globe-X reaches high visibility
- Some funds are paid to Cinar, and the explanation of the investments begins
- PricewaterhouseCoopers (PWC) Bahamas become investigators along with Usher and Brock
- Throughout April and May, investigation and accounting of assets continues in Nassau
- Globe-X fights to rebuild records and books to avoid the appearance of being half-assed
- Matteo assists in the recast

May 2000

- Cinar has been cease traded, delisted and is unable to file financial statements

June 2000

- Serious talks take place regarding buying out the Cinar position; more funds are paid to Cinar
- Government authorities move against Weinberg, Charest, Panju and Cinar

October 2000

- A payment schedule for retirement of Cinar debt is agreed upon

Spring 2001

- Globe-X defaults on payments and PWC begins to pursue liquidation
- Tom Muir and Bob Daviault begin to have a falling out, leading to Bob's departure
- Weinberg and Charest contest their accusations with Quebec Securities Commission (QSC) and the federal government
- Panju moves to England
- John Xanthoudakis tries to distance himself publicly from the problem, and reorganize hedge funds away from the Globe-X brand
- Cinar has now recovered $86 million of its $108 million invested, but continues to claim it is owed over $40 million

Summer 2001

- Bob Daviault vanishes to Canada
- Barry Usher departs Cinar and is replaced by Stuart Snyder
- Tom Muir sells Globe-X entities to Lowell Holden, a workout specialist in the U.S.
- PWC puts Globe-X in Bahamian Bankruptcy Court

and becomes the liquidator of Globe-X Canadiana and Globe-X Management

- Lawsuits are filed: Cinar vs. Norshield (Quebec), Norshield vs. Cinar (Quebec), Cinar vs. Mosaic (New York)
- Norshield makes Univest the primary hedge fund brand
- Norshield acquires First Horizon (Bank of Barbados)
- Norshield begins to attract large amounts of cash and new accounts in post-9/11 world
- Norshield/Mosaic expands on borrowings from Royal Bank of Canada (RBC)
- Total Return swap is executed, which moves Globe-X assets into Mosaic Composite
- Commax and Globe-X funds are largely converted into Balanced Return Fund and Univest
- Cinar decides to *not* return to operating company or public company status
- Cinar is on the block
- Cinar settles class action suit

November 2003

- Norshield is thriving, attracting new money and accounts, announces new products and develops new structure; returns on fund are good

March 2004

- Serious settlement talks between Cinar and Lowell Holden to end the conflict break down at 11th hour, prior to sale of business to Cookie Jar; part of breakdown is that Panju rescinds participation. Weinberg, Holden, Xanthoudakis are stunned

- QSC imposes $1 million fine on Weinberg and Charest (largest ever securities-related fine in Quebec)
- As part of Cookie Jar purchase, $5 million is set aside to pursue collection against Norshield et al.; funds are to be used for legal proceedings, accountants, public relations and private investigators, resulting in more funds for PWC Bahamas, Wes Voorheis, Inkster, Heenan Blaikie and many others
- Cinar purchase was financed by Toronto Dominion, who are Michael Hirsch's bankers

May 2004

- Norshield reveals the new Olympus UniVest fund. This fund has a special structure that includes Mosaic and guarantees underlying net asset value, liquidity, responsibility for leverage, cash reserves, foreign exchange, risk and settlement risk
- Mosaic is structured with large amount of RBC debt (up to $360 million), which is not specifically revealed to Olympus Univest investors, and the Mosaic balance sheet is strengthened with private assets of John Xanthoudakis and Tom Muir, including $150 million from BICE and $93 million from First Horizon (Bank of Barbados). The fund would be well received for its perceived performance, strength and ingenuity; its liquidity risks were not understood in the market, but were understood by RBC, the financier

July 2004

- PWC Bahamas would release a report claiming close links previously denied between Weinberg, Charest,

Panju and John Xanthoudakis, and claiming Norshield was involved in Cinar's Globe-X investments. The report accuses Globe-X and John Xanthoudakis of diverting assets away from them to the benefit of other investors
- Micheline Charest dies on the operating table while undergoing extensive plastic surgery
- CCE makes highlighted reports available to local and national press

August-September 2004
- Reports circulate about Norshield's role in Cinar situation
- Redemptions begin to exceed subscriptions

September 2004
- Francis Vailles of *La Presse* begins in-depth study of Mount Real business at urging of CCE
- Norshield/Olympus Univest is being starved out; executives bailing out, pipeline drying up

October 2004
- *La Presse* prints unfavorable story about Mount Real by Francis Vailles

Fall 2004
- Redemptions continue
- RBC loans are used to pay redemptions more than to reinvest in hedge funds

January 2005
- Bob Daviault deposition released by CCE; national and local press follows

April 2005
- Francis Vailles attends Mount Real annual meeting with photographer who is thrown out of meeting; nasty story follows

May 2005
- Norshield is forced to cease redemptions and monitor is named (RSM Richter)
- Wes Voorheis tells people Mount Real is his new target
- Lino Matteo throws CCE head Wes Voorheis out of his office

June 2005
- AMF announces investigation of Mount Real
- RSM Richter named receiver for Norshield entities

July 2005
- Royal Bank of Canada calls loans made to Norshield Financial Group et al.
- Redemptions of MRACS and RealVest notes accelerate and interest payments begin to fall behind
- MRACS and RealVest try to prepare brokers for a deferred interest period

September 2005
- MRACS and RealVest brokers try to keep clients calm
- Bob Daviault's second CCE deposition takes place
- Norshield offices close and public auction takes place

November 2005
- AMF raids Mount Real and affiliated offices, closing down all operations

- Richter reports finding only $8.8 million of Norshield assets out of $430 million invested
- John Xanthoudakis is assaulted by organized crime figures at his lawyer's office in Place Ville-Marie, downtown Montreal

December 2005
- André Allard begins effort to file a proposal in the bankruptcy court to bring Mount Real under protection and repay investors
- Strong opposition to the proposal surfaces from AMF and Raymond Chabot Grant Thornton (RCGT) to any proposal
- Local newspapers oppose proposal concept
- John Xanthoudakis begins in-depth interview with Bert Marotte of the *Globe and Mail*
- John continues to live with threats against his life, and is then tricked into a second encounter with assailants
- David Edwards, an American businessman, puts forward a reorganization proposal for Mount Real

January 2006
- The *Globe and Mail* prints an interview with John Xanthoudakis, stating much more than $8.8 million will be found
- The AMF, RCGT and local press besmirch David Edwards and Lowell Holden in their efforts to reorganize Mount Real and repay investors
- Judge Mongeau is forced out of Mount Real case

February 2006
- After numerous court sessions, David Edwards

withdraws proposal
- Three brokers have licences pulled and sanctions placed on them
- RSM Richter makes presentation to investors that "they stand by previous report," but now claim they've found $36 million, not $8.8 million; they never mention the $82 million guaranteed and reserved for by Industrial Alliance, nor a strategy for recovering Multi-Strat funds or from third parties

March 2006
- André Allard severely scolded in court by Judge Lalonde
- Mount Real placed in bankruptcy

January 2007
- Wes Voorheis becomes president of Hollinger, Conrad Black's former company

July 2007
- The OSC continues to bring charges against John Xanthoudakis and Dale Smith for the way they ran Norshield

August 2007
- Bill Brock wins decisively in court against Weinberg's suits and charges

February 2008
- The CCE and Weinberg settle their lawsuit out of court on a confidential basis, but Weinberg is pictured looking like he won the lottery

March 2008

- The Chartered Management Accountants find Lino and Paul D'Andrea to have engaged in fraud and place sanctions against them both

April 2008

- The terms of the settlement come gushing into public view because Weinberg pays $3.4 million to the CCE's bailiff who invests it in commercial paper that goes bad; so, the CCE doesn't get any money
- The AMF methodically continues to pursue the 24 sales agents that sold Mount Real commercial paper, bringing them to trial one at a time

Key Players

André Allard – Montreal bankruptcy trustee

In November 2005, Allard would begin an effort to become the receiver of the Mount Real business in liquidation. He would spearhead this effort through a proposal to bring the company out of bankruptcy and revive the business. His efforts were in concert with Lowell Holden and David Edwards, Minnesota and Washington State businessmen respectively. Allard's efforts would eventually fail and he would be severely reprimanded by Judge Lalonde.

Basil Angelopoulos – Montreal attorney

He represented Globe-X in its efforts to stabilize itself

and recover from the Cinar redemption demand. Basil and Bill Brock were former colleagues and friends, so it helped bring some civility back to a tense situation.

Wayne J. Aranha – PricewaterhouseCoopers, chartered accountant
He was named one of the Globe-X liquidators with Clifford Johnson.

Bill Brock – Litigation attorney at Goodman, Phillips & Vineberg
He arrived in Nassau with Panju and Weinberg to demand all of Cinar's money back. He would successfully lead the legal charge in the Bahamian supreme court and collect back from Globe-X $86 million of the $108 million invested. Diagnosed with leukemia in 2003, his health has been an issue since.

Maria Castrechini – Montreal businesswoman who was also John Xanthoudakis' sister-in-law
After doing a stint in the Norshield Montreal office, she would move to Nassau to work with Tom and Bob and tighten up administration of the Norshield International office. Post–March 2000, she would work with Steven Hancock as administrator of Cardinal International, the entity that administered all of John Xanthoudakis' deals, until its failure and closure in December 2004.

Micheline Charest – Co-founder and former co-CEO of Cinar
At one time she was "one of Hollywood's 50 most important women." Ousted with her husband, Ron Weinberg, she was fined by the

Quebec Securities Commission. In 2004 she would perish on the operating table during major cosmetic surgery.

Terry Corcoran – Former Montreal police officer, now a private eye and security specialist
He was responsible for John Xanthoudakis' safety after the death threats began.

Paul D'Andrea – CFO, Mount Real Corporation; also involved as an officer and in the accounting practices of MRACS and RealVest
Paul would function and work closely with Lino Matteo over the course of approximately eight years, mostly in administration and finance areas. His name would be cited in a variety of the suits and actions taken against Mount Real. Shortly after the November 11, 2005, collapse of Mount Real, Paul would quietly remove himself and start in another business.

Bob Daviault – Former CFO of Norshield Financial Group
He moved to the Bahamas to be CFO and partner to Tom Muir in Globe-X and Norshield International. Bob was the main liaison between Cinar and Norshield and would be the main person involved in cleaning up the financial records post–March 2000. Bob and Tom's relationship would erode in 2001, and Bob would leave to live somewhat secretly in western Canada. His depositions in 2004 and 2005 would completely contradict his deposition done in 2001.

David Edwards – Washington State businessman
He knew Lowell Holden and at one point was approached about the idea of becoming a director in Sterling Leaf. When he discovered that an American could not be a

director of that company, he immediately declined. There would subsequently be misinterpretation as to whether or not he was ever on the board. Edwards would be the businessperson behind the proposal to bring Mount Real back into existence for the purpose of retiring its debt to investors. Basically, the proposal intended to pay one hundred and fifteent percent on the investors' money over a span of five or six years. Edwards would be battered in the Montreal press, and in March 2006 would withdraw his offer and retreat to Washington.

Terri Engelman Rhodes – Headed the Chicago office of Norshield U.S. and structured cutting edge deals for the firm
She was the person who did the RBC borrowings with the New York offices of RBC. This would complete the structure allowing Mosaic Composite to be the financial underpinnings for the Olympic Univest products in 2004.

Jean Philippe Gervais – Montreal attorney, Gervais & Gervais
Gervais would be the attorney for André Allard, who would lead the effort in court to attempt to bring Mount Real out of liquidation and to reimburse the investors; despite Gervais' effective treatment of the file, he would be rebuffed and when Edwards withdrew the proposal, Gervais and Allard would be left with the severe reprimands of Judge Lalonde.

Alain Gutkin – Montreal attorney
Attorney of John Xanthoudakis after Torralbo's firm forced him to stop working on John Xanthoudakis' behalf.

Steven Hancock – President and CEO of Cardinal International

From 2001 to December 2004, Cardinal would be the "back office" and administrator for Norshield funds and activities throughout the world. His office in Nassau was on the top floor of the largest and most prestigious office building in the city. Cardinal was placed in liquidation in December 2004.

Steven Hart – Attorney

Hart was another attorney working on Norshield and Olympus Univest securities for John Xanthoudakis. It would be in his office in Montreal's largest office building that John would be assaulted. His firm would be purchased by Heenan Blaikie, the cce attorney.

Laurence Henry – President of MRACS and RealVest, and an officer/director in a variety of Mount Real related enterprises

Laurence would function in Lino's environment for a period of about ten years, both building businesses and operating businesses on Matteo's behalf. The collapse of mracs and RealVest would come as a devastating shock to Laurence Henry.

Michael Hirsch – Principal and CEO of Cookie Jar, the Toronto-based firm that would buy the assets of Cinar in 2003

He would be one of the beneficiaries of funds recovered by the cce if there ever were any.

Lowell Holden – Minnesota businessman

He would be introduced to Tom Muir by Matteo. Holden had extensive experience in workouts and turn-arounds. He thought he could negotiate a quick end to

Cinar's Globe-X claims, but failed. Five years later he remains embroiled in the situation. In late 2005 Holden would bring David Edwards into the Mount Real situation in an attempt to bring Mount Real Corporation out of bankruptcy.

Norman Inkster – Former head of the RCMP
Inkster would use his power and influence on behalf of the cce to eventually destabilize Norshield and bring down Mount Real.

Clifford Johnson – PricewaterhouseCoopers, chartered accountant
He was brought into the Globe-X companies by Brock to investigate the status of Globe-X investments. In 2002 he would become one of the liquidators of the Globe-X estate and remain in that position to the present.

Jeff Klein – Partner of Lino Matteo for 15 years as president of Honeybee Technology, a public company
Klein and Lino would serve as both officers and directors of the company for its entire existence, until Matteo's resignation in November 2005. Honeybee would function miscellaneously in a variety of businesses, including software development, software sales and the magazine sales and processing business (administering many of the magazine subscription and consumer installment contract sales that would become the core of the Mount Real enterprise).

Judge Lalonde – Bankruptcy Court judge in the Montreal circuit
Judge Lalonde would be the second judge to serve on the case of Mount Real. Assuming the case in December 2005, he would refer frequently to Jean Robillard as his

colleague and remind him that he (Robillard) had the authority and the ability to operate as a judge himself on the Mount Real case, with the exception of being able to send someone to prison. Lalonde would consistently find against the efforts of André Allard and Gervais and for the AMF and Raymond Chabot Grant Thornton. Eventually, Lalonde would strongly suggest that attorneys representing creditors proceed to place Mount Real into liquidation through motion and, ultimately, he would severely reprimand Allard for his efforts in the Mount Real situation.

Jaime Lao – Montreal investment broker, formerly with iForum
Lao would effectively network with the Asian community in raising significant amounts of money for Mount Real related investments.

Rick Leckner – Montreal PR man
He was a friend, PR person, adviser and investor in Norshield projects and John Xanthoudakis as a talent.

Don MacDonald – Reporter and columnist for the *Montreal Gazette*
He would be on the Cinar/Norshield story right from the beginning and seemed to always want to make the story seamy. He would, over six years, write the stories as they evolved and skirmish along the way with John Xanthoudakis and Lino Matteo. Eventually, his writings would help seal the fate of over six companies, including Norshield and Mount Real.

Michael Maloney – Journeyman and Montreal attorney
He was brought into the situation by Matteo to work on

legal issues primarily in the Bahamas and eventually on the Mount Real debacle in November 2005.

Bert Marotte – Montreal reporter for the *Globe and Mail*

Bert was on the Norshield/Cinar story from the beginning in March of 2000 and led the legal fight to open the hearings to the press. Bert would eventually get the first exclusive interview with John Xanthoudakis in December 2005 after the collapse of Norshield.

Bill Marston – Montreal investment broker, formerly with iForum

Marston would be the largest single source of money for the MRACS and RealVest investments tied to the Mount Real collapse. He would be the subject of many newspaper stories from both *The Gazette* and *La Presse*; the AMF would proceed to suspend his licence for securities and insurance sales. Marston is currently the defendant in several lawsuits by former clients. Marston would say, "I want to help people but cannot. When I read the obituaries and recognize a former client I know that I contributed to their last days of hell."

Lino Matteo – John's longtime friend and CEO of TSX-listed Mount Real Corporation

His overwhelming need to be in control of everyone and everything caused him to immerse himself in the Cinar/Norshield mess. He would become the main strategist in the financial cleanup and recasting, the legal strategist and eventually the main protagonist to Wes Voorheis of the CCE. By 2006, his businesses would be destroyed and

Matteo himself would become a poster boy for financial scandal in Canada.

Yves Mechaka – Key leader in iForum and former president of Norshield Investment Advisors

Mechaka would be a broker who would sell significant amounts of investments, including investments in Commax, Univest, RealVest and MRACS. Many of Mechaka's clients would be affected by the failure of Norshield and Mount Real.

Max Mendelsohn – Montreal attorney

He worked with Stuart Snyder and Bill Brock in an attempt to bring about an 11th-hour settlement in March 2004.

Tom Muir – Canadian businessman

He moved to the Bahamas in 1992 and founded the Globe-X entities, Commax, Norshield International (under licence) and other entities. Tom functioned primarily as a PR and sales guy, but held the title of president and was the beneficial owner of many of the entities, including BICE.

Claudine Murphy – A Montreal attorney operating as a sole practitioner

She was hired by the Mount Real entities to represent them in their court fight to revive Mount Real through a bankruptcy proposal. She would have a previous history with Judge Lalonde, and would attempt to have him removed from the case. Her attempts would be unsuccessful and ultimately Mount Real would withdraw its proposal.

Hasanain Panju – Cinar CFO

He was the mastermind with Weinberg of the financial shenanigans that would bring them and the company down. Formerly with Ernst & Young, he would rise to power as Cinar grew. In the post-dismissal period, he would quietly move his life and family to London, England, to enjoy the money he stashed away during the Cinar era.

Joe Pettinicchio – Served as president of Mount Real Corporation and iForum (for a period of about five years)

In that role, Joe would be primarily responsible for sales and the growth of iForum, and for investor and public relations for Mount Real. At the time of the Mount Real collapse, Joe had resigned from Mount Real and his functions and role there. Joe would continue to serve in his capacity with iForum through the seizure and delisting of the company by the AMF.

Mason Poplaw – Montreal attorney, McCarthy Tétrault

Poplaw would serve as the attorney for the AMF and Raymond Chabot Grant Thornton in the court actions held between November 2005 and March 2006. Ultimately, his points of view would prevail, due to the withdrawal of the proposal by André Allard and David Edwards.

Andrew Porporino – Cinar controller during the key period

Porporino came to Cinar as did the entire accounting and finance department: Ernst & Young, the auditors of Cinar. Porporino had a bird's eye view of Weinberg and Panju's antics and tricks in the late nineties.

Mario Ricci – The only person to actually work for each of the principals

A chartered accountant, Ricci worked with Mount Real until 1997, then worked for Cinar directly under Panju and Weinberg. In 1999 he would go to Norshield and work directly under John Xanthoudakis. Ricci would work with Muir and Daviault in the post-meltdown period, and become president of Olympus UniVest in 2004. He would depart in early 2005.

Jean Robillard – Chartered accountant, Raymond Chabot Grant Thornton

Robillard was named in November 2005 as the receiver for Mount Real Corporation, and eventually for the other corporations that have been dragged into the Mount Real situation, including RealVest, MRACS and half a dozen other entities. Robillard would vigorously fight the attempt by André Allard and David Edwards to revive Mount Real for the purpose of repaying the investors.

Harvey Sands – Accountant with RSM Richter

He would introduce John Xanthoudakis to Panju and Weinberg.

Gilles Seguin – Montreal attorney

Seguin represented Tom Muir and Bob Daviault in the June 2001 investigation of Globe-X by the Quebec Securities Commission (QSC). Both Muir and Daviault received immunity for their testimony; the QSC would eventually fine Weinberg and Charest $1 million (the largest fine ever in Quebec, and largest in history pertaining to securites).

Dale Smith – Norshield CFO and officer of First Horizon (Bank of Barbados)

He dealt with financial offerings and structuring throughout the late nineties and up to 2005. He would see through the last successful audit completed as of September 30, 2003.

Stuart Snyder – President of Cinar (from 2003 to March 2004)

Snyder would be the executive who would complete the transaction and sale of Cinar. He would be within an eyelash of completing a settlement with Holden in March of 2004; the settlement would have avoided the eventual meltdown and stopped the creation of the CCE.

Yves Tardif – Montreal investment broker, formerly with iForum

Tardif would be a major source of capital for MRACS and RealVest, and would bring many of his clients into the Mount Real fold. Tardif would be cited by the AMF and have his licence suspended for securities and insurance sales. He is also the defendant in several lawsuits against him by former clients.

Robert Torralbo – John Xanthoudakis' lawyer from 2001 forward

He would work on litigation and strategy regarding Cinar; eventually his firm would pressure him to cease working for John.

Barry Usher – Former insurance executive

He would become the Cinar CEO in early March 2000, after Weinberg, Charest and Panju were deposed.

KEY PLAYERS

Francis Vailles – Reporter for *La Presse*, a Montreal newspaper

Vailles would be fed information from the CCE and begin to write frequently on the situation with a special focus on Mount Real. He would pen a series of stories on Mount Real that would weaken the company and speed redemptions, stop subscriptions for its commercial paper and open an AMF investigation.

Robert Vineberg – Chairman of the Cinar board and senior partner in the major Montreal law firm of Goodman, Phillips & Vineberg

He would be instrumental in blaming the Weinberg, Charest and Panju trio for all of Cinar's problems and keeping the scandal away from the board of directors.

Wes Voorheis – Head of the CCE, an attorney who would pilot their collection efforts

Under his leadership, the CCE would recover little money, but would freeze the assets of Weinberg and Xanthoudakis, destroy Norshield and its funds, bring down Mount Real and six other entities it was involved in. The CCE would spend over $15 million on lawyers, accountants, public relations and investigators.

Ron Weinberg – Former CEO of Cinar and co-founder

He was ousted from the company in March 2000 after a series of events that caused a lack of confidence in him. In 2003 he was issued the largest fine in history by the Quebec Securities Commission. Today his assets remain frozen due to legal actions.

John Xanthoudakis – CEO of Norshield Financial Group and always in the middle of everything
He would offer advice to Panju and Weinberg, help Tom Muir get into business, move Bob Daviault to the Bahamas, manage the Globe-X Funds, bring in Lino Matteo to help clean things up, build Norshield to $1 billion under management, develop the Mosaic concept, borrow money from RBC, build Olympus Univest and watch it all collapse. By 2005, he was living with death threats and lawsuits, separated from his wife, with his financial empire in ruin.

Kathy Xanthoudakis – John's wife of 20 years and the sister of Maria Castrechini
She would push for separation and divorce in 2004. From this time forward John would never be the same businessman again. He would begin to miss meetings and not return phone calls; his focus diminished.